Boomers,

Xers,

and Other Strangers

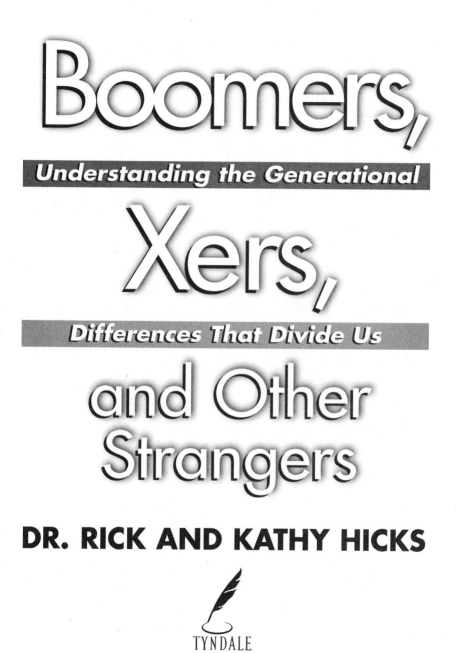

Boomers,

Understanding the Generational

Xers,

Differences That Divide Us

and Other Strangers

DR. RICK AND KATHY HICKS

TYNDALE

Tyndale House Publishers, Wheaton, Illinois

Library of Congress Cataloging-in-Publication Data
Hicks, Kathy,
    Boomers, Xers, and other strangers / Kathy and Rick Hicks.
        p.   cm.
    ISBN 1-56179-677-8
    1. Social values. 2. Conflict of generations. I. Hicks, Rick,
    1950-   . II. Title.
    HM681.H53   1999
    303.3'72—dc21   99-27725
                                                CIP

A Focus on the Family book published by Tyndale House Publishers, Wheaton, Illinois.

Unless otherwise noted, Scripture quotations are from the HOLY BIBLE, NEW INTERNATIONAL VERSION ®. Copyright © 1973, 1978, 1984 by the International Bible Society. Used by permission of Zondervan Publishing House. All rights reserved.

Some people's names and certain details of the stories in this book have been changed to protect the privacy of the individuals involved. However, the truth of what happened has been conveyed as accurately as possible.

Cover design: Bradley L. Lind
Cover photos: Rich Chartier and PhotoDisc

Printed in the United States of America

00 01 02 03 04/10 9 8 7 6 5 4 3

We dedicate this book to
our lovely daughter, Cora,
our resident member of the Net Generation
and a constant source of joy to her proud parents.

Contents

Section I: Developing Our Differences

Section II: Your Decade of Destiny

DEVELOPING OUR DIFFERENCES

I'm Okay—Why Aren't You Okay?

It was Christmas Eve, and the young girl was having trouble sleeping, anticipating the surprises that tomorrow morning would bring. She could hear the muffled voices of her parents downstairs, and her curiosity got the better of her. Sneaking onto the landing, she peeked through the banister to see what they were doing. There, spread out on the floor, were the parts of a new bicycle, but she could hear the frustration in her father's voice.

"There's no way I can put this together without the instructions," he was saying. "I don't even know which part this is!"

The girl's heart sank as she heard her mother try to calm her husband with a suggestion. "She's getting lots of other presents this Christmas. Why don't we just put it back in the box and hide it until her birthday? That will give us time to send for the instructions."

At that point, the girl noticed some large printing on the side of the box: www.kidsbike.com. She quickly retreated to her room, where she booted up her computer and logged onto the Internet. After accessing the company's Web site, she found the instructions for assembling the bike and printed out a copy. Tiptoeing back to the landing, she dropped the sheet over the banister so that it floated down to where her parents were doing one more thorough search before giving up. As she snuck back

3

to her bedroom, she heard her father exclaim, "Here they are!"

This IBM commercial, aired during the 1998 Christmas season, illustrates one way generations can differ from each other. It never crossed the parents' minds that they could get the instructions off the Internet, but the young girl saw it as an immediate solution to their problem.

Different Values

The differences between generations are more than just distinct ways of looking at things or new solutions for problems. They're gut-level differences in values that involve a person's beliefs, emotions, and preferences. More often than not, they result in misunderstandings, tensions, and open conflicts between family members, co-workers, and individuals in any setting where people of different ages try to get along or accomplish something together. Simple observation of the past several decades shows how values have changed step by step and issue by issue over time. Back in the 1920s, this country, for the most part, revolved around Judeo-Christian ethics. Now as we face the twenty-first century, our values have evolved to become radically different.

The values we develop in our youth are the foundation for what we believe as adults.

If we were to go back in time, we would see events happening in each decade that set the values for children growing up in those eras. Since we don't have a time machine, we'll have to depend on our historical records to help us understand what went on during those times. But this isn't just about catching up on our history. It's about learning what makes each generation tick. The values we develop in our youth are the foundation for what we believe as adults. Understanding this concept is the single most important tool we've ever seen to clearly identify why people of different generations hold different values. We are going to take an enlightening journey back to each decade from the 1920s through the 1990s to see what unique values each produced. With this insight, you'll begin to understand why your children or grandchildren think the way they do. Or maybe your parents' or grandparents' concerns and values will make more sense when you see where they came from.

Experiencing Differences

We all have values that differ from the values of others in our lives: those at work, our neighbors, those we encounter in civic organizations, those we worship with, and of course, the relationships that seem to affect us the most—our parents, children, and grandchildren.

If you're having conflicts with someone from a different generation, the cause is most likely rooted in the core differences of your values. It's incredibly important to understand how a younger or older generation developed its values and how they are put into practice.

Without an understanding of value development, you're walking into relationships blind to how individuals of other generations think, what they stand for, and why they do certain things.

Without that understanding, you're walking into the relationship blind to how individuals of other generations think, what they stand for, and why they do certain things.

Clashes or misunderstandings can arise from almost any issue where there are basic value differences. Topics can be as varied as financial decisions, fashion preferences, recreation choices, religious beliefs, musical style, food consumption, or morality concerns.

One enduring example of an issue that generations differ on is hairstyles. Rick's dad was raised in the '30s and '40s. Many men had shorter hair at that time. One reason is that the military (as of WW I) required short hair. They were changing from cloth hats to metal helmets, and all military personnel were required to have short hair so that their helmets would always fit. Dad and his generation grew up seeing their heroes return from war with short hair. So they identified short hair with positive character traits and kept their own hair short.

Rick grew up in the '50s and '60s. He was impressed with people like Jerry Lee Lewis, Elvis Presley, and the Beatles. They all had relatively long hair (except when Elvis was in the army, when he, too, had to wear a helmet). Well, when he got out of high school and away from the school's rules, Rick decided to let his hair grow long enough to put into a ponytail. Dad's first response when he saw the long hair was to tell Rick to "cut it off."

Rick countered with, "I should have the freedom to grow my hair as long as I like."

Then came the classic retort: "Only communists and radicals have long hair. Which are you?"

Dad grew up valuing short hair, and Rick grew up admiring long hair. This topic was a major battleground for them— as it might have been for some of you.

Another major values clash that started in the '60s occurs when unmarried couples decide to live together, either as a trial before marriage or as a lifestyle. This can cause turmoil between parents who believe that premarital sex is wrong and their young adult children who don't.

Values conflicts don't just relate to morality decisions. Sometimes, those who grew up questioning the ethics and actions of the government feel justified ignoring or breaking federal regulations or laws—especially if it's something they think they might get away with, such as tax fraud. A more public example would be burning draft cards. This type of defiance is unthinkable to those—usually the parents or grandparents of the previous group—who grew up in more patriotic times, when the government was trusted and counted on to get the country through difficulties. Conflicts regarding legal issues such as these may arise, especially if members of two generations find themselves in some type of business partnership where ideological differences come down to specific questions about how a financial or ethical situation should be handled.

Conflicts of a similar type often surface when an organization embarks on a new building project or other major financial endeavor. As the planning committee makes decisions about how the finances should be handled, those members who grew up during the Depression may suggest having cash in hand before proceeding. Meanwhile, younger committee members, raised during decades of prosperity, may see no reason the organization shouldn't take out a loan for the project.

Even what some consider small issues can become large ones when generational differences enter the picture. Kathy remembers her grandmother being concerned about her granddaughters using playing cards to play solitaire and other innocent card games, because her grandmother's values connected playing cards with the evils of gambling.

A person's experience and value system can determine that certain behavior is necessary. When Rick was a poor college student, he was invited to live with a friend's family. This upper-middle-class family was very gracious and generous to him. There were almost no limits on the food he was allowed to eat, and he ate well. There was just one limit set by the mother of the house: They could have only one small glass of orange juice at a time. She was raised during a time when orange juice was scarce and expensive and needed to be carefully rationed. That value stayed with her, even though she lived in Southern California and had orange trees in her backyard.

Understanding Differences

Understanding how values developed differently from decade to decade is like having a graduate-level course in human relations. In fact, this concept was the basis of a leadership class I (Rick) taught for a master's degree program through Azusa Pacific University. As part of the APU faculty, I was sent to eight different countries, where I taught the course to students who couldn't come to the United States to complete their graduate degrees. Through my studies in organizational and developmental psychology at Claremont Graduate School, where I earned my Ph.D., I was able to focus on the principles of value development. In my personal experience, this decade model has been the single most helpful concept in understanding people. It has enabled me to understand my family members; it has also served as a tool for leadership and ministry as I've worked with a wide variety of age groups.

I've been teaching this topic for over 15 years, in both family and organizational settings, and it never fails to grab people's attention. As they grasp the concept and understand the impact of the various decades, I see the light of understanding appear on their faces and hear comments like "That explains a lot" and "Wow, that makes a lot of sense. Now I see where that person is coming from."

Once, after sharing this material with a group of senior adults, a woman came to thank me for the new insight she had gained. "This has been so helpful for me," she said. "I've always felt that my kids were good kids, but I couldn't understand why they would do things that didn't seem right to me, like spending too much money. Now I realize it wasn't because they aren't good kids, but because they have different values than I do. Now I can see why they have that set of values and why those values are different from mine."

Another man said, "I've been frustrated with my son, who has finished college but can't seem to settle down and get a decent job. I thought he was just lazy, but now I have a better perspective of where he's coming from. I think I can be more understanding of his situation and even more helpful to him now, rather than just getting on his case."

I wish I could tell you that back when my dad and I were arguing over hair length, we had the tools to overcome our differences in values. We didn't then, which led to misunderstanding and tensions, but we do now. Perhaps you could benefit by gaining some understanding about ways to sort out value clashes in your own life to save yourself from the kind of predicament my dad and I were in.

If you have kids or youth in your family, or you relate to them in any setting, you'll benefit from current studies describing this newest generation in all its uniqueness. We'll look at a study that compares college freshmen during the last 30 years and see what radical changes have occurred in their outlook and behavior. We'll also take insight from the Coca-Cola Company's extensive marketing research on 27,000 12- to 19-year-olds worldwide. *USA Weekend*'s 11th Annual Special Teen Report, with 272,400 participants, will give us some interesting insights, too, as well as recently

This book has been written to give you hope. It is possible to get along with people of different generations. The biggest step toward that goal comes through understanding.

published books and articles addressing the topic of this new generation. In addition, we conducted our own survey of more than 1,100 high school students to learn about some of their attitudes, preferences, and trends. We believe all this information will be a useful tool for trying to relate to the young people in our lives. So read on to become better equipped.

Accepting Differences

Many people want—and need—to know how and why generations differ from each other. We'll always be confronted with generational differences. They existed in the past, we're dealing with them in the present, and they'll be a part of the future. When these differences are allowed to create conflicts within families, at work, or in any other setting, they can damage relationships.

This book has been written to give you hope. It *is* possible to get along with people of different generations. The biggest step toward that goal comes through understanding . . . understanding that we are different, how we're different, and how those differences came about. Once we have the knowledge, we can take the next step of acceptance—even if we don't always agree—which leads to overcoming the differences that often divide us.

Chapter 2

From High Chairs to Heroes to Hairstyles

"We couldn't believe what we were seeing! We had never seen so much money before. It was hard to believe it was real." The woman in my seminar on integrity was describing an incident her family had experienced that provided a test of values. "We were driving down the street on a Sunday evening when we noticed a cloth bag in the road. We stopped to investigate and found that it was a deposit bag from a local bank containing an enormous amount of cash. There was no one around to ask about it, no way to take it to the bank at that time of night, and no one who knew we had it. The only thing we could do was take it home with us. The kids were all excited, saying, 'We're rich! We're rich!' and 'This is our lucky day! Now we can buy that new car we need, right, Mom and Dad? Finders, keepers, right?' Well, my husband and I looked at each other and knew this would be a challenging situation. We really needed some financial help right then."

She paused in her story; others in the seminar started to react. One man said, "I know I would have kept the money. After all, no one knew you had it, and the banks are insured against those kinds of things. No one would have really gotten hurt, and your family would have really benefited."

"I disagree," a woman interrupted. "That would have been a terrible example for her children. They need to learn to be honest, so the money would have to be returned for the sake of their morality."

"But how did you know it wasn't God's way of providing for your needs?" someone else questioned. "It could have been a little miracle He sent to take care of you."

She assured them that many of those thoughts had crossed their minds that night as she and her husband decided what to do. Even though they could have really used the money, they finally decided they couldn't keep it. They valued honesty and integrity more than money, and they wanted to pass that value on to their children. "From the moment that money was in my house, I felt a combination of pressure, tension, nervousness, and guilt," she declared. "I couldn't wait to get it out of my house and back to the bank where it belonged.

This couple valued honesty, and that value helped to guide them through the situation and determined the outcome.

"The next morning I felt a tremendous sense of relief as I handed that bag of cash over to the manager of the bank. He expressed great surprise and relief that we would return the money, since there was no way they could have traced it to us. They gave us a small reward, but the real advantage for me was knowing that we had done the right thing."

This couple valued honesty, and that value helped to guide them through the situation and determined the outcome. If someone with other values had discovered the bag of money, the outcome could have been quite different.

Values are what we believe to be right or wrong, good or bad, worthy or unworthy. What we value is what we feel is worth fighting for or standing up for. It is what we believe in. Our values guide our lives. They give us direction, are a basis for decision-making, and help us make choices. Our lives are not just controlled by circumstances, habits, emotions, or random occurrences. Our values have a significant impact on all that we do and think.

Three Stages of Value Development

Learning how we develop our values is an important first step on our journey toward understanding. Values are not developed overnight. They are formed over time, as part of a developmental process. Morris Massey, in his book *The People Puzzle,* defines three important stages of value development. In very general terms, he describes what takes place during a child's formative years. It's helpful to look at these three stages (summarized in the "Value Development" chart on p. 14) to have a better understanding of how values are developed differently at various ages.

Children See, Children Do

One evening some friends came to our house for a visit. I (Rick) was roughhousing with their young son, Kyle. Throughout our friendly battle, I would affectionately call him a knucklehead as we teased and wrestled with each other. At the end of the evening, Kyle and his parents were in their car, pulling away from the curb. As we waved goodbye, Kyle leaned out of the window and yelled, "See you later, knucklehead."

The car came to a quick stop. "You shouldn't talk to adults like that," scolded Kyle's mom. "And you shouldn't call anyone names."

I came to Kyle's rescue. "It's okay, Angie," I explained. "We've been calling each other knucklehead all evening as an affectionate nickname."

Kyle didn't know the term could be considered an insult. He was simply copying what he had heard. He was in the first value-development stage identified by Massey as *imprinting.*

This first stage of value development takes place from birth to approximately seven years of age. Just as a foot leaves its imprint in the sand, the things a young child experiences affect his values. What he sees happening in his family and the world

around him is the "right" way for things to be done. There is no logic or reasoning involved. It is a matter of seeing, absorbing, and accepting.

Nature gives us obvious examples of imprinting. The movie *Fly Away Home* illustrates this principle well. A girl discovers a nest of goose eggs. Knowing that the mother goose will not be back, she transfers the eggs to her father's barn and cares for them. When the goslings hatch, she is the first being they see, so it is imprinted on their little brains that she is their mother and, thus, the one to be followed. They follow her around with great devotion, and she must show them how to be geese. The biggest challenge comes when they need to be taught to fly so that they can travel south for the winter. With the help of her father, she comes up with a creative solution involving an ultralight airplane.

> *What the child experiences is accepted, internalized, and considered to be right and normal.*

Although the imprinting process is not quite as obvious in people as it is in geese, the principle still holds true. What the child experiences is accepted, internalized, and considered to be right and normal. A child who grows up in a family where the father travels frequently assumes that all fathers are gone a lot. A child who grows up in a family with one parent and goes to child care much of the time assumes that all families are like hers.

I Want To Be Like ???

The second stage of value development described by Massey, called *modeling*, takes place from about age 7 to age 13. This is the most significant period of value development, because it is the stage when a child begins to make his own value decisions. Many of these choices stay with the person for the rest of his life.

At this stage, the child looks around his world, first at his parents and then outside his family. He is looking for people he admires—people he wants to be like. As he observes qualities he wants to emulate, he internalizes and imitates them. Heroes become significant at this stage.

Several years ago, I taught a graduate course in sociology to a group of Americans who were working in Taiwan. While focusing on this modeling stage of value development, I made the point that a child's heroes during these years can have a significant influence throughout his or her life. I then asked the students to tell me who their heroes were when they were about 10 years old. I was amazed to find out that 12 out of the 15 students in my class were pursuing careers similar to those of their childhood heroes! These were teachers, nurses, pilots, and missionaries. While this is an unusually high percentage, it illustrates the point. Those we look up to during this modeling period help to shape our values.

Who were your heroes when you were about 10 years old? Can you remember? I (Kathy) remember admiring our pastor's wife, Lois Lindley. She had many attributes I wanted to emulate in my own life. Some were beyond my ability, like her beautiful solo voice. I also admired the little cleft in the end of her nose and tried to create one in mine with my thumbnail! But I also was impressed with the way she shared in her husband's ministry and was committed to serving the church both in leadership and behind the scenes. For many years, when asked what I wanted to be when I grew up, I said, "A pastor's wife." Although I did not end up marrying a pastor, I did choose a man with whom I could participate in ministry and have had many opportunities to serve in various leadership and behind-the-scenes responsibilities.

> *Those we look up to when we are about 10 years old help to shape our values.*

While you may not end up doing something similar to what your childhood hero did, it's probably still true that that person has had a strong influence on your life.

When I (Rick) teach on this topic, I enjoy asking the various age groups present who their heroes were when they were 10. It's interesting to find that the older group, who went through this modeling stage of their lives before television, often have heroes who were family members or people from their communities—individuals they probably knew personally. Those who grew up with TV are more likely to have heroes who were sports stars, movie actors, or even fictitious characters. As we look at some of the celebrities, athletes, and leaders in our country today and see their lifestyles and values, we may rightfully be concerned about our children who are presently in this modeling stage. We'll deal with this issue in chapter 22 and give you some suggestions on how to make sure your child is exposed to positive role models.

But Everybody Else Is Doing It!

The third—and, for parents, often the scariest—stage of value development Massey calls *socialization.* These are the years from about 14 to the early 20s, when the family influence on young people diminishes. They go out into their peer group and society to try out their values. It's a proving ground, a final testing place for them to see how their values compare and which ones will endure. This is a time when they experiment, observe, and make decisions about what is right and what is wrong. They start making choices about what kind of people they will be and what they want to do in life.

Some of the earliest and most obvious signs of this stage are music, hair, and clothing preferences that are much different from their parents—and very much the same as their peers. Just think of how teenage hairstyles have changed from decade to decade. In the '50s, guys were combing their hair like Elvis and the girls were wearing ponytails. By the end of the '60s, the guys were trying to grow the ponytails. The '70s brought about more-styled long hair for guys. In the '90s, many of the guys went back to short hair—possibly to the consternation of their

They go out into their peer group and society to try out their values. It's a final testing place for them to see how their values compare and which ones will endure.

dads, who fought hard for the right to have long hair! Some combine long hair with shaved areas, often enhanced with bright colors like blue or green.

While some of these trends are short-lived, they still are indications that these kids are in the socialization stage and are testing their internal values as well. Teenagers often embrace the current social issues, believing their opinions to be more enlightened and superior to their parents' archaic views on life. Teenagers in the '60s tried to be more racially tolerant than their parents. Teens of the '80s were more in touch with the ecological needs of our planet. Teens of the '90s have been more politically correct and therefore much more tolerant of those who are different from themselves.

One of the current trends we find interesting is the increase in cigarette smoking among teenagers. With all the reports about the health hazards, the proof of nicotine addiction, the local ordinances limiting where people can smoke, and the example of people in their lives who are trying to quit, why would they even consider smoking? The obvious answer is peer pressure and their desire to show their independence from adults.

Teaching Old Dogs New Tricks

The socialization stage brings us to the end of our value-development process. At this point, our values are set. These values shape and guide us and are the basis for our decisions for the rest of our lives. There is, however, the possibility of adaptation of our values if we experience what Massey refers to as a "significant emotional event." This would be something that so deeply affects us that it causes us to reevaluate our basic values and makes us exchange one value for another. It involves more than a change in our behavior. It must also include a corresponding change of our beliefs. These significant emotional events can happen at any time in life, but the earlier they occur, the more significant the change will be.

I (Rick) experienced one of these significant emotional events at the end of my high school years. Because of the family I grew up in, my values were those of a nonreligious teenager of the '60s. Like many my age, I got involved in drinking, smoking, illegal drugs, and

A "significant emotional event" so deeply affects us that it causes us to reevaluate our basic values and makes us exchange one value for another.

a hippie lifestyle. I didn't care about school. In fact, my senior year was spent at a continuation school, where they send kids who are kicked out of public schools.

During the spring break of my senior year, a friend invited me to go to the Colorado River with him. It was the "cool" place to spend spring break in those days, so I went. When we got to Parker, Arizona, we ran into more friends from my old high school and hopped the fence of the campground to stay with them for free.

Since I looked older than the others, they all gave me money and sent me off to the local store to buy the beer. I returned with several cases of beer and an appetite. "What do we have to eat around here?" I asked.

The guys all looked at each other and shrugged. "I gave you all the money I had for beer," said one.

"Me, too," said another.

It turned out that every guy had given me every dollar he had.

"I can't believe it!" I said. "You gave me every cent you had, knowing that if I'd gotten caught trying to buy beer illegally, you would have lost it all, and nobody thinks to keep enough money out for food or even gas to get home?" This group had a lot of fun, but we were not known for planning ahead. "Oh, well," I said, "let's sit down and drink some lunch."

Next to us was a high school youth group camping with their youth pastor. They had come to talk about Jesus with anyone willing to listen, and they eventually got around to our group. After some of these girls tried to talk to us, they decided they needed reinforcements and brought in their youth pastor, Kent Hughes. As Kent talked with us, he discovered our foodless predicament and invited us to eat all our meals with his youth group.

At first we were skeptical, but hunger won out, and we eventually joined in. This was the first time I had spent a lot of time with a group of people who lived life according to values radically different from mine—Christian values.

At the end of the week, before my friends and I drove home on the gas Kent had provided, he explained that we could have personal relationships with God through faith in Jesus Christ. He asked each of us, "Do you want to accept God's free gift of forgiveness and salvation through accepting Christ's payment for your sins?"

At the time I said no. I wasn't ready to change my lifestyle, which I knew would be the result of that kind of decision. I believed in God but didn't want my values to be so restrictive. I wasn't ready to give up being cool to become like those nerdy kids in the youth group.

After graduating from continuation high school, I got kicked out of a community college (which took some effort on my part!) and decided to become a beach bum. With a year of doing nothing on my resume, my girlfriend's dad said, "Rick, cut off that ponytail, put on a suit, and show up to work at my office tomorrow. I have a job for you." Overnight I went from beach bum to junior executive at a photo engraving company in Hollywood, complete with profit sharing and a company car. For a while I felt as if I had really made it.

But it wasn't enough. One night, while stuck in a traffic jam on one of the Los Angeles freeways, I saw long lines of cars, which, from my position on a bridge, reminded me of ants going into an anthill. I realized that tomorrow they would all come out of their anthills, go to work, and then return home again in the evening. It all seemed so futile. I felt that there should be more to life than that, and I remembered the youth group that I had met at the river two years before. I realized they had the truth and meaning in life that I was looking for. That night I asked Jesus Christ to take charge of my life, and the resulting change was amazing.

Up to this point, I had always lived my life to get the most fun out of it. I had no desire to become a religious person. I clearly remember making a deal with God, in the brashness of my youth, saying, "I'm not going to give up the things in my life I enjoy just to become 'religious.' But if You have something better for me, then I will trade these things in for what You want me to have."

A couple months later, I was invited to a small graduation party for some friends of mine. When they were passing around the champagne for a toast, I tried to refuse the glass that was offered to me. Since I had been seeking to please God, I found I no longer had a desire to drink. When they kept insisting, I gave in, planning to have only one drink for the celebration. But that led to more drinks, and I wound up getting drunk.

When the joint of marijuana was being passed around, I realized I was losing my desire to smoke dope as well, but again, the badgering I received from my friends led to my joining in. As the party went on and everyone else was having fun, I remembered clearly the deal I had made with God. I realized that there was more peace, satisfaction, joy, and contentment in having a close relationship with God than in doing these things that had previously been the basis of my fun.

All at once I stood up, made apologies to my girlfriend, and said, "You may not understand this, but I really don't think God wants me to be doing these things. I'd rather follow what God wants me to do than do this stuff that used to bring me pleasure."

To my surprise, she did understand. It was almost as though she wished she had the same convictions. I left that party and that lifestyle forever.

I now had a completely different foundation for my values. Rather than doing what others were doing or doing what I thought would give me pleasure, I was basing my decisions and actions on a new set of beliefs. This significant emotional event caused me to exchange many of my previous values for new, biblical values that were part of my new Christian faith.

This change of values even affected my attitude toward education. This unmotivated student who barely made it through high school and got kicked out of community college ended up with a bachelor's degree, two master's degrees, and a Ph.D. in education and psychology!

Of course, there are other types of significant emotional events, such as divorce, losing a job, or a sudden change in health. Other potential value-changing events include the effects of war, the death of someone close to us, a financial crisis, or some form of significant enlightenment (such as a life-changing book, seminar, or even a conversation that influences how we think or act). These can all have an impact on our values if they lead us to change our beliefs about ourselves, God, significant relationships, or other things that are important to us. Apart from these events, however, our values tend to remain the same as they developed through the imprinting, modeling, and socialization stages we experienced as we grew up.

As we look more closely at the basis for value formation, begin to consider the world events that influenced the development of your values. Try to remember the details of the significant emotional events in your life—how they affected you and how your values changed as a result. Consider the experiences you had that tested your values, determining which ones would endure. As you put together the pieces of your own value-development puzzle, you'll begin to get a clearer picture of who you are and why you believe as you do.

Chapter 3

Pieces of the Puzzle

A major part of my (Rick's) growing-up years took place on my great-grandparents' farm in Kentucky. My parents sent my brother and me there every summer, from the year I was five until I was in high school, so we could help out. (I'm not sure who was helped more by this arrangement, my parents or my great-grandparents.) Daddy Hicks, as we called my great-grandfather, was the kind of man everyone listened to and respected, even an overactive, out-of-control kid like me. The values he had—and the way he lived his life and handled his affairs as a result—were quite different from how my parents lived their lives in California. Even a young kid like me noticed it.

I remember getting up early in the mornings and finding that Daddy Hicks had already taken his cup of coffee and surveyed the 144-acre farm, making a list of the jobs that needed doing that day. (Kathy has noticed that I will often take a cup of coffee and walk around the yard in the mornings, making plans for what I want to do there.) The job my brother and I dreaded most was mowing the lawn that constituted more than an acre. Daddy Hicks wouldn't say a word. He would simply reach down as if he were grabbing the starter cord on an old lawnmower and make a pulling motion. We knew that meant it was time for us to go to our lawnmowers—we used three simultaneously—and get started on the job. Although Daddy Hicks didn't say much, I believe I picked up from him a strong work ethic that wasn't typical of the kids I grew up with in the '60s. It is also unusual for a person with my playful, love-of-leisure temperament.

Daddy Hicks also taught me about money. "We don't spend money we don't have" was a principle he lived by. That became a strong value for me as well. In our family, we pay off our credit cards each month. We buy used cars and pay cash for them. It's a concept that is fairly unique in our "buy now, pay later" society.

One time I was in the market to buy a used pickup truck. I had $4,000 and was determined not to take out a loan. (This was obviously a few years ago!) I went to a used car lot and told the salesman, "I have $4,000, and I'd like to buy a truck. Show me what you have for that price."

He immediately took me to a truck that cost $7,000 and told me what a good deal he'd give me on a loan.

"You don't understand," I said. "I don't do loans. I want a truck I can pay $4,000 cash for. Do you have one?"

The salesman continued showing me trucks, talking to his manager and offering deals, all of which involved loans. I finally left the lot, saying, "If you come across a truck I can buy for $4,000, give me a call."

The next day I got a call from the salesman. "Hey, Rick," he said, "I was able to talk my manager down on that truck you wanted. I can sell it to you for only $5,000. We'll make you a good deal on a loan." He just didn't get it. I finally bought my truck for $4,000 from a man who lived near where I worked. It was a great deal!

Family members like Daddy Hicks play a significant role in helping to shape our values as children, but there are other significant factors, too. Each of these factors is like a piece of a puzzle that represents our value-development process. The key to putting a puzzle together is knowing how the pieces fit. In his book *The People Puzzle*, Morris Massey lists eight factors that contribute to our value development.

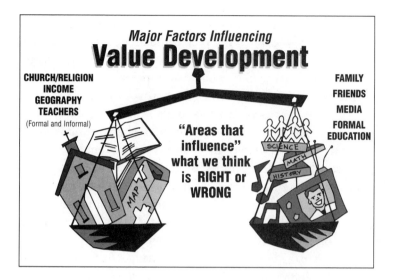

In this chapter we'll look at each of these factors (portrayed in the chart above) and see how it contributes to the formation of our values. As we do, keep in mind that although we experience these factors throughout our lives, it's when we're in the modeling stage—about age 10—that these factors have the greatest impact on our value development.

Family

As the story about Daddy Hicks illustrates, family is a key factor in value development. In fact, it's the primary source for the values we choose. Not only is it the first place we are exposed to value decisions, but it also has the strongest influence of all the key factors, particularly in the early years. The family is where we learn socially acceptable behavior and attitudes (manners, gender roles, etc.). Our family situation greatly influences the other key factors as well, such as our income level, our religion, and our geographical location.

The makeup of our family is important, too. Whether we grow up in a traditional two-parent family with siblings, a single-parent family, or a blended family has an effect on us.

The size of our family also makes a difference. Did you grow up as an only child who pretty much got whatever you wanted, or were you one of five kids who had to act quickly to get your share at the dinner table? Your parents may have been permissive or strict. The atmosphere in your home may have been accepting or critical. Unfortunately, there are many ways a family situation can be dysfunctional or abusive, and if yours was, this would definitely affect your value system.

Over the past few decades, we've seen major changes in the makeup and situations of families in our country with the increase of divorce, blended families, single-parent families, and even same-sex marriages. These changes have had a profound impact on the values of the younger generations.

One outstanding example of how changes in the family can affect a generation of people took place in the '40s and '50s. In 1946, Dr. Benjamin Spock published his revolutionary book on parenting called *The Common Sense Book of Baby and Child Care*. Previously, little had been written to help parents know how to treat their children. The few resources they had encouraged strict training schedules and discouraged "coddling" or showing affection. One source said that children should never be held on the lap, and that if they insisted on affection, kiss them on the forehead at night and shake hands with them in the morning. It was the "children should be seen—when behaving properly and for limited periods of time—and not heard" attitude.

Spock did families a service by encouraging parents to treat their children as little people with needs and telling them to follow their instincts in caring for them with compassion rather than sticking to strict standards of training and schedules. Apparently this new approach to child care had great appeal because it became the new rage. Parents everywhere bought it, bought into it, and applied Dr. Spock's principles to their families. Many took Spock's principles to the extreme, allowing much more freedom than ever before, becoming overly permissive and withholding discipline.

The results became evident when these babies grew up. In the '60s, when the first of Dr. Spock's babies went to college, they challenged the higher education system and the value system of the country. Between January and May of 1968, 40,000 students participated in 221 major demonstrations on 101 college campuses.[1] These were the draft dodgers and the hippies of the late '60s and '70s. The youth of America became involved in a value revolution as they displayed to the world their new, no-boundaries attitudes about sex, drugs, drinking, and conformity to the law.

In an article about the effects of Dr. Spock's book, Harry Stein, *Esquire's* ethics columnist, gives an interesting description of this generation:

> [Spock] has contributed to the making of a generation of adults less subject to regimentation than any that has come before; but, too, the pervasive misapplication of the new theories has resulted not only in literal millions of tyrannical infants and chronically unpleasant eight-year-olds and abusive teenagers, but, inevitably, in an extraordinary number of young men and women who are primarily concerned with their own gratification; people who, if the divorce statistics and the level of cocaine use and the number of self-help manuals crowding the best-seller lists are any indication, have contributed to an era of egocentrism unprecedented in this country's history.[2]

Formal Education

When you consider how many hours a day, how many days a year, and how many years total we spend in school during the value-development period, you realize how significant formal education is. Add to that the fact that the educational system has the power to reward those who perform well and penalize those who don't and you have a powerful force in the lives of students. Textbook content; the quality, philosophy, and attitudes of teachers; and the composition of the student body (racially, economically, etc.) are all elements that affect values. The atmosphere in school and how discipline is handled are also influential.

Textbook content became a big issue in our little town of Yucaipa, California, when our daughter, Cora, was in first grade in 1990. Maybe some of you remember the *Impressions* curriculum, which was the source of great debate in many school districts around the country. I (Kathy) remember going to a meeting at the school where the principal was trying to defend the new curriculum choice for the next school year. Concerned parents were up in arms about the dark, gory, and antisocial content of many of the stories and poems. During a time when all Christian content was being stripped from the public classroom, we were upset that the *Impressions* teacher's manual had suggestions for group activities that included having the students create their own witches' curses. This, of course, was a creative activity to enhance the study of the many poems and articles with themes about witches and mysticism.

"Actually, most of the material you are concerned about was not in the sample books the selection committee looked at," the principal tried to explain. "The publisher ended up sending us a revised version."

If this was supposed to make us feel better, it didn't work. I became increasingly concerned. Was there a hidden agenda in this textbook company's inclusion of this material, I wondered. I had recently read Frank Peretti's novel *Piercing the Darkness,* and the plot included school curriculum encouraging activities that led to demonic activity in children's lives. I knew my friends who were at this meeting with me had just finished reading that novel, too.

"Oh, no! It's happening in our little town of Yucaipa!" I whispered in their ears. We chuckled quietly but wondered uneasily. Would this curriculum desensitize our children to occult activities and make them seem more acceptable? We were afraid that requiring children to read stories about witches, spells, disobedience to parents, suicide, and gory violence as part of school—where truth is supposedly taught by people we tell them to respect—would send the message that these things are okay. We were concerned that this would turn our kids' values away from the ones we were trying to teach them at home.

In spite of months of meetings, newspaper articles, and threats of school board recall elections, the school administrators stood by their choice of curriculum, stating that they believed the content of the stories would be more exciting than other reading materials and would motivate the children to read. But because of the large number of concerned parents, they created "non-*Impressions*" classrooms in each school in our district at each grade level for the next few years. Eventually, the teachers seemed to use the curriculum less and less, and most avoided the questionable material.

Formal education, through content, relationships, and experiences, has a major impact on how values are developed and which values our children end up with. Some aspects of education will have positive results, and some may have very negative results.

Other Formal and Informal Teachers

In addition to schoolteachers, a variety of others also have the potential to influence us as we grow up. These could be scout leaders, Sunday school teachers, Little League coaches, or private music instructors. They are often people we have chosen to be involved with because of some common interest or a desire to learn from them that increases their potential for influencing us. Leaders of youth groups are particularly influential, since they are often perceived to be more "cool" and understanding than parents during the stage when teens are looking outside the family for values input.

One of the most significant teachers in my (Kathy's) life was my youth pastor at church, Kent Hughes (yes, the same man Rick and his buddies met at the campground in Arizona). The strength of his influence was affected by several factors. One was that my family strongly valued church attendance, and being involved in church activities several times a week was a deeply ingrained habit. This gave me many opportunities to be influenced by Kent. Second, my best friends were also in the youth group, so my most influential peer group was also under his teaching. The fact that Kent was only 10 years older than I was made him seem more "in touch" or "relevant" than my parents. Also, I was highly motivated to learn from him because he was my mentor in spiritual growth, which was a high priority in my life.

Religion

In the previous chapter, I (Rick) told you the story of how my new faith in God changed many of the values I had previously developed. Kathy, on the other hand, grew up in a family where religion was a natural part of her family life, so it was a key factor influencing her values.

Whether or not religion made an impact on your life as a child depends on the amount and quality of your exposure to religion. Those of you who were exposed to a consistent, life-influencing faith, especially in your families, were more likely to be significantly affected. Those of you with families who either were not involved in religion or were only superficially involved were not as likely to be affected. If your family's religion was extreme or even abusive, you may have developed negative opinions about religious values. Those of you who found your family religion to be a positive source of peace, unity, and growth probably placed a positive value on religion.

Whether positive or negative, over the decades it has been obvious that religion has had a dramatic impact on what people believe to be right or wrong, good or bad. One example of this comes from Dr. Louis Sullivan, Secretary of Health and Human Services (HHS), who on March 15, 1991, was addressing the Parents Resource Institute for Drug Education in Nashville.

When making the point that religious institutions have an integral part in shaping the character of children, he stated:

> One of the key factors influencing attitudes about drug use—the perception of risk, and the approval or disapproval of drug use—is religious influence. [HHS's 1990 National Household Survey on Drug Abuse studied] over 70,000 high school seniors [and] reaffirmed [that] involvement in values-creating institutions, like churches, correlates consistently with lower drug use.[3]

Our religious training/background does more than influence our beliefs about what is right and wrong. It often greatly influences major decisions in our lives. Significant and life-affecting choices, such as where to go to school, what profession to choose, or whom to marry are often greatly determined by our religious beliefs. The intensity of someone's faith can lead him to extreme actions, such as living a life of frequent sacrifice and service, going to war, and even martyrdom. At times, religion may be the most strongly felt value we possess.

Media

As we look at the relationship between media and values, we could spend the rest of the book just discussing this critical aspect of value development. The forms of the media have changed dramatically over the decades, from newspapers to radio to television and now the Internet. The media's increased impact on values is due, in large part, to the increase in their accessibility to children. This has taken much of the control of information out of the hands of parents, churches, and educators. In the past, the influential figures could direct the type and content of information that young people were exposed to. That is no longer true.

Several years ago my daughter, Cora, and I (Kathy) were watching a children's program on television. "We interrupt this program for a special news brief," said the voice on the TV. Then there was Magic Johnson, reading his statement announcing that he was HIV positive.

I looked at my daughter, wondering what she was thinking. I started picturing the kids at school the next day talking about Magic's announcement, since he was a sports hero. I knew this would probably be a hot topic on the playground and even in the classroom. What would be said? How far would the explanations go? How much misinformation would Cora hear?

I realized I was going to have to explain to her about AIDS—and the ways people get the disease—much sooner than I had planned. She didn't need to know all this stuff at her young age, but I wanted her to hear it from the viewpoint of our family values. I felt sad for her, and the loss of a little more of her innocence. Life was much simpler and friendlier when I was her age.

How did she respond? About the same way she responded when I explained the facts of life to her: "Yuck!"

Media influence our values. They are not a neutral source of information or entertainment. Producers of shows have agendas and messages they wish to get across to their audiences. News broadcasters make decisions about which stories will air and from whose perspective. Psychologist Dr. James Dobson, in one of his newsletters, expressed his disappointment about how the media completely ignored a pro-life rally in Washington, D.C., after thoroughly covering the pro-choice rally the month before: "It is clear that the media are not only biased in their presentation of the news, but that they have a specific agenda to promote."[4]

And what bias are the media presenting? Who are these people who are shaping our view of the world? Lichter, Rothman, and Lichter interviewed 238 influential American journalists. Their results showed that 86 percent reported that they attended church either seldom or never, and they came largely from highly educated, upper-class families. They also found that a high percentage of the journalists were from large cities, having little experience with small-town America.

"This group of journalists viewed themselves as being liberal in their viewpoints. Fifty-four percent reported that they were left of center, while only 17 percent claimed to be right of center. Only 15 percent felt that extramarital affairs were immoral. There appears to be a wide disparity, particularly in values, between media leaders and the general public."[5]

Then, of course, there are the advertisers, whose job it is to shape our values. There is a classic example from my (Rick's) childhood of television creating a market for merchandise. During the 1954–55 television season, Disney aired a three-part saga on Davy Crockett. Each of the programs aired about a month apart. This series sparked a craze among the children of our nation. In the seven months following the shows, over $100 million worth of Crockett items were sold.[6] I remember that my brother Rod and I both had to have our coonskin caps, and no one could separate us from them.

Friends

The influence of friends on our value development is most intense during the socialization stage. At this stage we compare what we have learned in our families with what others do and think, and see how our values hold up. Will we hang onto them or give them up for other values that make more sense to us? During the teen years, friends and peers often have more influence on us than our parents do.

Some people even believe that, other than genetic contributions, a parent has little or no influence on how a child turns out. The cover story of the September 7, 1998 issue of *Newsweek* reports on a new book by Judith Rich Harris entitled *The Nurture Assumption: Why Children Turn Out the Way They Do; Parents Matter Less Than You Think and Peers Matter More.* While this is considered to be a radical concept and has created quite a stir in the scientific psychological community, the fact that she can find enough studies to support her claims in a book shows that peer influence is a significant factor.

All we have to do is look at the clothing and hairstyles of teenagers and compare them to how their parents look to see who is having more influence on those kids. This is a time when teens are striving to establish their independence from their parents—to create a separate identity. This usually takes the form of identifying with their peer group and becoming more like them, internally as well as externally.

Dina and Jim, some friends of ours, stopped by the other night, and we got to talking about this concept of friends influencing our value development. Dina shared a story with us that clearly illustrates this point:

> I came from a family of five kids. Whether it was just to keep peace in the house or the result of a firm belief that children should be seen and not heard, my parents discouraged the expression of negative emotions, especially crying. If I was crying out of frustration with one of my siblings or from disappointment over a broken promise, I was told, "That is enough. Stop crying or you'll have to go to your room." Continuing to cry could occasionally bring about a spanking.
>
> Even as I got older, sensitivity and being moved to tears were not appreciated. This didn't seem to be a problem for my brothers and sisters, but I had a more sensitive and emotional temperament. If we were watching a movie on TV and there was a touching scene, everyone in my family would turn and look at me. I would try my best not to react, but often my eyes would fill up with tears, and someone would tease, "Look, Dina's going to cry." As a child I never saw my mother cry. The first time I did was as a young adult, and it was quite shocking for me.
>
> When I was in high school, I developed a friendship with two girls who taught me the value of expressing my

emotions. Maybe it was because we were a product of the '60s, which made us more analytical and sensitive about our feelings. I remember sitting in one of their bedrooms listening to the Carol King record, "You've Got a Friend."

"Why are you so quiet, Dina?" they asked.

I was struggling with something I was going through at home, and I sensed that I could communicate with these friends on a deeper emotional level than I could with my family. I poured out my heart to them, along with my tears, and found acceptance and emotional freedom. It was wonderful!

As our friendship grew over the years, we cried together over our heartaches, our joys, touching movies, and poetry. These girls had a freedom to express their tenderness, troubles, and hurt feelings in ways that I had not felt comfortable doing in my own home. Through these friends, I learned to appreciate, value, and express those qualities in my own life, and thankfully, so has the rest of my family more and more over the years.

As Dina was evaluating the values she experienced in her family, she compared them to those of her friends and found that her friends' value of free expression of emotion made more sense to her and better met her needs. She chose to internalize their value over the value of controlled emotions she had been taught as a child.

Income

Our family's income can have a significant impact on our value development as we are growing up. There is a truism that says, "What you grew up without, you will strive for, and what you grew up with, you will take for granted."

Rita, a friend and coworker, told us about her grandparents and great-aunts and great-uncles. "They lived through World

War II in Europe, which had an impact similar to the Great Depression here in the United States. It made them very thankful for what they had and very cautious about spending their money. They would only buy necessities and never spend money for their own pleasure. They saved cash for their old age in socks. However, for them, old age never came. They all died in their 90s, still saving for their old age!"

While income has a large influence on what our family has as far as possessions (type of house, number of cars, latest technology, type of vacations, etc.), a more significant issue is our family's attitude toward money. There are wealthy families who view their wealth as a sign of superiority and use their money as a form of power over others. There are other wealthy families who view their riches as a privileged responsibility and use their money to benefit others. Conversely, poor families can be so controlled by their desire for money that they would compromise other values, such as honesty, to get more. Other lower-income families would understand the value and potential of having more money and be motivated to work hard to increase their earning potential. Money values are taught—and more often, caught—by the children in families as they are growing up. The issue of money is not how much you have, but how you value it.

Geographic Location

If you have ever moved to a different part of the country, you know that geography influences values. When our family moved from Southern California to Georgia, one of the first differences we noticed was the way children talk to adults. If you ask a child, or even a teenager, a question, the answer will end in "ma'am" or "sir." This is unheard of in Southern California. If you did hear it from a teenager, it would probably be in a mocking tone.

Years ago, when I (Rick) was the head lifeguard at a conference center, I encountered another regionally influenced value difference. A group from Texas was coming through Southern California and was staying at the conference center. The leader of the group came to me and asked if we allowed "mixed bathing" in the pool.

"Oh, no, sir," I replied. (I just sensed that this man would want to be called "sir.") "We don't allow any bathing at all in our pool, only swimming." I had never heard of coed swimming referred to as "mixed bathing," and growing up on the Southern California beaches, I had never met someone who objected to it. The man explained that they didn't allow their men and women to swim in the pool at the same time and wanted to arrange separate times for them to swim. (I hoped that mixed lifesaving was allowed, since I was the only lifeguard available that weekend.)

If you drive around this big country of ours, you will find quite a variety of accents that are all "American." There are more differences between the people of the various regions of our country than just the way we each talk. Each group has unique values that affect those who are raised in that area and that may seem strange to those who aren't.

A Key Time for Key Factors

These are some of the key factors that affect our value development, but there are many others that can come into play, depending on our particular circumstances as we grow up. While some factors are more significant than others, perhaps the most significant element in value development is age. Many psychologists and sociologists would agree that the most influential period of our value-development process is around age 10. What happened to you and what was going on in society when you were 10 years old has shaped your values probably more than you realize. These factors that we've just looked at have the most impact on us when we're in this impressionable age. What we experienced in our families, at school, with our friends, through the media, and in every aspect of our lives at about age 10 had a greater influence on us than those same factors had at any other time in our lives.

This principle is the topic of our next chapter and the key to understanding why different generations develop values that clash with each other.

Chapter 4

The Wonder Years

As we flew across the country last summer, browsing through Delta's in-flight magazine, a one-page story about Chuck Norris caught our eye. Most of the article described his involvement in a real drug bust in Texas. (He actually is a legalized police officer, similar to his television role on the show *Walker, Texas Ranger.*) The paragraph that captured our interest quoted Norris saying that as a boy he "watched every western movie since time began. Those were my heroes growing up— James Stewart and John Wayne—men that I looked up to and idolized as a child."[1] What a great example of how the heroes we have during our modeling stage of value development (ages 7-13) can affect choices we make about our own lives.

Sometimes we tend to overlook this stage of development in a child's life. Kids this age aren't as dependent as younger children, so they don't need us to be quite as involved in all they do. But it's important for us to realize that this stage is crucial. Developmental psychologists acknowledge that children in this age range reach a pivotal point in their development.

Erik Erikson, in his study of psychosocial development (the changing ways we perceive ourselves individually and in relation to society), calls this stage *industry versus inferiority*. It's a time of mastering skills in all areas of life leading, hopefully, to a sense of competence that will be a basis for developing a strong sense of identity in future years.

Jean Piaget's theory of cognitive development places this age group in a stage called *concrete operational.* During this stage, children begin to develop clearer, more logical methods of thinking, and they become less egocentric, more aware of perspectives other than their own.

Lawrence Kohlberg's work on the development of moral reasoning states that starting at about age 10, children enter the *conventional* stage. This is when they base their moral judgments on the conventions of society and have a desire to conform. Something is considered to be "right" if it's something most people would agree with.[2]

This is also the key time when basic beliefs start to solidify. Although values can continue to develop through age 20, we will be using the concept of "about age 10" to refer to this very important time in the value-development process. What someone experiences at about age 10 will tend to influence who she is and what choices she makes for the rest of her life. Morris Massey describes what is going on during this significant phase: "The child shifts into intense modeling—relating to family, friends, and external 'heroes' in the world around him. People the child would 'like to be like' are carefully observed. Identification, or modeling, is one of the important factors in establishing our personality, standards, and goals."[3]

> *What someone experiences at about age 10 will tend to influence who she is and what choices she makes for the rest of her life.*

Another psychologist, Robert Goldenson, also agrees with the importance of this stage of identification and modeling:

> Identification is probably the most important factor in shaping the personality and establishing standards and goals. The process begins with the child's admiration for his parents. As the child develops, he gradually becomes

selective and adopts parental characteristics which seem most congenial to him. Soon group membership begins to exert its influence, and the child identifies not only with the play group or gang as a whole, but with certain individuals within it. New values and new goals must then be integrated with the ones he has absorbed from his family.

During the school years, the growing child also identifies in fantasy with the heroes of history, as well as characters in films, stories, and television. He gains vicarious satisfaction from associating himself with these heroes, and uses them as models in constructing his "ego ideal," the self he would like to become.[4]

At this age, kids move from simply accepting and absorbing the attitudes and behaviors of their families to becoming more selective. They hold on to what seems appropriate, but they are also checking out new ideas, attitudes, and values as they are exposed to them through school, media, community groups, and other influences. They are choosing the values and behavior patterns that appeal to them, and they are creating an internal idea of the kind of person they want to be.

Often kids this age choose a person or hero they want to grow up to be like. When President Dwight Eisenhower was a boy growing up on a small farm, he loved reading about history so much that his mother locked his history books in a closet. Ike used a wire to unlock the closet and retrieve them. He especially enjoyed reading about the Carthaginian general Hannibal, and he memorized Hannibal's battle moves. Eisenhower later became a general himself in the United States Army, acting as allied commander in chief in World War II. Three years after the war was over, he was elected president of the United States, significantly due to his successes in the battlefield strategy.

Events or circumstances can also make such an impression

during this stage that they help to shape future choices. When Joe Namath was a boy growing up in Pennsylvania, his father was a steelworker. One day his father took him to visit the steel mill. After experiencing the heat of the furnace and the ear-splitting racket of the machinery, Joe decided he would never work in a steel mill. He lived for sports, and his idol was Johnny Unitas, one of the greatest quarterbacks of all time (also from Pennsylvania). Joe wore Johnny's number, 19, his senior year in high school and led his team to an undefeated season. Joe went on to become, in the estimation of many, as great a quarterback as Johnny Unitas had been.

Sometimes a developing child's values and goals are more focused on a dream than a specific hero. Neil Armstrong, the first man to walk on the moon in 1969, as a boy actually had recurring dreams of being able to hover over the ground if he held his breath. He took his first plane ride when he was six years old, and he was hooked. He started taking flying lessons when he was 14, which he paid for himself by working at a pharmacy and a hardware store. He earned his pilot's license on his 16th birthday, before he even learned to drive a car. By age 21, he was a Panther jet pilot in the Korean War. Then, just before his 39th birthday, he flew to the moon and took that famous "one small step for man, one giant leap for mankind."[5]

Pete Maravich was another focused young man. Through his father, Press Maravich, the head coach at Clemson University in South Carolina, little Pete learned to love the game of basketball. As a young kid, he was inseparable from his basketball. He took it everywhere he went. At the movies, he would sit on the aisle so he could practice dribbling. He dribbled when riding his bike and even from moving

Because each decade is unique, those who grow up in a particular decade develop values that are different from those who grow up during other decades.

cars. His constant practice paid off in a fantastic basketball career, and in 1970 he broke the record and became college basketball's all-time leading scorer.[6]

The Decade Dilemma: Why We Are Different

Many of the influences we experience at this stage are major events that are happening to everyone in our society. These are wars, historical and political events, the financial climate, and the popular heroes. What we experience through the media in the form of news, popular songs, TV programs, and movies are all significant influences. While people of all ages are experiencing these things together, those who are in this value-forming stage are most significantly shaped by their influence. The adults have already established their values in previous decades and are filtering these elements through their existing value systems.

Because each decade is unique, those who grow up in a particular decade develop values that are different from those who grow up during other decades. Those who grew up in the '30s have very different values from those who were raised in the '60s, but they have similar values to those who were children in the same decade as they were. Because of this, we can look at each decade, see what unique events and circumstances were experienced by the 10-year-olds then, and determine how those defining experiences affected their values.

YOUR DECADE OF DESTINY

Chapter 5

"Some Limitations May Apply..."

In 1914 a nurse named Margaret Sanger wanted to do something about the plight of mothers who were overwhelmed by the demands of their families. She believed that birth control was an answer, but contraception was considered to be obscene. Her dream was to remove the stigma from contraception and set up a nationwide network of advice centers on birth control for women. One of the biggest obstacles she had to overcome was legislation, both federal and state, that prohibited the publication and distribution of information about sex, sexuality, contraception, and human reproduction. Contraceptives were also illegal, even for married couples, in most states. Throughout the '20s and the '30s, she fought for the reversal of the Comstock Laws. In 1937 it became legal to mail contraception information. At this time, birth control became a legitimate medical service to be taught in medical schools.

Now in the '90s, not only is it permissible for married couples to learn about and use contraception, but public high schools require health classes that teach about human sexuality and birth control. School districts have the option of distributing free condoms to students who are sexually active. When a concerned parent group in Philadelphia questioned the legality of these programs, the United States Court of Appeals for the Third Circuit upheld the program in the Philadelphia city schools, allowing schools to dispense condoms to students without parental consent.[1]

What a change in our country's values from 1920 to 1990! This dramatically demonstrates how values do change in our society over the course of time. In the 1920s, the values of most Americans closely mirrored Judeo-Christian ethics. The standards of acceptable conduct lined up with the teachings found in the Bible. Life looked pretty much the way we saw it portrayed on the TV show *The Waltons*. People worked hard; were honest, loyal, and trustworthy; valued family; and took care of their neighbors (or even strangers). Their faith in God and each other got them through the difficulties in their lives.

While many people today still hold the same ideals, I think it's safe to say that many common values today are radically different from those held in the '20s. But it didn't happen overnight. It's been a process, decade by decade, and that's what this next section of this book is about. In the next eight chapters we'll be looking at the events in each decade from 1920 through 1990 that helped to shape the values of those growing up during that time.

Our Disclaimers

Warning: The values we'll be talking about are primarily typical, white, male, middle-class values. As we address major trends that affected American society as a whole, we realize (so you don't need to write us) that we're making gross generalizations. As we've already mentioned, factors such as ethnic identity and gender influence our values and our interpretation of the significance of events. But space doesn't permit us to go into all the variations in values developed by different segments of society. So, to illustrate the principles of value development, we'll focus on the values of most of the people in the United States at a given point in time.

We also realize that we'll be leaving out factors in each decade that had significant ramifications for specific segments of American society but may have had a relatively small impact on the majority. For instance, although the Korean War had a tremendous effect on those who served and those who lost loved ones, its influence on American society as a whole was much less significant than the effects of World War I and World War II or the Vietnam War.

Mean Values and the Bell Curve

Remember when you were in school, and you were happy to know that your teacher would "grade on the curve"? She was referring to the bell curve. It meant that what was an A or a B or a C depended on how everyone else did on the test. C grades were determined by the mean score (the score most people got) and the other grades were determined by how the rest of the scores lined up on either side of this middle point. It created a bell-shaped graph like the one below. The benefit of this system was if everyone did poorly, those who did better than the rest still earned As and Bs, even if they did not score high on the test.

We want to use our old friend, the bell curve[2], to illustrate how the values of society tend to be the same for a majority, but there are always those who deviate in one way or another from the "norm" (see illustration below).

Normal Values of Society

Values Deviating from the Norm

Values Deviating from the Norm

We'll be talking about mean values, which are the values held by the most people during each time period. As we describe the values of the decade you grew up in, you might find that instead of having the values of the "norm," your values deviate one way or the other because of your personal circumstances. If you were raised in a conservative religious community or a liberal political environment, your values might fall on one side or the other of the "norm" section of the bell curve.

There could be many reasons why someone's values would fall outside the average range of society's values. (And remember, just because they are the most widely held values does not mean they are the best values.) As you look at the decade in which you were 10 years old, see if your values are typical or not; if not, see if you can identify what was unique about your environment that made a difference.

As we look at each decade, we'll see what historical, social, or cultural events took place that had an impact on the values being developed during that period. Any one event wouldn't have had that much effect, but when you put all the events of the decade together, you'll see the unique imprint each decade has on society.

In each decade chapter, we'll present a fictional story of a person or people who lived during that decade, giving us a snapshot of what events took place during that time. We'll also give a summary of important trends and events and comment on how they may have affected developing values. At the end of each chapter, you'll find a chart that helps to show the unique character of each decade, serves as a means of comparing one decade with another, and identifies how values have changed as the decades have progressed.

Are you ready for an educational stroll down memory lane? Are you prepared to learn about the events and factors that helped to shape those you have trouble understanding? We are about to show you the "Decade Dilemma," the reason we have differences that tend to divide us. Come along with us as we take you on a tour through the decades, beginning in 1920 and progressing through the 1990s.

Chapter 6

The '20s "Happy Days Are Here Again"

Charlie and his cronies at the rest home enjoy sitting around the recreation hall reminiscing about the "good old days." While they often have trouble remembering what happened yesterday, scenes from their childhood and youth in the '20s still seem vivid. This being Charlie's 88th birthday, he is feeling particularly sentimental. His granddaughter brought him a birthday cake, and the great-grandkids seem inclined to listen to his stories, so he embarks on a trip down memory lane.

"Bein' born in 1912 on my family's farm, I was just a little tyke when World War I was happenin'. But there are some things I do remember, like those somber announcements at the end of the Sunday mornin' services when Pastor Jenkins would announce that some family in our congregation had been notified about the death of a loved one in the war. There would be a kinda sad pride that someone we knew had made the ultimate sacrifice for the sake of makin' the world safe for democracy. Mama would always bake one of her special cakes an' take it to the grievin' family.

"One of the happiest days in our little town was the day we had the big parade down Main Street welcomin' home our soldiers at the end of the war. Flags were wavin', people were cheerin', and our hometown heroes marched in their uniforms singin', 'We won't come back till it's over over there.' We were so glad that the 'war to end all wars' was over an' life could get back to normal.

"But life didn't go back to normal. During the war my daddy had purchased some fancy new farm equipment on credit. He was thinkin' that crop prices would stay high, he could produce more crops, an' he'd be able to pay off the loan. But after the war the prices dropped so low that we fell on hard times an' we lost the farm. Like many folks in our community, we had to move to the city where my daddy could find work in one of the factories. At first we hated movin' off the farm, especially Mama. She missed bein' near her kin, cookin' for the church potlucks, an' bein' a part of the quiltin' bees. But eventually we joined a new church in the city an' got used to our new life.

"Even though our city house was smaller, it had electricity an' hot an' cold runnin' water. We didn't miss the old outhouse one bit now that we had indoor plumbin'. With electricity came all sorts of good things. With Daddy workin' hard at the factory six days a week, he soon made foreman, an' we were able to afford a new electric refrigerator an' vacuum cleaner.

"Those were Mama's favorite gadgets, but mine was the radio music box. At first Mama didn't want one in the house. Some people at the church said it was the work of the devil. Others thought radio waves could make you sick or start a fire in your house during a thunderstorm. But Daddy got his way, an' soon we were enjoyin' Will Rogers's witty comments on politics an' current events an' hearin' play-by-play accounts of baseball games an' boxin' matches. Mama's favorite was *The Fred Waring Show* because she liked the music of his band, The Pennsylvanians, an' the guest musicians he'd have on the show. It always tickled us that we could be listenin' to somethin' happenin' thousands of miles away. Somehow, listenin' to the radio made the USA feel smaller, an' we felt closer to Americans in other parts of our great big country.

"Back then, baseball was my favorite pastime. I'd just as soon play as eat. If I wasn't playin' it on a vacant lot after school, I was listening to it on the radio, especially if Babe Ruth was in the game. Even though the Yankees weren't our home team, we couldn't help but get excited and root for the Babe to hit another home run! When he hit his record 59 home runs in 1921, we thought we'd never see that record broken. But lo and behold, he hit 60 home runs in 1927! That record didn't get broken for another 34 years.

"Of course when I wasn't playin' baseball, I was goin' to school. More kids than ever were goin' to public school in those days. Before that, us kids were needed to work on the farms or in factories, an' schoolin' was considered more of a privilege for those who were better off. But with new machinery doin' more of the work, we weren't needed as much for workin', an' schoolin' was now considered one of our basic rights. When we lived on the farm, I'd just as soon stay home and work with my daddy and grandpa. But they told me if I worked hard an' studied well, I could better myself, an' even have a better life than my folks. They told us that at school, too. It was the American Dream—believin' that with enough hard work anyone could achieve the good life.

"We were taught to love an' honor our country an' to be wary of foreigners, especially communists. For a while after the war, everyone was afraid of communists, an' many people were unjustly accused. Many lost their jobs or were looked at suspiciously, but after a while people realized that communists were not taking over our country after all, an' this 'Red Scare' tapered off. There were also problems with the Ku Klux Klan in those days. They were out to harass blacks, Jews, Catholics, and foreigners. White, Protestant Americans as a whole were not very tolerant of people who were different from us.

"One day I'll never forget was when my daddy came home with our shiny, new, black Model T Ford! Mama wanted to know how Daddy paid for it, an' he said that Mr. Ford was lettin' people buy his cars on credit. I figured that was why half the cars in town were Fords. Well, it was my job to turn the crank to start the car, but Mama was always tellin' me to be careful. We heard stories of people who had sprained their wrists or even broken their arms from the kickback of the crank, so I was always ready to jump back if I needed to. We loved that old Tin Lizzy, even though she wouldn't start in the cold an' always rattled. We even had to back up some of the steep hills near our house, 'cause she had more power goin' backward than she did goin' forward. But one thing she *did* do was go 40 miles per hour on the straightaways, an' in those days that was a big thrill. There was even a rumor goin' around that if you traveled faster than that, it could do internal damage to your body. One of our favorite things to do after Sunday dinner was go for our Sunday afternoon drive. Sometimes we'd go out to our old farmin' community an' visit with our cousins. I always liked braggin' 'bout all the modern conveniences we had in the city. They *still* didn't have electricity or runnin' water.

"Of course, not everythin' about city life was good. There were changes goin' on in society that caused my parents much concern, mainly because of my older sister, Mildred. Millie, as she started calling herself, was completely enthralled with modern thinkin' an' new styles. I thought my mama was gonna faint when she came home with her hair bobbed in the latest fashion, wearin' lipstick an' rouge. She refused to wear the traditional long dresses with the high collars, an' started wearing the flapper dresses, which exposed her neck an' several inches of her legs! Mama and Daddy protested, but there didn't seem to be any way to control her. She had gotten a part-time job at a local department store, so she had her own dough to spend on the new fashions. If I said anythin' to her about the way she was acting, she called me a drip, said it was none of my beeswax, and told me to beat it.

"Some of the fads that Millie enjoyed seemed pretty harmless, like doin' crossword puzzles and playing the ancient Chinese game called mah-jongg. Even Mama got caught up in that new craze, playin' the game, which was made up of dominoes and dice, with her friends. It was also one of the things we all enjoyed doin' as a family. Of course, we enjoyed goin' to the movies together, too, even though they didn't have sound until 1927. My favorites were the westerns, but I also liked the comedies with Charlie Chaplin an' Buster Keaton.

"When the fellas started comin' around, it made Mama nervous. Instead of courtin' in the parlor, as she an' Daddy had done, Millie was goin' out in automobiles, which meant they were alone an' unchaperoned. This gave couples more freedom for neckin', which was gettin' very popular. Mama felt better when she knew they were goin' to one of the new dance halls, but only slightly. She thought the new dances like the fox-trot, the shimmy, an' the Charleston were indecent, but at least the dance halls were chaperoned. She just prayed that they weren't goin' to one of the 'blind pigs,' or speakeasies, in town, where illegal alcohol was served.

"They were called blind pigs because they were drinkin' establishments that were hidden behind false storefronts or businesses, since this was durin' the time of Prohibition. In January of 1920, the National Prohibition Act went into force, makin' it illegal to make, move, or sell beverages containin' one-half percent or more of alcohol. Instead of stoppin' the drinkin', it glamorized it an' created an underground racket. In front of these blind pigs would be lookouts that would let patrons in an' would weed out unsuspectin' people who wanted to do legitimate business at the dry cleaners, tobacco shop, or whatever else the cover might be. Before customers were let into the back, there was often a slidin' peephole where they had to give a secret password or show a membership card to get in. Once inside, they were told to "speak easy" so the noise wouldn't tip off the neighborin' businesses to what was really goin' on.

"Not only was alcohol bein' sold illegally, thousands of people were makin' it themselves. Why, you could actually go to stores an' buy stills an' everythin' else you needed to make moonshine, or bootleg gin, as it was called. I read that between 1921 and 1925 the government seized over 696,000 stills. In one area of Chicago they estimated that there was an average of 100 stills per city block! Although 500,000 arrests were made in the '20s, it didn't stop the illegal trade. Chicago Police Chief Charles Fitzmorris admitted at one point that 60 percent of his police force were in the bootleg business.[1] I guess it didn't matter if you did somethin' illegal, as long as you didn't get caught.

"Like most other things, Millie an' I were different in the kinds of people we admired. She was carried away by modern thinkers who thought that Freud's theories about sexual repression an' psychoanalysis were the cat's meow. She loved talkin' about the new scientific theories, like evolution. I, myself, was more impressed by Babe Ruth's home run record an' Charles "Lindy" Lindbergh's successful nonstop flight from New York to Paris.

"When I look back on my childhood, I think of patriotism an' faith as the American way of life. I think of Mama's homemade apple pie, her strong faith in God, an' her commitment to the teachin's of the Bible. I also remember the heartbreak of my parents when Millie started actin' like a flapper. Knowin' that she was goin' out smokin' an' drinkin' an' talkin' about things that proper young ladies wouldn't discuss was really hard on Mama an' my daddy. Home an' family were the most important things in our lives, an' her rebellious ways were very upsettin' to our traditional home.

"Of course, there was the excitement of all the new contraptions that made life easier, better, an' more modern. Between our Model T Ford, the radio, an' the movies, we were able to experience more than any other generation before us. It seemed like the good life that everybody was strivin' for was finally in reach. But then, when I was 19, the Great Depression hit, an' the good life was suddenly gone. Everything was a big mess, then—but that's a story for another day. I don't know about you, but I'd like another piece of that birthday cake."

A Closer Look

Charlie's crucial value-development stage—modeling—happened during the '20s, which was a very interesting time for a young kid. Let's look at some facts to better understand what happened during this time and then see what values he might have developed growing up in this decade.

■ ■ ■

During the '20s, the rural population decreased as the urban population increased, largely due to the financial difficulties of farmers. In 1920, for the first time, the census found the rural population to be smaller than the urban population. By 1930 the population was 56 percent urban and 44 percent rural.[2]

■ ■ ■

School attendance rose significantly during this time. In 1918, 25 percent of high-school-age kids attended school. In 1930, over 50 percent of high-school-age children attended school.[3]

■ ■ ■

Women voted in a presidential election for the first time in 1920.

■ ■ ■

From 1920 to 1929, manufacturing output rose by 64 percent due to factories becoming more efficient.
- Fifteen million automobiles were sold.
- Seven million radio sets were sold.
- Over three million new homes and apartments were built.
- Nearly nine million homes were wired for electricity.
- Six million telephones were installed in American private homes and offices.[4]

■ ■ ■

In the '20s, life expectancy rose from age 55 to 60. Some factors that contributed to this were public health programs—which helped to inoculate people—increased medical care, and refrigerated railroad cars, and home refrigerators, which allowed people all over the United States to have fresh fruits and vegetables year-round.[5]

■ ■ ■

In 1922, the first "radio music boxes" were sold at a cost
of $50 to $100 each. The first-year sales amounted to
$11 million. Sales doubled the second year and doubled
again the third year.[6]

■ ■ ■

In the 1920s, money spent on leisure activities such as
movies, dances, and sports rose by 300 percent.[7]

■ ■ ■

In the mid-1920s, movies attracted weekly audiences of
50 million; by 1930 that figured doubled, and even
more people went more often.[8]

■ ■ ■

The first feature-length "talkie" movie, *The Jazz Singer,*
starring Al Jolson, was released in 1927.

■ ■ ■

In the 1920s, the church faced competition in several
forms: psychoanalysis, science, and nagging questions
about war in relation to God's sovereignty. Sunday drives in
family cars also competed with church attendance. Atheism
grew, as well as the popularity of anti-Christian ideas like
nudist colonies, yoga, Ouija boards, and self-help philosophies. In spite of these trends, more than a quarter of the
American people believed in a literal interpretation of the
Bible. The term *fundamentalist* was coined in the 1920s.
Revival preachers like Aimee Semple McPherson and Billy
Sunday were popular during this time.

One of the major issues facing the church in this
decade was evolution. Fundamentalists worked hard getting state legislatures to pass laws making the teaching of
evolution a crime. In 1925 in Tennessee, the trial of high
school biology teacher John Scopes was a nationally
broadcast event. The whole nation listened in as the battle
between traditional beliefs and new scientific theory
raged. Although Scopes was found guilty of teaching

evolution, which was a crime at the time, the bigger impact on the national audience was the ridicule that William Jennings Bryan, who defended the traditionalists' belief in "everything in the Bible," suffered at the hands of Clarence Darrow, Scopes's defender. Darrow said that his purpose was to prevent "bigots and ignoramuses from controlling the education of the United States." In a time when scientifically derived truth was revered, the traditionalists began to look very old-fashioned.[9]

■ ■ ■

Automobile ownership increased.
- In 1920, one in 13 people owned an automobile.[10] In 1929, there was one car for every six Americans.[11]
- In 1920, 1.9 million cars were produced. In 1929, 4.8 million cars were produced.[12]
- In 1923, one out of every two cars sold was a Ford.
- Mr. Ford helped Americans buy cars by paying his workers a huge wage ($5 per day) and allowing his cars to be purchased on credit.
- In 1924, a new Ford cost $290.[13]

■ ■ ■

Prohibition, which began in 1920, glamorized alcohol use and increased its abuse in some areas. By 1927 in Chicago, arrests for drunk driving had risen 476 percent, and deaths from alcoholism had risen 600 percent.[14]

■ ■ ■

According to a national poll taken in 1926 to determine the nation's attitude toward Prohibition:
- 49.8 percent believed the law should be modified.
- 31.3 percent believed the law should be repealed.
- 18.9 percent were satisfied with the law.[15]

Kids like Charlie who grew up in the aftermath of World War I were raised on patriotism and were loyal to the American way of life. In spite of a short dip in the economy right after the war, most were experiencing some level of prosperity by the end of the decade. This confirmed to them that hard work leads to rewards. They watched their hardworking parents reap their benefits as they were able to bring home new automobiles and appliances. They were encouraged to go to school and to educate themselves, with the belief that they could grow up to be better off than their parents. They were getting close to achieving the good life, as there was more money for leisure and entertainment, like movies and radios—until the Depression hit.

Families and traditional values were still very important to the majority of the people, in spite of the rebellious faction of young people who became flappers and those who ignored Prohibition laws. Those kids who were aware of the thriving illegal alcohol businesses under Prohibition received a message that said, "It's okay to do something illegal, just don't get caught." (Incidentally, Richard Nixon turned 10 years old in 1923.) But for the most part, the values passed on to this group of kids were very much like those passed on to their parents—very traditional. At this point, the family was still the most influential source of values.

A Portrait of the '20s

Demographics in 1920
Population: 106,491,000
Farmers: 30%
Life expectancy:
Men: 53.6 years
Women: 54.6 years

Money Matters in 1920
GNP: $91.5 billion
Federal budget: $6.4 billion
National debt: $23.7 billion
Prime interest rate: 5.4%
Average annual salary: $1,236

Cost of Living in 1920
Eggs: 68¢ (doz.)
Milk: 17¢ (qt.)
Bread: 12¢ (loaf)
Coffee: 47¢ (lb.)
Round steak: 42¢ (lb.)

Key Events

1920　First presidential election in which women nationwide were allowed to vote; Harding elected

1920　Prohibition begins; Babe Ruth joins the Yankees

1921　Tomb of the Unknown Soldier is established

1922　Rebecca Felton of Georgia is the first woman to serve in the Senate

1923　President Harding dies in office; Vice President Calvin Coolidge becomes president; Ku Klux Klan is strong

1924　President Coolidge reelected

1925　John Scopes convicted of illegally teaching the theory of evolution in Tennessee

1926　Henry Ford introduces the shorter 40-hour workweek

1927　Charles Lindbergh makes first solo nonstop transatlantic flight

1927　Babe Ruth hits 60 home runs, setting new world record

1928　Amelia Earhart becomes the first woman to fly across the Atlantic

1928　Herbert Hoover elected president

1929　Stock market crash leading to the Great Depression the following year; Admiral Byrd flies over South Pole

Fads/Trends

Mah-jongg—a popular Chinese game

Flappers

Flagpole sitting

Dance halls

Dance marathons

Dances: the Charleston and the shimmy

Crossword puzzles

Speakeasies and blind pigs (for illegal drinking)

Freudianism and psychoanalysis

New Inventions/Technology

Vitamins E and D discovered
Whooping cough (pertussis) vaccine developed
The electric shaver patented
All-electric phonograph developed
Telephones become widely available
Transatlantic phone service
Radios (in more than half of homes by late '20s)
Movies with sound by end of decade
Increase in electricity and running water in homes
    (especially in urban areas)
The birth control movement begins

Radio

1921	First church broadcast; band concert; farm news
1922	First presidential broadcast; World Series; commercials
1923	*Eveready Hour* (variety); *Happiness Boys* (comedy)
1924	Radio sales jump from $60 million to $350 million
1925	Broadcast of John Scopes evolution trial
1926	Betty Crocker recipes; *Allen's Alley*
1927	First national broadcast—Rose Bowl game
1928	*Real Folks; Main Street* (first drama); *Chase & Sanborn*
1929	*The Back Home Hour; Amos 'n' Andy*

Hit Songs

1920	"Avalon"; "When My Baby Smiles at Me"
1921	"Secondhand Rose"; "Ma, He's Making Eyes at Me"
1923	"Yes, We Have No Bananas"; "Who's Sorry Now?"
1924	"Somebody Loves Me"; "California, Here I Come"
1925	"If You Knew Suzy"; "Sweet Georgia Brown"
1926	"Bye Bye Blackbird"; "Baby Face"; "One Alone"
1927	"Ol' Man River"; "Me and My Shadow"; "Bill"
1928	"You're the Cream in My Coffee"; "Crazy Rhythm"
1929	"Happy Days Are Here Again"; "Singin' in the Rain"

Publications

1920	*Age of Innocence*
1921	*Reader's Digest* begins publishing
1922	*Tales of the Jazz Age; Babbitt; To the Last Man*
1923	*Etiquette* from Emily Post
1923	*Time* magazine begins publishing
1925	*Yorker* magazine begins
1925	*The Great Gatsby; In Our Time; Arrowsmith*
1926	*The Sun Also Rises; Torrents of Spring; Early Autumn*
1927	*Elmer Gantry; The Bridge of San Luis Rey*
1928	*The Bishop's Wife; Swan Song*
1929	*A Farewell to Arms; All Quiet on the Western Front*

Movies

Movie attendance = 33 million weekly

1920	*Dr. Jekyll & Mr. Hyde; Pollyanna; Mark of Zorro*
1921	*The Kid; The Sheik; Little Lord Fauntleroy*
1922	*Robin Hood; Sherlock Holmes; Oliver Twist*
1923	*The Hunchback of Notre Dame; The Ten Commandments*
1924	*The Thief of Bagdad; Beau Brummel; Babbitt*
1925	*The Phantom of the Opera; The Gold Rush*
1926	*The Scarlet Letter; Don Juan; Son of the Sheik*
1927	*The Jazz Singer* (first "talkie"); *King of Kings*
1928	*The Last Command; The Crowd; Street Angel*
1929	*The Taming of the Shrew; The Broadway Melody*

Fashion

Women:
Men's styles (blazers, shirts, ties, fitted suits)
Hair cropped short at the ears with waves
Curves of the body suppressed by cylindrical corsets
       to achieve hipless and bosomless silhouette
Felt cloche (helmet-shaped) hats, flapper dresses

Men:
Knickers, padded shoulders, narrow lapels
Oxford shoes replace high-buttoned style
Wristwatches replace pocket watches

Heroes

Babe Ruth	Charles Lindbergh
Amelia Earhart	Rudolph Valentino
Jack Dempsey	Richard Byrd
President Calvin Coolidge	

Chapter 7

The '30s "Brother, Can You Spare a Dime?"

What was so "great" about the Great Depression anyway? It was a catastrophic time for our country. Economic failure and natural disasters caused unemployment, homelessness, and hopelessness for millions of people. It definitely was not great, as in "being superior," but if we take the definition of *great* to be "remarkable in magnitude," the term certainly fits. This historical event was great in its scope, as it significantly impacted the lives of people at all levels of society (with the possible exception of those very rich who were too calloused to care about the plight of those less fortunate than themselves). It was great in the impact it had on our government, causing it to take on functions, duties, and responsibilities for American citizens that it had never taken on before. It was great in duration; to those who lived through it, it seemed endless. Promises that prosperity was "just around the corner," and that, in time, this financial fiasco would turn itself around through natural events eventually were proven quite false.

Perhaps the most accurate reason for calling the Depression "great" is the dramatic impact it had on the value development of those who lived through it—and the effects were not limited to those who were about age 10. This event became a significant emotional event (thus a value-changing occcurence) for all who experienced it, no matter what their ages. The Great Depression of the 1930s was probably the most significant value-influencing factor in American history. Among other things, it changed the

The Great Depression of the 1930s was probably the most significant value-influencing factor in American history. Those who lived through it still talk about it, while those who didn't experience it will never quite understand.

way people viewed money, security and government. Those who lived through it still talk about it, while those who didn't experience it will never quite understand.

I (Rick) didn't even know what the Great Depression was until I was in high school. I just thought it was a year that everyone got really depressed! While we can study the events and facts to learn about what happened during those influential years, we will never be influenced by the Depression the way those who experienced it were.

Take Robert, for example. Now about to turn 80, he experienced the Depression right as he was turning 10. Since his wife died, he has been living in an apartment at the back of his daughter's house. Today he is enjoying a visit from his cousin Dorothy, who has been spending time visiting various relatives around the country since her retirement from teaching school and the passing of her husband. Robert and Dorothy had been pretty close as kids, since their families lived together during the Depression. Dorothy, being a few years younger, had always looked up to Robert like an older brother.

"I bet it's nice for you to be here close to your kids and grandkids," Dorothy says as she looks around his apartment.

"There were times when being this close to the grandkids was noisier than I prefer, with their music and friends coming and going all the time. But now they're off at college most of the time, and it's more peaceful. Actually this suits me just fine, since it saves me money and allows me to live on my pension," he explains as he pours them each a glass of iced tea.

"If I remember correctly, you were always thrifty and good at saving. And you did well in business. I'll bet you have a sizable nest egg and don't need to worry about living on just your pension." Dorothy gives him a knowing smile as she helps herself to a sugar cookie from the plate on the coffee table in front of her.

"Well, I hate to use it, not knowing what the future will bring." He hands her a glass of tea. "Besides, the way my daughter and son-in-law spend, they may need some help if times get rough again—like in the '80s when they needed a loan because business was slow for a few years. It made me think about the old days. Thank God it didn't get anywhere near as bad! But you never know when it might happen again."

"Hopefully, it never will happen again," says Dorothy. "It was so unbelievably terrible. Like living in a nightmare. In all my years of teaching, I could never completely communicate to my students what it was like. And we lived on the farm through most of it. I know it was even worse for you when you were living in St. Louis. I was pretty young when you and Mary and your mom came to live with us on the farm. I never quite understood why your father left your family to fend for yourselves like he did."

"It was tough for me to understand too, especially at the time. We were so scared, so desperate. I was angry with him for so many years. But as I got older, had a family of my own, and felt the weight of responsibility, I gained a little more perspective. As I thought back over the circumstances of our life and started to see them through my father's eyes, I began to understand a little better, and a lot of the anger was replaced with sympathy. I still don't think I'd have left my family in the same circumstances, but they were desperate times. People did things they'd never imagine doing in order to survive. I think he probably knew we'd end up on the farm with you if he left us. It was probably the only way we could have survived."

"The details have always been foggy in my mind. Just what

did your family experience before you came to the farm?" asks Dorothy

Robert is thoughtful for a moment as he sips his tea. "When we moved to St. Louis, I was only two years old. My father went to work for an army buddy of his that he had kept in contact with since World War I ended. I think it was selling insurance, or something like that. I was too little to understand what it was. I just remember that when I was about 10, a few months after Wall Street crashed, my father's job crashed, too. He tried to get work other places, but no one was hiring. People were losing their jobs all around us. The lucky ones who kept their jobs usually got a cut in pay, and a lot of them got their hours cut, too. Everyone was panicked.

"I remember Father coming home very upset one day after he tried to get some of our savings out of the bank so he could pay the mortgage. The government had closed the banks. They called it a bank holiday, but it lasted for several days. So many people were trying to get their money that the banks couldn't come up with the cash. Some of the banks reopened, but the one my parents had their savings in didn't.

"With no savings and no job, things got pretty desperate around our house. We did everything we could to save money, like turning off the heat and eating very simple meals. We even had to go without electricity after a while. Father finally gave up trying to find a job and tried selling apples on the street. Some apple growers had donated much of their crop so people with no income could sell them and have a little money. They went for a nickel apiece, but the few who were buying couldn't support the hundreds who were trying to sell them. Mother took in ironing and sewing jobs. I shined shoes, ran errands, and did anything else I could to earn a few cents.

"But it wasn't enough. The bank that held the mortgage on our house foreclosed, and we were out on the street. We slept in the park with other homeless families, keeping warm by huddling together under newspapers we called 'Hoover blankets.'

People were pretty upset with President Hoover's lack of action to help the hungry and homeless. There were shantytowns, with houses made of anything people could find to protect themselves from the cold and rain. We called them 'Hoover towns.' "

"How did you feed yourselves, and what happened to all your belongings?" Dorothy is starting to realize how sheltered their life on the farm was in comparison to this.

"The bank sold all the furniture and anything else of value. We only had what we could wear and carry with us. Most of our clothes were already pretty worn, because we hadn't been able to buy anything new for a long time. I had a handful of toy soldiers and some marbles in my pocket, but that was all I owned. Mary had a doll that eventually became bald and eyeless, but she hung onto it with loving desperation. We spent most of our day standing in bread lines and waiting to get into soup kitchens run by the charities in town. My father never smiled anymore. Now I understand that he must have felt like such a failure, to allow his family to become destitute like that. He'd been so proud of our house and the nice things he was able to buy for us. Then it was like he could hardly bear to look at us. He spent a lot of his time talking with the other unemployed men, trying to figure out what to do and who to blame.

"Eventually the word started spreading that there was a bill before Congress proposing that a bonus promised to the veterans of World War I be paid to them early—to help with the desperate financial situation they were in. The bonus amounted to one dollar per day of military duty, which was invested in the mid-1920s and was intended to accumulate interest until 1945. With the interest, it would have amounted to about a thousand dollars for each veteran. But with the current crisis, people needed their money just to buy food and shelter, so support for the bill intensified. My father decided to go with the other men to show their support of the bill. No one we knew had a car or money for travel, so they hopped freight trains to get there. This was pretty risky. The conductors often beat the hobos when they got caught. But some of the conductors were veterans themselves, and word got around which trains were sympathetic to the cause. In June of 1932, 22,000 veterans from all over the country showed up in Washington, D.C., calling themselves the Bonus Army, singing war songs and carrying signs.

"They camped along the river and in abandoned government buildings. Their common war experience, and now common cause in lobbying for their bonuses, brought a sense of unity and optimism—especially when the bill passed in the House. But when it was defeated in the Senate, their hopes were defeated with it.

"Most left to return to the desperate situations they had left behind. But about 8,000, including my father, decided to stay as a protest and reminder to the government. This became quite an embarrassment for President Hoover, who set a deadline for all the veterans to leave the city. When they didn't leave, he resorted to force. One day, at the end of July 1932, General Douglas MacArthur and Major Dwight Eisenhower marched up Pennsylvania Avenue with infantry, cavalry, and tanks. They actually used force against their own veterans, routing them from the buildings and chasing them from their camps, which they burned. Rioting broke out and tear gas was used to bring the situation back under control.

"My father sent a letter describing all this to us. He gave it to one of the men who came back to our area to find his family. This man told us that my father had given up hope and become even more depressed and beaten than before. He wasn't coming back to us. He couldn't bear to face the situation and watch us suffer. Mother was numb to the news at first. I think she was in shock, or maybe it was what she had feared or expected. We weren't the only family around that had been deserted. At least Mary and I still had Mother. Some parents abandoned their children so orphanages would take them in. I would overhear Mother and some of the other deserted wives talk about this sometimes, and then I would lie awake at night wondering if

Mother would ever get desperate enough to do that. But she was a strong woman emotionally, even if she was frail and half starved physically.

"One day she called Mary and me together for a family council. 'Children,' she began, 'now that we know your father is not coming back, we need to do something to take care of ourselves. We know there is no work or place for us to live here. My sister, your Aunt Barbara, and her husband, Jim, live on a farm in Kansas, not too far past Kansas City. They didn't have a mortgage on their farm, so I'm pretty sure they'll still be there. They can grow most of their own food, so they're probably doing better than most. I know if we can get there, they'd be happy to have us. We can help out around the farm so we won't be too much of a burden to them.' "

"How could Aunt Margaret even think we'd consider you a burden?" exclaims Dorothy.

"Every mouth was a burden in our situation, no matter how well loved it was."

"Well, how did you ever make it from St. Louis to our farm?"

"Mother knew that the train ran along the Missouri River most of the way to Kansas City. She had been told that people camped in groups along the river and train tracks. Sometimes you could hop a train, and sometimes you could hitch a ride in a car. When we couldn't do either, we walked a lot. Most towns had bread lines and soup kitchens, and sometimes you could find scraps of food that had been discarded from grocery stores and restaurants. We ended up doing all those things along the way. People would help us out when they could. Sometimes we'd find people going the same way we were, and we'd travel together for a while. It was a pretty risky trip, but we had nothing to lose. There was nothing for us in St. Louis, and some hope in Kansas."

"I can still remember my mother's reaction when she saw you ragamuffins coming down our road to the farmhouse.

'Here come some more beggars,' she said from her rocking chair on the porch. 'I guess we can find a few scraps for those poor wretched souls. That woman is as skinny as a beanpole.' When your mother called out her name, and said 'It's me—Margaret,' my mother gasped, dropped her knitting, and ran to embrace you all. She'd been so worried about you. The last we heard, you were losing your house, and then not a word. We didn't know how to find you."

"And we couldn't afford even a stamp to send you a letter. I remember that day well. We were so relieved to find that you were still there on the farm and that you'd let us stay."

"Of course we let you stay. You were family, and even though we didn't have much ourselves, we wouldn't think of not taking you in. Actually, once we heard your horror stories, we felt well off in comparison. Besides, once we got you fed and healthy, you really helped out with the farm. You became the son my father never had."

"It was good for me to have a man in my life again, too. But my days as a farmer didn't last long, as you remember."

"That's right. At first we were able to hang on, in spite of the fact that prices were so low that we couldn't afford to take the crops into town to sell. At least we had eggs from mother's chickens that we could eat and sell. And we were able to grow or raise enough food to get by on. Our clothes were getting pretty worn, but so were everyone else's."

"Remember those great days when the egg money added up to enough that your mother would let us go to the movie while we were in town? That was really a highlight for me."

"For me, too. I remember watching Shirley Temple and thinking how wonderful it would be to have curls like that."

"I think *King Kong* was my favorite. I preferred the adventure movies. The same with the radio. I loved lying on the rug in front of the radio, listening to *Flash Gordon, Dick Tracy,* and *The Lone Ranger.* I'd lay there with my eyes closed just imagining it all."

"Sometimes we thought you'd fallen asleep." Dorothy

smiles at the memory. "Those were happy times, in spite of the financial hardship. At least we had each other."

"And at least we had no mortgage to foreclose like so many of the other farms in the community. Remember the 'penny auctions' when the banks sent auctioneers to sell off all the foreclosed farmers' possessions? The neighbors would scare off all the real buyers and then we'd refuse to bid more than a penny for anything. The auctioneer had to sell the items for a penny. Then, when it was over, we'd all turn around and give the stuff back to the owners." They both chuckled at the memory. "They still lost their farms, but at least they didn't lose everything."

"What finally did us in was the drought and then the dust storms in 1936. Our topsoil just blew away in a big black cloud of dust, and there was nothing we could do about it. Not even the chickens survived. There was nothing to do but pack up the car and truck and head west, hoping to find some work."

"I'm glad we decided to head toward the Northwest rather than California. Uncle Jim didn't have too much trouble finding a job in a lumber mill. I heard it was pretty bad in California, with so many displaced farmers showing up and no place for them to farm. Many ended up as migrant workers—or looking for jobs that didn't exist in the cities."

"It wasn't too long after we settled in Oregon that you left us to go into the Civilian Conservation Corps."

"As soon as I turned 18 and was old enough to go! It seemed like the best way for me to help the family. Not only was my food and housing provided, but I was also able to send $25 a month home to help all of you. I loved working outdoors in the national parks, and we had a real sense of camaraderie among the fellas. Actually, we lived in an army-like encampment. I didn't realize then that I was being prepared for the time I would soon spend in the army during the war."

"Now there's another chapter of our lives we could have done without." Dorothy shakes her head and sighs.

"I think we've had enough reminiscing for the time being,"

says John. "I just heard my grandsons arrive home. I want you to see how they've grown into such fine young men since you saw them last. I just wish they didn't do such strange things to their hair."

A Closer Look

It is impossible to comprehend or communicate all that happened during this devastating, yet extremely influential time in our nation's history. Here are a few more facts to help further describe what those who lived during the '30s experienced and were shaped by.

■ ■ ■

After the historic stock market crash in October 1929, the economy was unable to recover. Within months four million Americans were out of work. By the beginning of 1931, eight million Americans were unemployed. By the end of 1931, 13.5 million could not find jobs. Those who managed to keep jobs experienced as much as a 50 percent cut in pay and a reduction in the number of hours per week they were allowed to work.[1] Although in 1929 only 3 percent of the workforce was unemployed, by 1933 that figure had risen to 25 percent. From 1930 to 1933, the number of workers who lost their jobs averaged 75,000 every week.[2]

■ ■ ■

In addition to loss of income, many also lost whatever savings they had when banks were forced to close. In 1930 alone, more than 1,300 banks closed.[3] One-fifth of the nation's banks closed during the decade. Nine million families lost their life savings. The banks that were left foreclosed on unpaid mortgages. By 1934, two-fifths of the homeowners in 20 major cities lost their homes.[4]

■ ■ ■

Some families economized by sharing rented homes or apartments with other families. Many had nowhere to go and joined the growing ranks of the homeless, living anywhere they could find or create shelter. In northern cities during the cold months, the homeless even crowded into the municipal incinerators at night for warmth, even though this meant sleeping on top of garbage.[5]

■ ■ ■

Food became very scarce for many people. Those who had some kind of meager income survived on stale bread and canned vegetables. Those who were unemployed lived on handouts from bread lines and soup kitchens. Those in the middle class did not usually go hungry, but many had to suffer the hardship of adjusting to a greatly reduced style of living.[6]

■ ■ ■

The effects of the Depression on the middle class varied, depending on location and occupation, but everyone suffered. Between 1929 and 1933, for example, the incomes of lawyers and doctors dropped as much as 40 percent. The salaries of the highest-paid stenographers in New York decreased from $40 per week to $16.[7]

■ ■ ■

In 1930, the U.S. had 6.3 million farms. A quarter of the population either lived on a farm or had grown up on a farm.[8] Because of prices dropping so dramatically, farmers were not only unable to make a living, but banks also foreclosed on many. By 1935, 750,000 farms had been foreclosed on.[9]

■ ■ ■

The emotional and financial strain of the Depression had a devastating effect on many families. Unemployment and the inability to provide for their families according to the standard of living that they had been accustomed to devastated the self-esteem of many men. This was compounded by the fact that most men (80 percent according to a Gallup Poll survey) did not want their wives to work, but this often became a necessity.[10]

■ ■ ■

While the cost of divorce caused the divorce rate to drop, the pressures of the situation caused a dramatic climb in the rate of desertion. Not only did fathers leave their families, but parents also deserted children. Between 1930 and 1931, the number of children in orphanages increased 50 percent. By 1932, there were 20,000 children in institutions because parents were unable to support them. It was also estimated that 200,000 children wandered cities and towns as vagrants after their families split up.[11]

■ ■ ■

Churches in this decade were affected in many ways by the current events. In trying to help the poor, they, like every other charitable institution, were overwhelmed by the need. Church attendance dropped; eventually only one-third of the population attended services once a week. Financial contributions declined 36 percent between 1926 and 1936 for churches overall, and in more rural areas, like the South, contributions dropped even more drastically (54 percent for the Southern Baptists).[12]

■ ■ ■

The various churches and religious communities struggled with many of the national and international issues of the day, often lining up on different sides. These issues included Prohibition, the New Deal, the persecution of European Jews, and whether the United States should get involved in the events leading up to World War II. Many regretted their support of World War I and were promoting pacifism and isolationism. Although many were distressed at the persecution of the Jews in Europe, none imagined the extremes to which Hitler would take it, and no one could figure out how to stop it short of going to war, which most wanted to avoid.

■ ■ ■

The number of transients caught illegally riding trains on the Missouri Pacific Railroad jumped from 13,745 in 1929 to 186,028 by 1931. The Southern Pacific Railroad removed 700,000 vagrants from its trains in 1932.[13]

■ ■ ■

Between 1928 and 1930, the U.S. gross national product fell from $104 billion to $74 billion. National income dropped from $88 billion to $40 billion.

■ ■ ■

The Hoover administration's hands-off philosophy of economics was replaced by President Roosevelt's New Deal, which created government relief programs and other legislation and safeguards to help the nation's desperate situation. Most people were relieved to see the government finally doing something to help.

■ ■ ■

One of the most popular federal relief programs was the Civilian Conservation Corps. Young men age 18 to 25 were taken from the cities to work on reforestation, irrigation, and other conservation projects in national parks, in forest reserves, and on other federally owned land. It provided room and board and $30 per month, $25 of which was sent back to their families. This program employed 2.75 million men between 1933 and 1942.

■ ■ ■

Other significant parts of the New Deal included the Securities Exchange Commission, which regulated the operations of the stock market and ended the abuses that had led to the big crash of 1929. The Federal Deposit Insurance Corporation provided federally funded insurance for bank accounts up to $2,500. The Social Security Act coordinated state and federal old-age pensions and unemployment compensation, which up until that time had varied widely from state to state.

■ ■ ■

Those who were not constantly fighting for survival found ways to distract themselves with affordable pleasures and entertainment. Many stayed home and entertained themselves with games like chess, checkers, dominoes, bridge, and the new board game craze, Monopoly. In 1935, 20 million Monopoly sets were sold in one week.[14] Bingo also became very popular, as well as other means of winning cash, like chain-letter schemes and the Irish sweepstakes.

■ ■ ■

Radio continued to be a very popular and economical form of family entertainment during the '30s. A study done in 1937 reported that people spent an average of 4.5 hours a day listening to the radio.[15]

■ ■ ■

Media had a tremendous influence on social trends. In 1934 this could be seen in the effect that Clark Gable had on men's fashion through the movie *It Happened One Night*. In one scene, he took off his shirt, revealing that he was wearing no undershirt. Almost overnight men stopped wearing undershirts. In fact, sales dropped so dramatically that knitwear manufacturers and garment workers' unions were reported to have sent delegations to the movie producers asking them to cut that scene from the film![16]

■ ■ ■

Movies also glamorized cigarette smoking, and are believed to have contributed greatly to its increase in popularity. In 1910, fewer than 9.7 billion cigarettes were produced in the United States. In 1930, production was up to 124 billion.[17]

■ ■ ■

Another movie trend was the popularity of Shirley Temple products. In spite of the financial crisis of the nation, mothers scraped together enough money to have hair-dressers put Shirley Temple curls in their daughters' hair. Six million Shirley Temple dolls were sold per year, in addition to many other products adorned with her perky face.[18]

If it is true that what you have been deprived of you strive for, then the '30s were responsible for providing great motivation for those who grew up in this decade. What they were most deprived of was security: financial security, the security of family relationships, the security of property ownership, and job security. Because of this, they are highly motivated to act in ways that they believe will provide security for themselves and those they love.

These people are usually careful about spending and big on saving. Even today you can hear them saying, "Save it for a rainy day" and "You can never tell when there will never be another depression." Some are hesitant to trust the banking system and stash money around their homes. They prefer paying cash, rather than "buying on time" or using credit cards.

A friend of ours came back from the settlement of her father's estate amazed. "We couldn't believe it," she said, shaking her head. "We always were so careful with our money, like we barely had enough to get by. Now we find out that my father had over a million dollars in assets. Yet he always lived like he just came out of the Depression."

In addition to the high value placed on security, the '30s also influenced American views on the role of government, particularly in financial matters. Although not everyone agreed with Roosevelt's New Deal, most believed that its policies and the resulting agencies helped to save the economy and get Americans back on their feet. Government involvement was generally seen as necessary, positive, and welcome.

Heroes during this time were often all-American athletes or media personalities (real or fictitious), such as Buck Rogers, Superman, Little Orphan Annie, Gene Autry, and Shirley

Temple. Their lifestyles promoted virtue and traditional values. Plots and story lines proved that rewards came to those who lived good, clean lives.

By the end of the '30s, things were just starting to turn around financially, but now there was something else to worry about. In 1939, Germany invaded Poland, and Britain and France declared war on Germany. Although President Roosevelt tried to keep the United States out of World War II, the bombing of Pearl Harbor by the Japanese in 1941 made it impossible to stay out.

As terrible as war is, this one had one positive aspect to it: It revived the sickly American economy. Within a few months, three million new workers were hired by war-related industries. During the four-year period of the war, five million people would reenter the workforce. Full employment was achieved by 1943.[19] As the bombs came down, the economy went up. World War II brought the financial relief that Americans had been seeking for the past decade. In the '40s, for the first time, many began to experience the long-sought-after "good life."

A Portrait of the '30s

Demographics in 1930
Population: 123,188,000
Farmers: 24.9%
Life expectancy:
Men: 58.1 years
Women: 61.6 years

Money Matters in 1930
GNP: $90.4 billion
Federal budget: $5.46 billion
National debt: $16.9 billion
Prime interest rate: 3.6%
Average annual salary: $1,368

Cost of Living in 1930
Eggs: 44¢ (doz.)
Milk: 14¢ (qt.)
Bread: 9¢ (loaf)
Coffee: 47¢ (lb.)
Round steak: 42¢ (lb.)

Key Events

1930   The Great Depression begins after stock market crash in 1929

1930   Unemployment rises sharply; Bank of U.S. closes all 60 branches

1931   Hunger marchers are turned away from the White House

1932   12,000 Vets march on Washington, D.C. to demand war bonus; turned away by troops led by Gen. MacArthur

1932   President Hoover voted out of office; Franklin D. Roosevelt becomes president; unemployment reaches 24%

1933   The Depression peaks—56% of blacks and 40% of whites (13 million) unemployed

1933   President Franklin D. Roosevelt initiates the New Deal

1933   Prohibition repealed because it was unpopular and impossible to enforce

1933   The Black Blizzard windstorm destroys farmland in the Midwest

1934   Midwest drought continues

1935   Social Security Act passed; Alcoholics Anonymous organized

1936   President Roosevelt reelected

1936   Continued drought and dust bowl cause mass migration of farmers to the West Coast; major flooding in Northeast

1937   Dirigible *Hindenberg* crashes, killing 38 people; Amelia Earhart vanishes over Pacific on flight around the world

1938   "War of the Worlds" radio broadcast causes widespread panic as audiences believe Martians are attacking the U.S.

1939   France and Great Britain declare war on Germany after invasion of Poland, beginning World War II

Fads/Trends

Backgammon, Sorry, and knitting
Dances: jitterbug, swing, boogie-woogie, Lindy hop
Astrology
Monopoly (board game)—an instant success
Miniature golf
Swallowing goldfish at colleges
Bingo—started in movie houses, popular with charities
Chain-letter moneymaking schemes
The Irish sweepstakes
Fairs—both local and world's fairs

New Inventions/Technology

Pluto (the planet) identified	Camera flashbulb patented
Nylon invented	Zippers invented
Vitamin K discovered	Spam introduced
Helicopter invented	Teflon developed
Scientists split the atom	DDT developed

First wearable hearing aid (weighing 2 1/2 pounds)

Radio

1930	Walter Winchell; *Ripley's Believe It or Not*
1931	*The Ed Sullivan Show; Buck Rogers; Little Orphan Annie*
1932	*George Burns and Gracie Allen Show*; Jack Benny
1933	FDR's fireside chats; *The Lone Ranger*
1934	*Kraft Music Hall* (host: Bing Crosby); *Bob Hope Show*
1935	*Fibber McGee and Molly; Dick Tracy; Flash Gordon*
1936	*The Kate Smith Show; The Shadow; Chase & Sanborn*
1937	*The Guiding Light; Our Gal Sunday*
1938	"War of the Worlds" broadcast causes panic
1939	*The Milton Berle Show; Lil' Abner; Aldrich Family*

Hit Songs

1930   "I Got Rhythm"; "On the Sunny Side of the Street"
1931   "Life Is Just a Bowl of Cherries"; "All of Me"
1932   "April in Paris"; "Brother, Can You Spare a Dime?"
1933   "We're in the Money"; "Smoke Gets in Your Eyes"
1934   "On the Good Ship Lollipop"; "I Only Have Eyes for You"
1935   "Cheek to Cheek"; "Summertime"; "Red Sails in the Sunset"
1936   "Pennies from Heaven"; "I've Got You Under My Skin"
1937   "Thanks for the Memory"; "The Lady Is a Tramp"
1938   "A-Tisket, A-Tasket"; "Whistle While You Work"
1939   "It Don't Mean a Thing"; "Over the Rainbow"

Publications

1930   *The Maltese Falcon; The Woman of Andros*
1931   *The Good Earth; The Road Back; Sanctuary*
1932   *Tobacco Road; Brave New World*
1933   *Winner Take Nothing; To a God Unknown*
1934   *Goodbye, Mr. Chips; Tropic of Cancer*
1935   *Tortilla Flat; Taps at Reveille; Pylon*
1936   *Gone with the Wind; The Crack Up*
1937   *Of Mice and Men; How to Win Friends and Influence People*
1938   *The Yearling; The Citadel; Northwest Passage*
1939   *Grapes of Wrath; All This and Heaven, Too*

Movies

Movie attendance = 90 million weekly
1930   *All Quiet on the Western Front; Animal Crackers*
1931   *Dracula; Frankenstein; Cimarron*
1932   *Tarzan, the Ape Man; Grand Hotel; Mata Hari*
1933   *Alice in Wonderland; Little Women; King Kong*
1934   *It Happened One Night; Stand Up and Cheer; The Thin Man*
1935   *Mutiny on the Bounty; Top Hat; Bride of Frankenstein*
1936   *The Great Ziegfeld; A Tale of Two Cities; Swingtime*

1937   *The Life of Emile Zola; Stage Door; Topper*
1938   *Boys' Town; Jezebel; Snow White; Bringing Up Baby*
1939   *Gone with the Wind; The Wizard of Oz; Pinocchio*

Fashions

Sophisticated Garbo look: Broad shoulders (3" shoulder
        pads), a small bosom, streamlined hips and normal
        waistline
Hair and hems are longer than in the '20s (mid-calf).
Makeup: red lipstick, rouge, plucked and penciled
        eyebrows, false eyelashes, and fingernail polish
Military look introduced in mid-'30s.
Feminine shape enhanced by undergarments with "uplift."
By the end of the decade, feminine suits have tight
        jackets and pleated, flared, or straight skirts.
In the summer, bare midriffs and Carmen Miranda
        turbans are popular.

Heroes

President Franklin D. Roosevelt
Shirley Temple
Babe Ruth
Jesse Owens
Dizzy and Daffy Dean
Joe Louis
Bing Crosby
Johnny Weismuller
Time magazine's Man of the Year in 1938—Adolf Hitler

Chapter 8

The '40s
"Praise the Lord and Pass the Ammunition"

Betty was born in 1932 in Detroit. While her parents and grandparents struggled through the Great Depression, her most vivid memories begin after the worst years, when the country's financial situation started looking up. Her most intense value-development stage corresponded with the beginning of World War II. Now in her retirement years, she enjoys telling her grandchildren what it was like to live during that time.

"I still remember the day everything changed in my world. I was nine years old. It was December 7, 1941—the day Japan bombed Pearl Harbor. My parents looked like they were in shock as they listened to the report on the radio. Mother started crying and Father tried to comfort her, but he was worried too. There had been lots of talk about war. Father had even registered for the selective service the year before. But the wars in Europe and China had seemed so far away. Everyone had thought, and hoped, that the United States wouldn't have to be involved.

"It seemed like no time at all before Father, like so many others, decided to do his part and joined the Army Air Corps. I remember watching him pack the day he left, stuffing his gear into his duffel bag. He looked so handsome in his uniform. My emotions were a jumble of pride, worry, and loneliness as I anticipated not seeing him for a long time. 'How long will you be gone, Father?'

"Hearing the pain in my voice, he stopped packing and took me into his arms. 'I don't know, sweetie. We have a big and important job to do, and it could take a long time. But I will come back just as soon as I can. And I'll be thinking about you and your mother the whole time. I need you to be brave and help your mother while I'm gone, okay?' I couldn't trust my voice, so I just nodded and gave him a hug. I desperately wanted to be brave for him, to give him a happy send-off, but happy wasn't among the many emotions I was feeling.

"Then I saw him reach into his pocket and pull out his grandfather's pocket watch, which was one of his prized possessions. 'I want you to take care of this while I'm gone,' he said as he placed it in my hands. 'I'm going to need it when I get back, so put it in a safe place. Whenever you wind it, say a prayer for me, okay?'

"After we took Father to the train station to see him off, I put his pocket watch in a little jewelry box on the nightstand by my bed. Most of the time I kept it in there, but sometimes, when I was missing my father, I would hold it as I was going to sleep. The ticking of the watch comforted me, and I would imagine it was the beating of my father's heart, all safe and sound somewhere. It made me feel better to know he was a B-17 pilot. I hoped that meant that he was just flying over all the fighting on the ground and wouldn't get hurt.

"It seemed like everyone we knew had someone from their family fighting in the war—fathers, big brothers, uncles, or cousins. Everyone got involved with what was called the war effort. We all seemed to feel that if we were going to be in this war, we would do everything we could to help win it. It affected every area of our lives. After Father and the others left their jobs at the car factory to go overseas, the company started making M-3 tanks around the clock and needed more workers. While a lot of blacks from the South came north to fill some of those jobs, it wasn't enough. My mother, like many of my friends' mothers, began working in the factory, making those tanks.

"It seemed funny at first, our mothers doing 'man's work,' but the president said it was their patriotic duty and the best way to support their men. It turned out that the women were very good at these jobs and enjoyed contributing to the cause. Everyone was talking about Rosie the Riveter, a real lady who could install over 3,000 rivets a day. She was an inspiration for all of us, and especially for the other women who were working in the factories. When I saw the Rosie posters around town, it made me think about the work my mother was doing, and it made me proud that our family was helping in the effort. After the war, it was reported that the United States produced 85,000 tanks, 295,000 airplanes, 70,000 warships, and 5,500 merchant ships[1]—and my mother helped!

"Of course, with so many of the mothers working, life changed for us kids, too. A lot of the little ones ended up in new day care centers and kindergartens that the government helped to start. Most of us older kids ended up being on our own after school, unless a neighbor or grandma was around to watch us. At school we were taught to make some simple dishes like oatmeal, scrambled eggs, and butterscotch pudding so we could help take care of ourselves. But being on our own didn't mean we didn't have plenty to keep us busy.

"Even us kids were involved in the war effort. I remember working with Grandmother in our victory garden. Everyone we knew had one. We lived in an apartment, so we planted ours in a vacant lot down the street. Some people even planted them in public parks. We were encouraged to grow our own vegetables so the troops could have the produce that the farmers were growing. It was hard work for a 10-year-old girl like me, but whenever I started to complain, Grandmother reminded me that I was helping to feed my father and the other soldiers, and that made me feel good. I missed my father terribly, and working in the garden made me feel a little closer to him.

"Victory gardens weren't the only way we kids helped in the war effort. We were told that we could help our soldiers by collecting materials that could be made into weapons and supplies that they needed to fight the war. Grandmother, Mother, and I cleaned out our closets. Jimmy and Sally, who lived next to us, had a wagon, and we took it door to door collecting paper, rubber, metal, and silk stockings. It seemed like almost anything could be reused in the war somehow. I remember scrap parades when trucks full of collected items would drive down Main Street, and we'd all line the street and cheer.

"Mother would even save the fat that was left over from cooking and take it to Mr. Grady's meat market. Mr. Grady turned in the fat so that the government could make explosives with it. He would pay mother for the fat with ration points so she could buy something for us. You see, we couldn't just buy anything we wanted in those days. Through school we were given ration books, one for each person in the family. These books had stamps that allowed us to purchase specific items, but only a certain number of those items.

"First it was food items like sugar, coffee, and meat. We had 'meatless' Tuesdays and Fridays. Then gasoline, fabric, and shoes were limited. We were only allowed three pairs of shoes a year. Our favorite shoes—sneakers—were no longer available because all the rubber was used for the war effort. I remember one year when my feet grew so fast that I outgrew my three pairs of shoes. I remember my mother giving me one of her shoe stamps so I would have shoes to wear to school.

"Even our fashions were affected by the war effort. The government made rules about how much fabric could be used in garments. We couldn't have pleats, more than one patch pocket, decorative trims, or zippers. Hems couldn't be more than two inches deep, and cuffs were out. To conserve cotton, silk, and wool for the troops, new fabrics like rayon and nylon were developed. Because Mother couldn't get silk stockings anymore, I remember her drawing lines with eyeliner on the backs of her legs to make it look like she was wearing stockings! Of course, that was when she was wearing skirts. A lot of the women started wearing slacks, especially to work in the factories. It was much more practical for the kind of work they were doing.

"While my father was away, I would write letters to him often, because his letters always said how much hearing from me meant to him. He would tell us about missions he'd flown in Europe, and we would mark them on a map on our kitchen wall. We would listen to the news reports on the radio, hoping to hear something about Father's division, the 101st Airborne. On June 6, 1944, President Roosevelt came on the radio to tell the American people about the D-Day invasion of Normandy. At first people were cheering the news, church bells were ringing, and factory whistles were blowing. We had been anticipating this invasion and helping to prepare for it, and the time had finally come. But then the reality of the situation hit, and Mother and I got real quiet. We didn't have to say anything; we knew we were both thinking the same thing: Would my father be okay? We sat hugging each other on the couch while the president led the nation in a prayer over the radio that night. I remember I didn't sleep very well, and Father's pocket watch stayed in my hand all night.

"The next day we were relieved to hear of the success of the invasion. Although the number of British and American casualties that first day was close to 5,000, it was considerably less than the 75,000 that some of the planners of the invasion had feared. Mother and I were relieved and proud to hear about the success of the 101st Airborne division in the attack. We hugged and laughed and cried, all at the same time.

"Because of the gas rationing, we didn't go many places. We read books, played card games, and enjoyed listening to the radio. I loved the big band sounds of Tommy Dorsey and Glenn Miller, especially when Bing Crosby or Frank Sinatra would sing. We laughed through shows like *Fibber McGee and Molly* and were on the edge of our seats listening to *Dick Tracy*. We also walked to the movie theater in the middle of town every chance we got to see stars like Abbott and Costello, Gary Cooper, Bette Davis, and Ingrid Bergman.

"Although we had to give up a lot of things, we all felt it was honorable to go without since it was for the war effort. We had a saying, 'Use it up, wear it out, make it do, or do without.' The government had regulations that affected much of our lives, but that was okay because it was solving problems for the common good.

"Finally the day we had waited so long for had arrived! Father had wired us what train he'd be on, and we were waiting at the station for him as his train pulled in, along with what seemed like a million others who were just as anxious as we were. I searched the windows, trying to get a glimpse of him in the midst of all the hands waving and people calling to each other. All of a sudden I was picked up and swung around in a big hug. He had found me first. Then he and Mother had a good long hug and kiss before we all walked home together, hand in hand. "Oh, I have something for you, Father," I remembered as I reached into my coat pocket. Then I did what I had looked forward to and imagined many times since my Father had left for the war. I happily placed his pocket watch back into his hands. It was so good to have him home.

"We had grand parades welcoming our soldiers home. Mother and I were very happy to have Father home again, but many of my friends had lost fathers, uncles, and brothers. It was both a happy and a sad time. In addition to the sadness of lost loved ones, we also were stunned to find out about the horrors of the Nazi concentration camps. There had been some reports about them earlier in the war, but they had sounded so unbelievable, most thought they were exaggerations or rumors like the ones that had gone around during WW I. Now that the facts were revealed, we were all appalled. How could this have happened? Why didn't we do something to stop it? What could we have done? There seemed to be many questions, but not any good answers. In the end, most were just shocked into silence and grief.

"With all the men coming home, the factories started laying off the women and blacks who had been working during the war. They were told that the returning soldiers needed the jobs. This made many people mad. *Now* the women were told that it was unwomanly to work for money. *Now* the patriotic thing to do was give up their jobs and go back to keeping house. My mother was frustrated and disappointed at first because she liked the extra money she had been able to save while working. But she soon became pregnant with my little brother, and then my little sister, so it worked out for the best. A lot of babies came right after the war. It was part of what was called the baby boom.

"With our family growing so fast, we needed more room than we had in our apartment in the city. We had been able to save quite a bit of money during the war since Mother was working and rationing didn't allow us to buy much. Our savings, plus the GI Bill, allowed us to buy a brand-new home in the suburbs. Most of our friends moved out there too, some of them to the same area.

"Living in the suburbs was different than living in an apartment in the city. We all had backyards and garages, and there were lots of families with lots of kids like ours. Instead of walking to the corner grocery store, we had to drive to the shopping center. That meant we needed a car, so we bought a brand-new 1947 Oldsmobile.

"Another change that happened in our family was we started to go to church more. Father had been given a Bible by a chaplain during the war and said that when he felt overwhelmed by the horror of the war, talking to the chaplain and reading his Bible helped him to get through. Even at home, I had seen people from the local churches helping the families that were grieving over the loss of their loved ones. Plus it was the accepted thing to do. Good people went to church. And it didn't seem to matter so much anymore that people went to different kinds of churches. People were more accepting of different beliefs; they were more interested in getting along.

"After the war there were all kinds of new inventions and products to buy, and most people had the money to buy them. One of the most exciting events for our family was the arrival of the television set. Even though it was only black and white, and there weren't too many shows at first, it was wonderful and exciting for us. My favorite program was *The Howdy Doody Show*, while my parents' choice was *Milton Berle's Texaco Star Theater*.

"Yes, my childhood was full of hard times and good times. Through the hard times, we looked to our government for leadership, and it came through for us. President Roosevelt led us into the war and helped to organize and carry out the war effort. We all made sacrifices and worked together for the common good, and together we won the war. After the war, we celebrated our victory and enjoyed the fruit of our labors. The good life had arrived, and we knew we had earned it!"

A Closer Look

Betty's story illustrates what the world looked like in the '40s. Let's look at some facts from that period, and see what values a 10-year-old would develop as a result of growing up during those times:

■ ■ ■

During World War II, 40 percent of the vegetables consumed were grown in victory gardens, leaving more of the commercial crops for the troops.[2]

■ ■ ■

Because of gas rationing, people found ways to entertain themselves at home. In addition to listening to the radio and reading, playing cards became very popular. Sales of playing cards rose 1,000 percent during this time.[3]

■ ■ ■

In general, people were very patriotic and positive about the government's leadership. Through following the government rules and guidelines and all pulling together, not only did they help to win the war, but they experienced many financial and technological benefits as well. Most trusted the government to take care of them by making good laws to protect them. This decade saw the creation of new laws guaranteeing a minimum wage, Social Security, collective bargaining for labor, a five-day workweek, stricter child labor laws, and banking reform.

■ ■ ■

Reports about the Nazi concentration camps and the murdering of the Jewish people appeared early in the war (1942), but they were not front page news and seemed so preposterous that most people viewed them as anti-German propaganda like they had seen during World War I.[4] There was also quite a bit of anti-Semitism in the United States. American Jewish leaders pleaded in vain for some type of rescue efforts by the U.S. The government rejected proposals to bomb the camps or the rail lines to them, because that would require too much reordering of war priorities. In 1944, the Roosevelt administration established a War Refugee Board, which restructured immigration policy and attempted to rescue East European Jews. They managed to rescue about 111,000 Jews (mostly Hungarian.) But for six million Jews (and three million other concentration camp victims), it was too late. The end of the war reports and graphic photographs stunned the American people with grief, unbelief, and perhaps guilt for their lack of response. There ended up being little public discussion (mostly private grief), and the decade passed with little reflection on the Holocaust. However, future writers would bring the horror to life and cause the American public to deal with it in the future.[5]

■ ■ ■

In 1945, the year the war ended, 18,610,000 women were employed outside the home. The Women's Bureau reported that 80 percent of them wanted to continue their jobs after the war.[6] (This marks the beginning of the breakdown of the traditional family, where mothers stay home while fathers work outside the home.) Most wanted to continue their jobs after the war, but many were laid off to provide jobs for returning veterans.

■ ■ ■

The huge increase in American industry and productivity required by the war produced tremendous growth in the economy. The standard of living of Americans increased greatly. Compare the average American family income before the war and during the war:

	1938	1942
Washington, D.C.	$2,227	$5,316
Hartford, Conn.	$2,207	$5,208
New York City, N.Y.	$2,760	$4,044[7]

■ ■ ■

During the war, Americans had saved billions of dollars, which they proceeded to spend after the war on new homes, cars, and appliances.[8]

■ ■ ■

After the war there was a mass exodus from the cities. According to *Esquire* magazine, "In the 1940s, the 12 largest cities saw an 81 percent rise in suburban population."[9]

■ ■ ■

After several years of decline during the Depression, churches experienced an increase in participation after WW II. Before the war, about 43 percent of the people went to church. That rose to 55 percent being members of religious groups by 1950. This increase was partly due to the effects of the war, but was also attributed to post-war social pressures and affluence. Churchgoing became part of the suburban lifestyle, a sign of community, and protection against suspicions of communist sympathies. The three major religious groups in America—Protestants, Catholics, and Jews—all went through radical theological reconstruction in the '30s and '40s to better harmonize their doctrines with the intellectual concepts and mores of modern society. The Nazis and the Holocaust discredited religious intolerance. The human potential for evil was obvious through the violence of the war. In general, religion became more liberal, more ecumenical, and more tolerant.

There was, however, a fundamentalist movement also happening in the 1940s. In 1942, the National Association of Evangelicals was founded, becoming a broad coalition of Protestant conservatives attempting to encourage inter-fundamentalist unity. By 1947, it included 30 denominations. In 1943, Youth for Christ was organized. In 1947, Fuller Theological Seminary in Pasadena, California, was founded as a center for scholarly fundamentalism. In 1949, the Evangelical Theological Society was formed, committing itself to teaching scriptural inerrancy and the promotion of evangelical scholarship. That same year, Billy Graham conducted a highly publicized revival and crusade that brought him and his ministry to public attention.[10]

■ ■ ■

In the late 1940s, there was an explosion in TV sales:
- 7,000 sets were sold in 1946
- 172,000 sets were sold in 1948
- 5,000,000 sets were sold in 1950.[11]

■ ■ ■

In 1946, the baby boom began. The birthrate increased 20 percent over the 1945 birthrate, and 74 percent of couples had their first child during their first year of marriage.[12]

■ ■ ■

In 1949, the first Baby Boomer children reached kindergarten age. Educators estimated a 39 percent increase in school attendance the following year.[13]

The victory gardens, scrap drives, andz rationing taught the children of this decade the value of teamwork. Everyone pitched in and sacrificed for the war effort, and together they won the war.

Rationing taught this group to delay gratification and develop discipline. As they submitted to the authority of the government and conformed to the wartime regulations, they experienced success in winning the war. This taught them to trust and respect the government and created a patriotic loyalty.

The entrance of masses of women into the traditionally male workplace sent more than one message to society. One was that women could contribute much more to the commercial endeavors of society than was previously thought or allowed. Rosie the Riveter was a bona fide hero during the war, and the contribution of the women in the workforce was critical to winning the war. On the other hand, when the war was over, the message that the woman's place was in the home was heard loud and clear. While their contribution to the war effort was greatly appreciated, it was considered an exception to the norm, an emergency provision, no longer necessary or desirable once the men returned from the war.

The "good life" experienced by Americans after the war taught these kids that sacrifice, discipline, and hard work bring rewards. The savings accumulated by their parents during the war provided them with new homes in the suburbs, new cars, and new appliances. One of these new appliances, the television, created its own impact on this impressionable group. This was the beginning stage of values coming into their lives from a source outside their home and immediate community.

As this group of 10-year-olds was observing the world around them and forming their values, a new group was arriving in mass quantity. The dramatic increase in the birthrate, beginning in 1946 and continuing for almost three decades, has been named the baby boom. The sheer size of this group, called the Baby Boomers, makes them a factor to contend with both for those who came before them and those who follow after them.

A Portrait of the '40s

Demographics in 1940
Population: 132,122,000
Farmers: 23.2%
Life expectancy:
Men: 60.8 years
Women: 68.2 years

Money Matters in 1940
GNP: $99.7 billion
Federal budget: $13.2 billion
National debt: $43 billion
Prime interest rate: 0.6%
Average annual salary: $1,299

Cost of Living in 1940
Eggs: 33¢ (doz.)
Milk: 13¢ (qt.)
Bread: 8¢ (loaf)
Coffee: 21¢ (lb.)
Round steak: 36¢ (lb.)

Key Events

1940   FDR reelected for third term as president

1941   Pearl Harbor attacked; United States declares war on Japan; Germany and Italy declare war on the U.S.

1941   Rationing begins

1942   Japanese-Americans are placed in camps to isolate them until the war is over; coffee, sugar, and gas rationed

1943   Polio epidemic in the United States—almost 1,200 die, thousands are crippled

1944   FDR reelected for fourth term; GI Bill passed; first details of mass murder of Jews revealed

1945   FDR dies in office; Vice President Harry Truman becomes president; Hitler commits suicide; Germany surrenders

1945   Atomic bomb used to end the war with Japan; World War II ends

1946   Dr. Spock publishes his book *The Common Sense Book of Baby and Child Care*; Nuremberg trials held

1947   Red Scare (fear of communism) leads to blacklisting and loyalty investigations
1948   President Truman is reelected
1949   Billy Graham holds first major crusade

Fads/Trends

War effort: victory gardens, rationing, and scrap drives
Playing cards
Slumber parties, pep rallies, beach parties
Music: big bands, swing, bebop, rhythm and blues
Dances: swing, Lindy hop, jitterbug, Congo, fox-trot
Baby boom starts: 1946 birthrate up 20% over 1945
Many move from the cities to the suburbs
McDonald's is started in 1940
The saying "Kilroy was here"
Daylight savings begins
Bible sales increase 25%
Roller derbies
Cowboy and Indian suits and toys
Toni home permanents

New Inventions/Technology

1942 Radar used, bazookas developed
1942 First electronic computer developed
1942 Magnetic recording tape developed
1943 DDT introduced as a boon to farmers
1944 DNA is isolated
1944 Jets (propless planes) developed
1945 Atomic bomb created
1946 Xerography process invented
1946 Start of television sales boom
1947 Transistor invented
1948 Long play (LP) records
1948 Garbage disposals
1949 Carbon dating developed
1949 Polaroid Land camera

Radio

1940   *Superman; Truth or Consequences; Quiz Kids*
1941   *The Red Skelton Show; The Inner Sanctum; Duffy's Tavern*
1942   *People Are Funny; It Pays to Be Ignorant*
1943   *The Army Hour; Perry Mason; Meet Your Navy*
1944   *Roy Rogers; The Adventures of Ozzie and Harriet; The FBI*
1945   *Queen for a Day; Arthur Godfrey Time; Topper*
1946   *Twenty Questions; The Bing Crosby Show*
1947   *You Bet Your Life; The Jack Paar Show; Lassie*
1948   *Stop the Music; This Is Your Life; Our Miss Brooks*
1949   *Dragnet; Martin Kane, Private Eye*

Hit Songs

1940   "When You Wish Upon a Star"; "Eight to the Bar"
1941   "Chattanooga Choo Choo"; "There! I've Said It Again"
1942   "White Christmas"; "Don't Sit Under the Apple Tree"
1943   "Oh, What a Beautiful Morning"; "Oklahoma"; "GI Jive"
1944   "Don't Fence Me In"; "Too-Ra-Loo-Ra-Loo-Rah"
1945   "Sentimental Journey"; "If I Loved You"; "Let It Snow!"
1946   "Chiquita Banana"; "Zip-a-Dee-Doo-Dah"; "Tenderly"
1947   "Almost Like Being in Love"; "Peg o' My Heart"
1948   "Nature Boy"; "Lazy River"; "It's Magic"
1949   "Mona Lisa"; "Some Enchanted Evening"; "Ghost Riders"

Publications

1940   *For Whom the Bell Tolls; You Can't Go Home Again*
1941   *My Friend Flicka; The White Cliffs of Dover*
1942   *The Robe; Dragon Seed; The Moon Is Down*
1943   *Thirty Seconds Over Tokyo; The Song of Bernadette*
1944   *A Bell for Adano; Here Is Your War; Anna and the King of Siam*
1945   *Animal Farm; Cannery Row; Friendly Persuasion*
1946   *The Common Sense Book of Baby and Child Care*
1947   *The Diary of Anne Frank; Tales of the South Pacific*
1948   *Walden Two; The Ides of March; The Naked and the Dead*
1949   *1984; Dinner at Antoine's; The Greatest Story Ever Told*

Movies

Movie attendance = 80 million weekly

1940	*Grapes of Wrath; Rebecca; Fantasia; The Road to Singapore*
1941	*Citizen Kane; How Green Was My Valley; The Maltese Falcon*
1942	*Bambi; Casablanca; The Road to Morocco; Tortilla Flat*
1943	*For Whom the Bell Tolls; Lassie Come Home*
1944	*Going My Way; Meet Me in St. Louis; Double Indemnity*
1945	*The Bells of St. Mary's; National Velvet; Lost Weekend*
1946	*Song of the South; Best Years of Our Lives; The Big Sleep*
1947	*Miracle on 34th Street; Gentleman's Agreement; The Egg and I*
1948	*Treasure of the Sierra Madre; Hamlet; Key Largo*
1949	*Cinderella; Sands of Iwo Jima; Twelve o'Clock High*

Popular TV Shows

(TVs weren't widely distributed until 1946, programming was limited in the beginning)

1940	Republican National Convention is telecast
1945	Macy's first Thanksgiving Day Parade
1946	Wrestling; *Faraway Hill* (first TV soap opera)
1947	*Meet the Press; The Howdy Doody Show; Kraft Theater*
1948	*Milton Berle; Candid Camera; Bigelow Show*
1949	*The Lone Ranger; The Original Amateur Hour; Mama*

Fashion

Trousers and military garments for women

Day dresses with aprons and pinafores, South Seas sarongs

The new concept of "separates," interchangeable items of clothing

Shoulder-length hair with big curls, piled on top of head with curls or pompadours, or curled into a sausage in the back

"Butch" and crewcut hairstyles for men

Bobby socks and rolled up jeans for teens

"Zoot suits" for teen boys

Postwar: feminine dresses with full skirts, sashes, and ruffles

Heroes

Rosie the Riveter	Jackie Robinson
President Franklin D. Roosevelt	General George Patton
General Douglas MacArthur	General Dwight Eisenhower
Audie Murphy	Joe Louis
Joe DiMaggio	Frank Sinatra

Chapter 9

The '50s "Rock Around the Clock"

Those of us who have memories of this time remember the decade of the 1950s with fond nostalgia. We enjoy restaurants with '50s themes and dressing up in poodle skirts, rolled-up jeans, and T-shirts for costume parties. Many of the songs played on jukeboxes in soda shops can still be heard on our oldies-but-goodies radio stations around the country today. The early Baby Boomers turned 10 during this decade, and many of us who didn't enter our teens until the '60s still have lots of '50s memories from our earlier childhood.

Barbara was one of the first Boomers, born in 1946, the year after her dad returned from fighting in World War II. He had gotten a job as a clerk in a bank in Chicago. At first their family lived in an apartment downtown, but it wasn't long before they'd saved enough money to join the throngs of families moving to the suburbs with the help of the GI Bill. That cozy little bedroom community that Chicago businessmen commuted home to each night is the place Barbara thinks of as home when she remembers her childhood.

Now in her mid-50s, she enjoys selling real estate, a career she started once the kids were all off to college. She likes the flexible schedule, allowing her to attend her grandkids' school programs and have tennis dates with "the girls," as she calls her group of friends. Today they are having lunch together at Mimi's Café after their friendly morning match.

"So, how was the awards ceremony yesterday? Did Justin make the honor roll again?" Carol asked Barbara as they handed the menus back to the waitress.

"He sure did. That little guy is one smart cookie. Of course, his mother deserves some of the credit. She gives him a lot of attention—takes him to those hands-on displays at the museum, plays learning games with him, things like that. I don't know where she finds the time, working like she does. But she manages to squeeze it in. She calls it 'quality time.' "

"I think that's great," affirmed Judy as she stirred some sweetener into her iced tea. "My kids are the same way with my grandkids. They actually take time to play with them. Do any of you remember your mothers playing with you?"

"You know, I was just thinking about that the other day. Although most of the moms in the neighborhood were home during the day, I don't really remembering our parents playing with us," remarked Barbara. "There were lots of kids in the neighborhood, and we'd play in each other's yards and houses, or in the vacant lots at the end of the street. I don't even think our mothers knew where we were most of the time. They just counted on the other mothers to send us home at dinnertime. Parents didn't worry about constantly supervising their kids like they have to today. They didn't have to warn us about not talking to strangers. They were more concerned that we'd be polite."

"Of course, it took our mothers longer to get the housework done in those days," Nancy, the fourth member of their tennis group reminded them. "Although they were excited about all the shiny new appliances they were acquiring, they still had a lot less than we have today. I remember my mom hanging the laundry on the clothesline, and then having to iron everything. And meals took a lot longer to fix, without microwaves and all the prepared foods we now have. I remember how excited we all were the first time we had frozen TV dinners!"

"Mom and us kids thought they were great. But I remember my father wasn't too impressed," laughed Judy. "I remember him telling Mom that after a hard day at the office, he needed to have a 'real meal.' So Mom saved the TV dinners for the baby-sitter to fix for us on the nights Mom and Dad went out. Sometimes we'd have them on the nights he went to the Elks Club meetings."

"For us it was bowling league night. Especially when my mother had PTA meeting on the same night. We'd all have our baths early, get into our pajamas, and be eating our TV dinners on trays in front of the TV when the baby-sitter arrived." Carol smiled at the memory.

"Did your parents ever take you to the drive-in movies in your pajamas?" Nancy asked. "They'd bundle us up with our pillows and blankets in the back of the station wagon, and we'd sleep through the second feature, which gave them a chance to watch it in peace. I guess it saved them having to get a baby-sitter."

"Life seemed so much simpler in those days, didn't it?" Barbara asked almost wistfully. "We didn't have to worry about drugs and AIDS and child abuse. I guess some of that was happening then, but we just weren't aware of it. All the families we knew seemed normal and happy and went to church. In fact, in those days it was the unusual family who didn't go to some kind of church or temple. I don't know if they were all going for the right reasons. It was definitely the socially acceptable thing to do."

"I think some were going to help their image. I remember my father telling my mother that his company let it be known that one of the qualities of the ideal employee was church membership in a respectable denomination. In fact, there was someone at the office who was suspect because he didn't go to church." Judy leaned forward, lowered her voice and raised her eyebrows, mimicking how shocking this news would have been in the '50s. "The rumors began to circulate that he was a communist."

"Boy, that rumor was the kiss of death in those days," remembered Nancy. "Everyone was afraid that communist spies were infiltrating our society and stealing our technological secrets for the Russians. Senator McCarthy ruined a lot of reputations with his accusations—government officials, teachers, and even people in Hollywood."

"I remember one teacher at our school that none of the kids liked. We actually tried to start a rumor that he was a communist, hoping the school would get rid of him!" Judy laughed and shook her head at the memory.

"Did it work?"

"Unfortunately not," Judy sighed. "But a bunch of us kids sure got ourselves in trouble."

"Speaking of the Russians, remember how we were so afraid of them coming and dropping bombs on us? Did any of your families build a bomb shelter?" Carol asked.

"We did," said Barbara. "My dad got the instructions out of an issue of *Popular Mechanics* and built it in our backyard. My mother stocked it with enough food to last for 14 days, since that was how long the government believed the fallout would be the most dangerous. They actually made it pretty comfortable, and I ended up using it for a playhouse. My brother would take it over sometimes and have "no girls allowed" club meetings in it. But they usually got in trouble because they would get into the food supplies, and mother wouldn't let them back in for a while." Even after all those years, Barbara still experienced a sense of triumph over her brother's restriction.

"We didn't have a bomb shelter," remarked Judy, "but my mom and dad made sure we knew where all the public bomb shelters in the community were. Remember those yellow and black signs they used to have on the buildings that they thought would be safe? There was one on the church at the end of our street, and our family planned to go to that church basement if we were home when the air raid sirens went off. Of course at school, we always practiced crouching under our desks during the air raid drills. It seems silly now that we thought that would actually protect us if an atomic bomb was dropped."

"Oh, I know!" Nancy broke in. "I was cleaning out my

mother's attic a couple of months ago, and I came across a booklet the government produced in the early '50s called "What to Do in Case of an Atomic Bomb Attack." It was laughable. It assured you that hiding behind a thick wall would save you from radioactivity, even if you were close to the blast. It even suggested that men wear wide-brimmed hats to protect their faces from the heat flash, in case they were caught outside when a bomb was dropped. I don't know if the government was that naive or was just trying to give us false confidence that we would survive an atomic blast!"

"I guess it worked," said Barbara. "Even though we were concerned, it seemed like most people were fairly optimistic that if we were prepared, we'd survive okay. I guess we were in ignorant bliss until later years when the real effects of atomic war were realized."

There was a break in the conversation as the waitress brought their lunches and they sorted out their orders. After the typical comments about how big the portions were and how good the food tasted, Carol brought up a subject that had been on her mind before the arrival of the food. "One thing I've always wondered about was the Korean War. We always hear so much about World War I and World War II, and of course Vietnam, but not so much about Korea. Did any of your fathers fight in Korea? Do you understand what it was about?"

"My dad was a veteran of World War II, and I remember hearing him make comments about Korea being a 'police action'—not a real war like the two world wars," Barbara explained. "Apparently the U.S. troops were just sent over to push the North Korean communists back to where they belonged and keep them from taking over South Korea. It wasn't expected to take long, but the Chinese came to help the North Koreans, and it ended up taking three years. Apparently there were mixed emotions and thoughts about the war. Some, like General MacArthur, felt that all of Korea should be freed from communism, and he wanted to go on and finish the job. On the other hand, many, like President Truman, felt that anything more than liberating South Korea would be the beginning of World War III. Since we knew that we weren't the only ones who had the atomic bomb, no one wanted that. It was the first war fought merely for containment and didn't feel like a real victory. It was kind of confusing and frustrating for the American people, so it didn't make as big of an impression as the previous wars had."

"Enough of this dismal talk about wars and bomb shelters," complained Nancy. "I like to remember the fun and happy parts of the '50s, like neighborhood barbecues and hula hoop contests. Do you remember when Disneyland opened? It truly seemed to be a magic kingdom to us. I remember how proud I was to have my own pair of Mickey Mouse ears with my named embroidered on it. I would wear it every day after school when I watched *The Mickey Mouse Club* on TV. And watching the Disneyland show on Sunday nights was a family ritual we just wouldn't miss! Mom would make a big batch of popcorn for us. I can still remember the scraping sound of her shaking that big pot over the burner of the stove while the corn was popping. I wonder if anyone still makes popcorn like that?"

"Not if they have a microwave," replied Barbara. "I remember my first trip to Disneyland. It was really a big deal for us, living near Chicago. We had taken several family vacations by car to national parks, but this was the first time we made it all the way to the West Coast. We stayed in campgrounds most of the way so we could save money. But when we got to Anaheim, we splurged and stayed in a motel across the street from Disneyland. I loved every bit of it, but my favorite was the Dumbo ride."

"Oh, my favorite was the Peter Pan ride. I loved the part when you look down on that little town, like you were flying high over it," remarked Nancy. "Did any of you find the Snow White ride to be scary? I used to have nightmares about the part when the witch jumps out at you holding the red apple."

"Yes, I always thought that was pretty scary for a ride for little kids," agreed Barbara. "Fantasyland was definitely my favorite, but we always had to spend a lot of time in Frontierland for my brother. He thought he was Davy Crockett, and we could barely drag him away from that fort on Tom Sawyer's Island. He had all the Davy Crockett paraphernalia, including the coonskin cap."

"My brother was a little older than me, and he wanted to be Elvis Presley," said Carol with a chuckle. "He slicked his hair back and would practice singing and gyrating in front of the mirror when he thought we weren't watching. He'd get so embarrassed when he'd hear me and my girlfriends giggling that he'd throw his hairbrush/microphone at us!"

"And did we all watch Elvis on the *Ed Sullivan Show?*" asked Barbara.

"Of course!" they all answered in unison.

"Although it was a bit of a disappointment when they only showed him from the waist up," admitted Nancy. "I don't know how many nickels I put in the jukebox listening to his songs. Hanging out in the soda shop was one of my favorite things to do on Saturdays, unless there was a sock hop or a good movie at the drive-in. During the week after school, I loved watching *American Bandstand* with Dick Clark. It was great hearing all the latest rock 'n' roll tunes and learning the newest dance steps."

"Hey, didn't I see Dick Clark hosting something on TV the other night? It seems like he'll just go on forever. He's amazing," interjected Judy.

"Well, now that we're back to the present, I need to get going. I have a 2:00 appointment to show a house. Who's got the check? I have the calculator," interrupted Barbara, as she reached into her purse.

"Here it is, and don't forget to add in the tip this time," reminded Carol.

A Closer Look

If we took a vote for the most ideal decade, the '50s might win. A time of relative peace and prosperity, many look back at its simplicity with longing and nostalgia. World War II was over, and the good life was being lived out. Let's look at some of the features of this time that created these feelings and influenced its youth.

■ ■ ■

This was a decade of unprecedented population and economic growth. In the five years between 1948 and 1953, more children were born than in the previous 30 years, and this baby boom continued into the mid-'60s.[1]

■ ■ ■

A family could buy a home with modern appliances, individual bedrooms, garages, and lawns for as little as $6,000, and the GI Bill provided low-interest loans to make it even easier to afford.

■ ■ ■

The automobile industry could hardly keep up with the demand for new cars. In 1945, only 70,000 cars were built. By 1950, production soared to eight million. The number of cars on the road had doubled from 1945 to 1955, totaling about 52 million.[2]

■ ■ ■

Greater mobility allowed more freedom to travel, and the National Highway Act of 1956 provided $26 billion to build interstate roads that connected major cities across the country. National parks became popular vacation sites to drive to in the family car. As families spent more time exploring our scenic country, other businesses and services sprung up to meet their needs, such as picnic and rest areas along the highways, gas stations, motels, restaurants, and campgrounds. The increase in mobility that started after World War II continued to build during the '50s.

■ ■ ■

On Sundays, more people than ever went to church. While in 1940 less than half of the population belonged to a church of any kind, in the late '50s more than 63 percent listed themselves as church members.[3]

■ ■ ■

In 1954, a Gallup Poll reported that 94 percent of the population believed in God.[4]

■ ■ ■

The Christian faith was strongly felt in society. Popular movies had religious themes, like Cecil B. De Mille's *The Ten Commandments* (1956) starring Charlton Heston as Moses. In 1959, Heston also starred in William Wyler's biblical epic *Ben-Hur*. Popular songs with religious themes were heard on the radio during this decade. "I Believe," "It Is No Secret What God Can Do," and "*Vaya con Dios*" made it to the hit parade. In 1954, Congress added the words "under God" to the pledge of allegiance. Schools preceded athletic events, assemblies, and graduations with prayer. "In God We Trust" was added to the American currency.

■ ■ ■

A *Look* magazine poll on moral attitudes reported a moral relativity based on group acceptance: One should do whatever he wants as long as it would be accepted by the neighbors.[5]

■ ■ ■

Housekeeping and raising a family were considered the ideal roles for women in the '50s. Because of this emphasis, couples began to marry at a younger age. By 1953, almost a third of all 19-year-old women were married to men who were only about 22 years of age. The divorce rate, which had been slowly climbing since the 1920s, leveled off in the '50s.[6] Divorce became socially unacceptable.

■ ■ ■

Kids had it made in the '50s. Their sheer numbers caused them to attract the attention of society. By 1958, one-third of the population was younger than 15 years old.[7]

■ ■ ■

Affluent parents indulged their children, wanting the kids to have it better than they did growing up. These kids had

spending power, and industries catered to them. The popularity of western movies and TV shows led to heavy sales
of cowboy hats, guns, and holsters (and of course the
Davy Crockett coonskin caps). Slinkies, Silly Putty, and
Frisbees came out during this time. One of the biggest
fads was the hula hoop, of which 100 million were sold
around the world in 1958, the year after it was introduced.[8] Barbie made her debut in 1959 (but her inventors
were told at the toy manufacturer's trade show that she
would never sell). Walt Disney opened Disneyland in
1955, and *The Mickey Mouse Club* became a popular
afternoon TV show.

■ ■ ■

As the kids grew into teenagers, their parents indulged
them with their own bedrooms where they could listen to
their own music on their radios and record players. Boys
would devour their comic books, and girls would write in
their diaries. Parents would build them recreation rooms
in basements and garages where their friends could come
over and entertain themselves playing Ping-Pong, pool,
and darts.

■ ■ ■

Early marriages meant early dating, and this often
revolved around school activities, such as sock hops
(dances) in the gym after football and basketball games
and formal proms. Drive-in movies became a popular
date, and teens continued to frequent soda shops with
jukeboxes playing their favorite hit tunes.

■ ■ ■

While the teens of this time were declaring their uniqueness from adults, it was still a time of conformity to each
other. In general, they were nonpolitical, and few questioned authority (unlike the teens of the next decade). The
few nonconformists on the fringe of this youthful society
were called "beatniks," and they seemed to congregate in

places like San Francisco in California and Greenwich Village in New York. They were poets, writers, artists, and musicians who were rebelling against the conformity and monotony of suburban living. They typically dressed in khaki pants, sweaters, and sandals and expressed themselves through folk songs, poems, and long evenings of philosophical discussions over bottles of wine. The Maynard G. Krebs role in *The Many Loves of Dobie Gillis* is probably the best-known characterization of a beatnik.

■ ■ ■

Although television became popular in the late '40s, its distribution and influence increased incredibly in the '50s. In 1950, 3.875 million households (9 percent) owned a TV. By 1960, TV ownership increased to 45.75 million households (87.1 percent).[9]

■ ■ ■

By 1959, the average American was watching television more than five hours a day.[10]

■ ■ ■

Movie theaters experienced a dip in attendance during the '50s due to the popularity of television. Movie financiers became more careful, only willing to back a "sure thing," so fewer movies were produced. More than 400 movies came out in 1951, but only 154 in 1960.[11] In addition, many free-thinking writers and actors were blacklisted as suspected communists, and major studios experienced financial problems.

■ ■ ■

To combat all this and save the industry, movie magnates decided to do things in movies that TV couldn't do. From 1952 to 1955, 3-D movies were produced. Moviegoers wore paper and cellophane 3-D glasses to see the special effects, as objects appeared to fly off the screen toward them. Another development was "Cinerama," which used larger screens and multiple speakers placed around the audience. Moviemakers also pulled Americans away from their beloved television sets by including more sex appeal in movies than was permitted on TV. *Gentlemen Prefer Blondes,* with Marilyn Monroe, and Brigitte Bardot's *And God Created Woman* are examples of this.

■ ■ ■

From 1930 to 1952, school enrollment remained basically the same, but when the Baby Boomers hit school age, enrollment increased between 1.5 to 2 million students each year. From 1950 to 1960, the number of students in elementary school increased 50 percent.[12] Government funded new school buildings and hired more teachers, but they could never quite keep up with the demand.

■ ■ ■

In addition to the increasing number of children, another factor that promoted education as a priority during this time was the Cold War and the race into space with the Russians. When the USSR released two Sputnik satellites in 1957—before our first Explorer in 1958—Americans were concerned. We realized that in addition to our American virtue of hard work, we were going to need intelligence, too, to remain the world superpower that we had become. Increased availability and quality of education became a national concern.

■ ■ ■

The government convinced us that it was their responsibility to ensure military superiority, that our military must be unequaled. Thus began the arms race with the Soviet Union. We became anxious about international spies stealing our new technological secrets. Fear of communist infiltration was rampant, and in 1950, Senator Joseph McCarthy announced he had a list of 205 State Department employees who were Communist Party members.

Trials and investigations ensued. Suspicion and accusations ruined many lives until the Senate finally censured McCarthy in 1954.

■ ■ ■

Mass destruction was not the only scientific advance of the '50s. More productive uses were found for atomic power, such as making electricity and powering ships and submarines.

■ ■ ■

The polio epidemic in 1952, with 58,000 cases of this crippling disease causing 1,400 deaths, motivated the creation of the polio vaccine. Synthetic penicillin was developed, and the first contraceptive pill was produced.

■ ■ ■

Microchips were invented, leading to the development of the modern computer. Transistor radios and stereophonic records were introduced and distributed to enthusiastic consumers. Although color television was not widely distributed until the '60s, the technology was invented in the '50s.

The kids who were growing up in the '50s experienced a very different world from the world their parents grew up in. These kids knew nothing but the good life. They had no reason to believe that prosperity wasn't going to continue, so they expected to be well off. Rather than becoming security-minded adults, like those who experienced the deprivation of the Depression, they assumed that the good life would continue and didn't do much in the way of saving. They were consumers at heart, responding enthusiastically to television advertisements and fads.

These kids were used to getting their way. Because of their sheer numbers, society was catering to them and their needs. Dr. Spock encouraged parents to set aside previous strict, disciplined, structured, and almost unemotional child-rearing practices and see their children as human beings entitled to understanding, respect, and emotional nurturing (a unique concept at the time). This new concept appealed to parents who were already inclined to indulge their children in reaction to the deprivation of their own childhoods. These indulged kids learned to value immediate gratification rather than the delayed gratification learned by kids in previous decades.

This was the first group of kids who had television as a major influence in their value development. For the first time, a source outside the child's community was having tremendous influence on the values that child was embracing. Advertisers were helping to develop a great appetite for their products, creating a generation of avid consumers. Kids developed an expectation not only of immediate fulfillment of their desires, but also of immediate solutions to problems, as they watched program after program that contained the solution of a problem in 30 or 60 minutes. Through TV, they also became more aware of issues and topics that had previously been limited to the realm of adulthood, as political and news coverage became more prevalent. In retrospect, it's not surprising that these kids grew up with strong political opinions, demanding immediate solutions, like stopping the war in Vietnam in the '60s and '70s.

Another effect of television on values was that kids began to identify with TV characters as heroes instead of, or in addition to, real people. This meant that they were exposed to values and lifestyles they would not encounter through their families, churches, or communities. In some ways this was good, as it expanded their knowledge and experience of the world and introduced them to people with attitudes different from their own. But it also exposed them to values that were in conflict with some of those held by their parents, leading to friction between the generations.

Heroes like Davy Crockett embodied an adventurous, independent spirit. Other heroes of the day included Elvis Presley,

James Dean, and even the Lucy Ricardo character from the hit show *I Love Lucy.* These all were rebels against the conventional rules of behavior of that time. Lucy was constantly going against her husband's wishes, getting herself into hot water, and being anything but the well-organized and efficient housewife and mother respected by the adult society of the '50s.

But there were other, more traditional heroes, such as John Wayne, who usually played very positive roles. Kids of the '50s also looked up to President Dwight Eisenhower and General Douglas MacArthur, real war heroes. President Eisenhower was helping to protect Americans and the rest of the world from the threat of communism. His government was winning the arms race and trying to keep up in the space race. The kids of this decade were being assured that, with the proper understanding and preparation, they could survive the threat of nuclear attack, and willingly they tried to believe (at least for a while).

Like the teenagers just ahead of them, these kids also grew up identifying themselves with rock 'n' roll music. It expressed what they were feeling and believing, and their parents didn't like what they were hearing. Lyrics included themes like disobeying authority (parents, school, etc.), the fun and excitement of sex, going against the rules of society, and the concept of "us against them" (referring to the older generation). Identifying with the lyrics and passion of the songs influenced the values of these kids, who grew up challenging the establishment and bringing about the sexual revolution.

This was the beginning of the generation gap. The combination of permissive parents, the influence of national media, and the powerful influence of this group based on their size were significant factors. Add to that their increased education and the fact that these kids grew up in affluence rather than subsistence and we end up with differences in values so great that adults and emerging youth could hardly understand—and would rarely accept—each other's viewpoints.

A Portrait of the '50s

Demographics in 1950
Population: 149,188,000
Farmers: 15.3%
Life expectancy:
Men: 65.6 years
Women: 71.1 years

Cost of Living in 1950
Eggs: 72¢ (doz.)
Milk: 21¢ (qt.)
Bread: 14¢ (loaf)
Coffee: 55¢ (lb.)
Round steak: 94¢ (lb.)

Money Matters in 1950
GNP: $364.8 billion
Federal budget: $39.6 billion
National debt: $257.4 billion
Prime interest rate: 1.5%
Average annual salary: $2,992

Key Events

1950	Korean War starts when North Korean troops invade South Korea; U.S. sends troops
1952	Polio epidemic: 58,000 cases lead to 1,400 deaths and thousands crippled
1952	General Dwight D. Eisenhower is elected president
1953	An armistice is signed to end the Korean War; Salk polio vaccine is developed and put into use
1954	Supreme Court unanimously decides that racial segregation in public schools is unconstitutional
1955	Interstate Commerce Commission bans segregation on interstate trains and buses
1956	President Eisenhower is reelected
1957	Russian satellite *Sputnik I* is launched; Americans are concerned about being behind in space race
1958	Beatnik movement begins
1958	First U.S. satellite, the *Explorer I*, is launched
1959	Alaska and Hawaii become the 49th and 50th states

Fads/Trends

Comic books, Silly Putty, Chutes & Ladders, Slinky
3-D movies, bowling
Flying saucer watching, hula hoops, pogo sticks, Frisbees
Davy Crockett coonskin caps and other merchandise
Beanie caps with propellers
Stuffing phone booths and cars
Dances: the cha-cha, the merengue (adults)
         the stroll, bunny hop (teens)
American Bandstand
Barbie doll introduced in 1959
Pizza
Waterskiing, go-carting

New Inventions/Technology

1951	The hydrogen bomb is developed
1951	Color TV introduced in U.S.
1951	UNIVAC, business computer
1952	TV dinners introduced by Swanson
1953	First successful open-heart surgery
1953	The Salk vaccine is developed
1954	First atomic-powered ship, the *Nautilus* submarine
1954	The microwave is invented; first color TVs are sold
1954	Seamless nylon stockings are produced
1955	Velcro and Dacron are produced
1956	Disposable diapers (Pampers)
1957	Sony introduces the first pocket-size transistor radio
1958	Stereophonic records are invented
1958	Launch of first U.S. satellite, *Explorer I*
1959	Pan American Airlines begins first passenger service encircling the globe

Radio

Rock 'n' roll music stations

Popular TV Shows

1950 *What's My Line?; Burns and Allen*

1951 *I Love Lucy; Red Skelton; Superman; Wild Bill Hickok*

1952 *The Jackie Gleason Show; Dragnet; I've Got a Secret*

1953 *You Are There; Romper Room; The Tonight Show*

1954 *Father Knows Best; Disneyland; Lassie*

1955 *The Lawrence Welk Show; The $64,000 Question; Gunsmoke*

1956 *As the World Turns; The Huntley-Brinkley Report; The Price Is Right*

1957 *American Bandstand; Have Gun, Will Travel*

1958 *The Donna Reed Show; 77 Sunset Strip; Rifleman; Lawman*

1959 *Rawhide; Bonanza; The Twilight Zone; The Many Loves of Dobie Gillis*

Hit Songs

1950 "Goodnight, Irene"; "Tennessee Waltz"; "Autumn Leaves"

1951 "Hello, Young Lovers"; "Unforgettable"; "Tell Me Why"

1952 "Your Cheatin' Heart"; "Lover"; "Glow Worm"

1953 "Secret Love"; "Ebbtide"; "Doggie in the Window"

1954 "Shake, Rattle, and Roll"; "Rock Around the Clock"; "*Cara Mia*"

1955 "Sixteen Tons"; "Maybelline"; "Only You"; "Earth Angel"

1956 "Blue Suede Shoes"; "Love Me Tender"; "Hot Diggity"

1957 "April Love"; "Jailhouse Rock"; "Peggy Sue"; "Tammy"

1958 "All I Have to Do Is Dream"; "Purple People Eater"

1959 "Personality"; "Sound of Music"; "I'm Just a Lonely Boy"

Publications

1950 *Betty Crocker's Picture Cookbook; Martian Chronicles*

1951 *Catcher in the Rye; From Here to Eternity*

1952 *Mad* comics; *Old Man & the Sea; East of Eden*

1952 *The Holy Bible, RSV* (Best Seller '52–54)

1953 *The Robe; A Man Called Peter; Angel Unaware*

1954   *Lord of the Flies; Fellowship of the Rings*
1955   *Gift from the Sea; Man in the Gray Flannel Suit*
1956   *Don't Go Near the Water; Peyton Place*
1957   *Kids Say the Darndest Things; The Cat in the Hat*
1958   *Dr. Zhivago; Breakfast at Tiffany's; Ice Palace*
1959   *Exodus; Hawaii; The Ugly American; The Mansion*

Movies
Movie attendance = 60 million weekly
1950   *All About Eve; Father of the Bride; Harvey*
1951   *A Streetcar Named Desire; African Queen; American in Paris*
1952   *High Noon; Greatest Show on Earth; Singin' in the Rain*
1953   *Gentlemen Prefer Blondes; From Here to Eternity*
1954   *On the Waterfront; Sabrina; Dial M for Murder*
1955   *Rebel Without a Cause; Lady and the Tramp; Oklahoma*
1956   *The King and I; The Ten Commandments; Around the World in 80 Days*
1957   *Bridge on the River Kwai; My Fair Lady*
1958   *Gigi; South Pacific; Cat on a Hot Tin Roof*
1959   *Ben-Hur; Sleeping Beauty; Some Like It Hot; Gidget*

Fashion
Lipsticks: pink and white
Madras plaid shirts, poodle skirts, toreador pants
Ponytails, poodle and pixie cuts, bouffant hairdos
Cinched waistlines and full skirts with petticoats, empire waists
Miss Clairol hair color (especially platinum blonde)
Shifts, chemises, raccoon coats, mohair, paisley
Rolled-up jeans, T-shirts, black leather jackets
Sideburns and greased-back hair, flattops, ducktails
Beatniks: khaki pants, sweaters, and sandals

Heroes

Elvis Presley

James Dean

General Douglas MacArthur

Dr. Benjamin Spock

Ricky Nelson

President Dwight Eisenhower

Sugar Ray Robinson

Roy Rogers

Chapter 10

The '60s
"The Times, They
Are A-Changin'"

During the '60s, California was the happening place to be, even if you were still in grade school like John. Born in 1950, he was soaking in the influences around him as the new decade began. At first the '60s didn't look very different from the '50s. Family-centered, affluent suburban life continued as it had been for the first few years, but dramatic changes were on the horizon. Those changes greatly affected those who experienced them, as well as those who watched.

As John and his coworkers sit around the table in the executive lunchroom, the songs of the oldies station that play over the intercom prompt memories that make for lively conversation. As they share their growing-up experiences, reactions range from peals of laughter to somber reflection to amazement at the changes they've been through during their lives.

As "The Times, They Are A-Changin'" started to play, Greg, one of the younger directors in the company, looked up from his Cobb salad. "So John, how much of the '60s do you remember? I heard George Carlin say that if you remember the '60s, you weren't really there!"

"Oh, I was there all right," chuckled John. "I may not remember it all, but I remember enough."

"Well, tell us what you do recall, and educate us youngsters about what we missed," Beth teased. "I love to hear about history from those who lived it firsthand!"

"I grew up in a pretty normal family. We weren't born hippies and radicals, you know. We lived in a nice house in the suburbs, Dad went to the office every day, and Mom helped in the PTA and played bridge with the ladies in the neighborhood. In those days, people didn't worry about 'stranger danger' and kids were allowed to go places on their own. I remember walking to the local movie theater, which had to be a couple of miles away. For 35 cents I'd see a double feature plus cartoons. I watched movies like *Spartacus, West Side Story, Mary Poppins, How the West Was Won,* and a bunch of Elvis movies. It seemed like all his movies had the same plot, just with different songs. Between the movies, they'd have drawings and give away prizes. I'd buy a hot dog for lunch, and by the time I'd get home, it would be dark.

"I remember watching a lot of TV with my brother and sister. Sometimes we'd fight about what to watch, so Dad came up with a plan to help keep the peace. We had a weekly schedule, and my days were Tuesday, Thursday, and Saturday morning. (I was the youngest, so Saturday morning cartoons were my favorites.) On our days, we got to choose which shows to watch. *Howdy Doody* was my favorite when I was little, and *The Mickey Mouse Club.* We all wanted to watch *Engineer Bill* at dinnertime. We'd save our glasses of milk so we could play red light, green light with him. When he said, "Green light," we'd all drink as much milk as we could until he said, "Red light." Then we stopped until he said, "Green light," again. I guess the goal was to see who could finish his milk first. I've always been pretty competitive. Maybe that's when it started! Anyway, it was a clever way to get the kids who were watching to drink their milk!

"Some shows even Mom and Dad watched with us. I remember Dad coming home from work early sometimes to watch Soupy Sales with us."

"Who or what was Soupy Sales?" interrupted Beth.

"He was a comedian who lived in a little house and had visits from some furry dog friends called White Fang and Black Tooth. They didn't speak any intelligent words, only made funny noises, and all you ever saw of them was their paws. They would play tricks on Soupy and get him in trouble. It sounds pretty dumb now, but we all thought it was hilarious. I also remember all of us climbing onto my parents' bed, watching *The Beverly Hillbillies* on the little TV they had in their bedroom and laughing together. We'd even talk about the show the next day at school with our friends, because they all watched it.

"Another big TV event I remember was the Kennedy-Nixon debate. It was the first time two presidential candidates faced each other on national television, and it was a big deal. We watched it as a family, and my parents told us that this was the first time they had a chance to hear the candidates talk about their views before an election. I remember thinking, *Wow, here I am at my age, getting to see the presidential candidates on TV. TV really brings life to us. From now on, we can really know what's going on.* These days, we may be hearing more than we want to about what is really going on.

"But sometimes, knowing what was going on was scary, like the Cuban missile crisis. When President Kennedy announced on TV that the Cubans were building missile bases for Soviet missiles that would be able to reach a lot of our American cities, everyone was worried. In schools we practiced getting under our desks in case of an attack, even in California! Kennedy had put the air force on alert, readied our own missiles, and sent Polaris nuclear subs toward Soviet waters. Then he set up a blockade of ships east of Cuba to prevent Soviet ships from coming to deliver missiles. There was an air attack planned, but Khrushchev cabled an offer to Kennedy saying he would dismantle the missile bases if the United States promised not to invade Cuba. The offer was accepted, war was averted, and Kennedy became a hero. We all breathed a little easier after that. Just telling you about it now brings back the memories of how scared I was back then.

"TV coverage also brought pictures and issues into our homes that had been easily ignored up to that point, like civil rights for black Americans. Civil rights legislation to desegregate schools and public transportation was passed in the mid-'50s, but we weren't affected much by the civil rights demonstrations until we started seeing coverage of them on TV in the early '60s. When we saw women and kids in those marches being attacked by police dogs and knocked down with water from fire hoses manned by police, we were shocked! All they were doing was asking for the rights they were already given by law. They weren't being destructive or violent, just standing up for themselves. It was easy to ignore the problem until you saw real people being hurt on TV."

As John was saying this, George from accounting joined them in the lunchroom.

"George, tell us about your memories of the civil rights events of the '60s," encouraged Greg. "Was anyone in your family directly involved? How did it affect you as a black person growing up during that time?"

"I had an older cousin who was a freedom rider in the South in the early '60s," he began. "He volunteered to be a part of a group of blacks and whites who rode buses into the South. They wanted to bring attention to the fact that although the new laws said that all passengers were to be treated equal and that segregated facilities were illegal, these laws weren't being obeyed or enforced. The blacks in the group would ride in the front of the bus, and the whites would ride in the back. When they came to towns and bus stops, the blacks would try to use the facilities reserved for whites only. They were trained not to be violent, just persistent. Their purpose was to force the issue, bring attention to the injustice they knew would result, and start people thinking about solutions for the problems."

"What happened to them?" Beth asked, full of concern.

"Sometimes they were met by crowds of angry people who beat them up with the permission of the local police chiefs," George winced at the memory. "Once, the bus was set on fire. Often they were led away to jail singing the old spirituals to encourage each other. It was pretty scary for my family, especially my aunt, but my cousin was determined to stick with it. I was very proud of him."

"Did their protest work?" asked Greg. "Was it worth all that they went through?"

There was a moment of thoughtful silence as George finished a bite of his sandwich. "At first it didn't seem to. Dr. Martin Luther King Jr. and the other leaders, who were mostly clergymen like him, kept encouraging our people to stick to nonviolence—but they realized that they needed to make a bigger impact. So they decided to have a protest march in Birmingham, Alabama, the city that was proud to be known as the most segregated city in America. They wanted to make a significant impact. And they sure did!

"The march that affected my family the most was the March on Washington, D.C. the summer of 1963," remembered George. "We lived in Los Angeles and couldn't afford to go, but we watched it on TV. About a quarter of a million people marched from the Washington Monument to the Lincoln Memorial singing, 'We shall overcome.' I remember singing along in our living room as all our relatives huddled around the TV. When Dr. King gave his 'I Have a Dream' speech, I remember looking at my mama and seeing tears running down her cheeks as she listened to his words of hope for the future. Her favorite part of the speech was:

'When we let freedom ring . . . we will be able to speed up that day when all of God's children, black men and white men, Jews and Gentiles, Protestants and Catholics, will all be able to join hands and sing in the words of the old Negro spiritual, 'Free at last! Free at last! Thank God almighty, we are free at last!'[1]

"But not everyone agreed with Dr. King's nonviolent protests. Many were getting impatient and angry, and leaders like Malcolm X were becoming popular. Even though he was murdered in 1965, his influence through his books and followers led to groups like the Black Panthers who advocated 'black power,' black pride, and demanding rights by force.

"I'll never forget the Watts riots in August of 1965. It was five days of rioting, burning buildings, and looting started by an incident of police brutality. Something just snapped in the community, and pretty soon everything was out of control. It was hopeless rage and violent despair. We lived on the outskirts of it, and I was scared to death. Mama made us all stay inside, away from the windows. We packed some suitcases in case our apartment started to burn and we had to get out of there fast. Our neighbor owned a store in the middle of the rioting area, and even though he put a sign in the window saying that blacks owned it, it was looted and destroyed just like the rest of the businesses. For months after it was over, I had nightmares about waking up in a burning apartment."

"How awful!" murmured Beth.

"I remember it, too," inserted John. "We lived about 30 miles away in Long Beach, and it seemed to go on forever! My dad had us get out the hunting rifles and load them, just in case. It all seemed so crazy and out of control, we couldn't tell what would happen next."

"It finally ended with about 35 dead, more than 900 injured, and 4,000 arrested. It took years for the community to recover," George explained sadly. "And it led to similar riots in other cities. I read somewhere that between 1965 and 1968 there were over 100 riots in American cities, with more than 8,000 people killed or injured."

"And the blacks weren't the only group that were protesting their plight," added John. "College students started having sit-ins at the colleges, starting the free speech movement, and the feminists were starting NOW, the National Organization for Women. Feminists were holding their own protests by burning their bras and picketing the Miss America Pageants. The environmentalists also got started in the '60s. There were causes to join everywhere!"

"Wow, the '60s really was a time of protest, wasn't it?"

exclaimed Greg. "There were also all those Vietnam War protests, too, right?"

"That's right," nodded John. "The evening news was full of reports of violence in the war and violence in opposition to the war here at home. The protesters were questioning the government's motives and justification for going, and there never seemed to be any good answers. I remember it really hitting home to me the summer before my senior year in high school. My friends and I were realizing we had one more year before we were eligible for the draft, and we needed to decide what to do.

"We had this friend, Steve, about a year older than us. He knew he was going to be drafted, so he enlisted in the Marines. He was only in Nam a few months when the boat he was in tipped over. He was always looking out for the other guy, and he was helping everyone else get into the rescue boat. By the time everyone else was in the boat, he was tired and couldn't hold on any longer. The weight of his gear pulled him under, and he drowned. He lost his life, and we didn't understand why. I remember going to his funeral. We were still in high school, and we were asking each other, 'Why did Steve have to die? Why was he even in Vietnam?' His death seemed so meaningless and really made the issue personal for us.

"No one seemed to know why we were fighting this war, yet if we became eligible for the draft, we would be expected to fight. A lot of guys were planning to go to college, because that would mean a deferment from the draft. Some talked about going to Canada to escape the draft. Our attitude toward this war was so different from the way my dad and grandfather talked about World War I and II. They told stories about how young guys would lie about their age so they could enlist early and go and fight. People at home were all patriotic, helping with the war effort by making sacrifices for the cause and calling the soldiers heroes when they came home.

"Vietnam was a totally different story. Instead of lying about their age to get into the army, guys were lying about their nationality to avoid the draft. Others were burning their draft cards, trying to avoid going to war. Instead of getting behind the cause, a lot of Americans questioned and protested the war. Instead of coming home as heroes, Vietnam vets were often looked down on. I remember watching the news one evening and seeing a group of soldiers getting off a plane, just having returned from Nam. The protesters were yelling at them, carrying signs, and some were even spitting on the soldiers as they walked by."

"That's so sad. It all sounds pretty depressing. Was anything good going on?" Beth wanted to know as she pushed the last few bites of salad around on her plate.

"Yeah, there were the Beatles and the Beach Boys and a lot of other great groups." The change in topic seemed to perk John up. "My brother and sister and I were really into music, because my grandfather had a jukebox in his restaurant. When he got the new releases, he gave us the old 45s, so we had quite a collection. But when the Beatles arrived on the scene, our interest intensified, and we started buying our own records. We could hardly wait for the next one to come out."

"Weren't the parents kind of worked up over the Beatles and all that 'Beatlemania' stuff?" asked Beth.

"They were, and it's funny to think about it now," chuckled John. "Everyone was talking about their long hair, but if you look at their first albums, they looked pretty clean-cut, and their hair wouldn't be considered long at all now. Their music was about teenage romance, and some of it was pretty mellow in the beginning. In fact, some songs like 'Til There Was You' and 'Michelle' are played in dentist offices and elevators now as Muzak. But as the decade progressed, their music and lifestyles changed, and we changed right along with them. As their hair grew longer, they also became more radical and got into drugs and Eastern religions, and so did many of us. I even took meditation lessons from a maharishi at one point. The Beatles definitely had a significant influence on society, and my life mirrored that in many ways."

"So, were you a hippie, and did you live in a commune, have 'love-ins,' and talk about 'flower power'?" Greg was starting to see John in a whole new light and was amused by his mental picture of John with shoulder-length hair, wearing a headband, love beads, and bell-bottoms.

"I didn't move to San Francisco with flowers in my hair, but I did have psychedelic flowers painted on my VW bus. I experimented with a lot of stuff, just like all my friends, and life was 'groovy' in those days. We were into rejecting everything that was connected with 'the establishment,' which was basically our parents, school administrators, big business, and the government. We wanted to be free from meaningless traditions and rules and be free to do our own thing. Through drugs, mysticism, and just plain truth-seeking, we believed we were achieving a higher level of consciousness, a new level of freedom. We basically tried to create a new culture based on love and enlightenment."

A pause in the conversation allowed the group to hear the song that was playing on the radio. The singer was asking if anyone had seen his old friend John, who had freed a lot of people, but now was gone. It seemed to him that the good die young.

"So, what about Kennedy's assassination? Do you remember when it happened?" asked Greg.

"That's one of those moments in history when everyone who was old enough to understand what was going on remembers where they were and what they were doing. I was in junior high at the time. My teacher announced that the principal was going to make an important announcement over the speakers in our rooms. When he told us that President Kennedy had been assassinated, several kids gasped, and we were all stunned. Some of the girls started crying. When we went to the cafeteria for lunch, everyone was subdued and quiet.

"I kept thinking, *Why couldn't the government with the Secret Service men protect the president? If he isn't safe, am I safe?* Then my next thought was, *Who killed him?* I really believed that the Russians killed the president and that nuclear war was about to start. Of course it didn't, and for several days, all we did was watch the coverage of the whole event on TV. The replays of the shooting in slow motion, the swearing in of Lyndon Johnson as the new president, and of course, the funeral procession. I don't think anyone will ever forget the sight of little three-year-old John-John saluting his father's casket as it went by. Then Martin Luther King and Robert Kennedy were assassinated. It seemed like all the heroes were being shot.

"I think that was the beginning of my questions about the government. The government's inability to protect the president and other leaders concerned me. But then I saw civil rights protesters being treated harshly by police and started hearing about the protests against the government's involvement in Vietnam. There were dissenters and activists on every side, and I was watching them and listening to them."

"Sounds like it was a rough time for the government," commented Beth. "Was anyone happy with anything they were doing?"

"We got pretty excited about the space program," said George, rejoining the conversation. "We had been racing those Russians with their cosmonauts for years, and it seemed like they were always a step ahead of us. But when we were the first to land a man on the moon, we were all really proud and excited."

"That's the other moment in history where everyone remembers where they were," interjected John. "I was 19 and working at McDonald's, but the boss had brought in a TV set so we could watch it. There was hardly any business, because most people were home watching their TVs, too."

"I remember that it was a Sunday evening," added George, "and we were supposed to be singing in the youth choir in the church service. But we didn't want to miss seeing this historic event! Mama was a little upset with us for not going, but Papa said, 'Church is there every week, but watching the first moon landing is a once-in-a-lifetime experience.' So we all sat there with the rest of the world and watched Neil Armstrong take that historic step and say, 'One small step for man, one giant leap for mankind.' It was a moment of glory for Americans and a positive event to help close such a turbulent decade."

"Well, on that positive note, I think we'd better end this reminiscing and get back to work." Greg started collecting food containers to be tossed. "Thanks for the history lesson, guys. I'll never listen to '60s music quite the same way again."

A Closer Look

The '60s was a decade of change. Virtually every value and area of life was examined and challenged by some segment of society. Let's take a look at some of the statistics and events that affected those of us who were developing our values during this time.

■ ■ ■

In the first half of the '60s, salaries were up (increasing 20 percent), inflation was stable (1 to 2 percent), and unemployment was low (5 to 6 percent).[2] People had more money than ever before, were experiencing the good life, and continued to indulge their kids.

■ ■ ■

By 1969, 58 million of the nation's 62 million households had television sets (94 percent).[3] By the mid-'60s, stations began broadcasting in color, and by 1969, 40 percent of TVs were color sets.[4] Daily newscasts gave people a new awareness of current issues and world events. This had the simultaneous effect of shrinking the world into a global village that could be experienced, to some extent, through the miracle of television. It expanded people's universes beyond their homes and neighborhoods, and they were confronted with issues that had not touched their lives before.

■ ■ ■

Blacks and sympathetic whites protested to encourage the enforcement of civil rights laws that were passed in the

1950s. Peaceful in the beginning, these protests became more militant and eventually led to violent rioting in cities across the nation. Television coverage of the events led to increased support from other sectors of American society.

■ ■ ■

Feminists like Betty Friedan, author of *The Feminine Mystique,* brought attention to women's issues such as sexual discrimination in the workplace and abortion. NOW was established in 1966. The increased use of the birth control pill helped to end the baby boom and gave women more control over their lives and sexual freedom. The number of working women increased by about 50 percent during this decade.[5]

■ ■ ■

One of the most momentous movements of the decade was the turning of the youth against their parents' values. Everything was questioned and suspect. Materialism was seen as the corrupting force of society. Greed and lust for power were seen as the reasons behind the social inequities being experienced by minorities and women and as the motivation behind the imperialistic foreign policy that led to involvement in Vietnam. Many of the youth lost respect for authority and did not feel obligated to obey authorities they did not respect. "Never trust anyone over 30" was a common statement. This was due, in part, to the belief of young people that adults lied to them. The government lied about things that were going on in Vietnam. Adults told them that marijuana would kill them. Blacks were promised equalities that were still being denied them. Products that were supposed to help the environment, like DDT, turned out to be harmful. The youth responded by rejecting adult values, which included the good life their parents had worked so hard to obtain for them. They demanded freedom from old rules, free speech, free sex, and freedom to do their own thing. In

1969, a total of 448 universities either experienced student strikes or were forced to close. Student demands included revision of admissions policies and the reorganization of entire academic programs, in addition to antiwar and civil rights issues.[6]

■ ■ ■

Like so many of the traditional values that were challenged by the youth of this decade, religion was also affected. The mainline Protestant churches saw an 11 percent decrease in attendance. However, conservative, evangelical Protestant groups, including Pentecostal churches, actually grew in number and respectability during this time. The Roman Catholic Church experienced great change through Pope John XXIII's Second Vatican Council held in 1962 to reform the church. This brought about changes such as masses performed in local languages rather than Latin. Some of the results of Vatican II included greater acceptance for Catholics and their doctrines in American society. In addition, many priests and nuns left their orders, and parishioners became more willing to act independently of the church in religious and moral matters, especially when it came to birth control.

Many young people became interested in Eastern religions, such as Buddhism, Hinduism, Zen Buddhism, and Krishna and spiritual practices such as transcendental meditation. Islam was embraced by many blacks as part of the "black is beautiful" movement.

■ ■ ■

The popular fashions of the young mirrored their rejection of adult values. Instead of the neat, orderly fashions of adults, the youth chose outrageous outfits with bright colors and designs. Bell-bottom pants with patterned, colored shirts, headbands, sunglasses, and beads (both men and women); loose-flowing, ethnic-style (especially East Indian

and African) clothes; and secondhand clothes decorated
with fringes and patches became popular. Men grew big
sideburns and let their hair grow long. Women and girls
also wore their hair long and often used an iron to
straighten it.

More conservative dressers were wearing bell-bottoms,
pantsuits, mini-, maxi-, and midi- (mid-calf) skirts. The
"mod" look was in (from England).

■ ■ ■

Organ transplants (heart, lungs, livers, pancreas, kidneys)
were accomplished successfully during this decade. Vaccines were introduced that prevented measles and rubella,
and oral polio vaccines were used. Radiation and
chemotherapy were being used against cancer. Cigarettes
were identified as a leading cause of cancer, heart disease,
and other fatal illnesses. Tobacco companies were forced to
stop TV advertising and required to put warning labels on
cigarette packs and printed ads.

■ ■ ■

Rachel Carson, in her book *Silent Spring,* described a
world in which nature has been destroyed by the use of
pesticides. It was instrumental in stopping the production
of DDT and was the beginning of the modern environmental movement. In 1961, Congress passed the Water
Pollution Control Act, which forced many polluters to
stop dangerous practices. Concern about polluted air led
to a federal clean air act in 1963 and another in 1967 that
set standards for what could be emitted from
smokestacks.[7]

■ ■ ■

Several factors during the '60s affected behavior and attitudes about sex and marriage. The feminist movement
became popular and vocal, and marriage rates for women
of all ages leveled off or fell during the '60s and '70s.
Feminists also lobbied for changes in divorce laws, which

partially accounted for divorce rates nearly doubling
between 1968 and 1972. With all the emphasis on freedom and rights, divorce was not viewed as distastefully as
it had been.

Youth tended to postpone marriage for several other
reasons, including rejection of traditional values and the
greater acceptance of premarital sex. The availability of the
Pill made birth control easier and more effective. Sex outside of marriage became more common and more graphic
in movies and song lyrics. Although the traditional view of
premarital sex being wrong was still held by most people,
the trend was definitely heading toward looser attitudes
toward sexual behavior. In 1969, a Gallup poll reported
that 74 percent of women believed that premarital sex was
wrong. Just a few years later, only 53 percent of women
surveyed shared that belief.[8] This "sexual revolution" and
"free love" had ramifications. By 1967, many colleges in
the country had coed dorms. Venereal disease greatly
increased among the youth.

■ ■ ■

To stop the spread of communism from North Vietnam
to South Vietnam, the U.S. government chose to support
the South Vietnamese cause by sending military advisors.
In 1962, the U.S. government told those advisors that
they could fire in self-defense if attacked. In 1964, Congress passed the Tonkin Resolution approving presidential
action in Vietnam after the North Vietnamese were
accused of firing on a U.S. ship. In 1965, continuous
bombing of North Vietnam began. On October 15 and
16, war protests were held in 40 American cities. In 1967
war protests increased. In 1968, Vietnam became the
longest war in U.S. history. In 1969, 250,000 antiwar
activists marched on Washington, D.C. In 1969, the first
draft lottery was held. Serious questions about the U.S.
government's goals, motives, methods, and truthfulness in

reporting made this war very unpopular, particularly with the youth of the nation. The "score" in 1969 was:

- U.S. troop strength: 484,000
- U.S. dead: 39,893
- U.S. wounded: 250,000
- U.S. missing: 1,400
- Enemy dead: 568,989

■ ■ ■

The music of the '60s was an important form of expression for the youth. The music changed dramatically from the beginning to the end of the decade, reflecting the experience and concerns of those producing it. The most obvious example of this would be the evolution of the Beatles' music and their lifestyles—from "I Want to Hold Your Hand" to their "Magical Mystery Tour" album.

The music was definitely the teens' own, unique from that of their parents, and the lyrics reflected their passions (love, sex, drugs) and their sentiments (antiwar, anti-establishment, pro-environment). Of course, within the youth music, there was a variety of sounds: The Beatles, The Beach Boys, Simon and Garfunkel, Sonny and Cher, The Fifth Dimension, Diana Ross, Bob Dylan, The Mamas and the Papas, The Rolling Stones, Janis Joplin, Glen Campbell, The Righteous Brothers, The Monkees, Jimi Hendrix, Jefferson Airplane (we could go on and on).

Not only was music something to be listened to on your transistor radio or record player, it was something to be experienced. Rock concerts often drew 50,000 or more fans and would go on for hours with lots of drug use, especially marijuana. Probably the most historic rock festival was the Woodstock Festival, held in Bethel, New York, in August of 1969. An estimated 400,000 people showed up; it lasted for several days, and it rained a lot. It could have been a disaster, but the spirit of community and sharing prevailed, and even the police spoke well of the fans. They listened to hours of music by Jimi Hendrix, Country Joe and the Fish, Janis Joplin, Joe Cocker, and many more. Not all concerts were as amiable, however, and drug overdoses were common occurrences.[9]

■ ■ ■

The race into space that began in the 1950s when Russia launched the first satellite, *Sputnik*, continued into the '60s. Russia launched two dogs into space in 1960, and the United States followed with a chimpanzee. On April 12, 1961, the Russians launched the first man into space, followed by the first American in space on May 5, 1961. JFK challenged Congress with the goal of a man on the moon by the end of the decade, and the space program made amazing advances during the decade, resulting in the first lunar landing on July 20, 1969.

The decade of the '60s was a turning point in American society. It's impossible to adequately represent all that occurred during that time and all the ramifications we experienced in the values that were developed. Obviously the biggest result was the huge gap that became evident between the values of the youth and the values of the adults. One factor that influenced this was that most young people were more educated than their parents. This group of kids was raised in a time when education was a high priority, and the economics of the country could better provide an education for them. This increase in education gave them a different perspective and perhaps the attitude that their perspective was more accurate.

These kids spent the first half of the decade watching what was going on, largely through television. They learned that, because of their sheer numbers, they were a force to be reckoned with, to be catered to, to be listened to. Dr. Spock told their parents to listen to their needs, respond to those needs, and let them express themselves as individuals, which they did. Industries catered to them as the huge group of consumers they were.

The government had to make room for them, building new schools, supplying more teachers, and so on. They had clout, and, as they grew up during the second half of the decade, they learned to use it.

This group of kids was more aware of the issues and problems in society than any other developing group because of the exposure they received through television. They became aware of the many groups who were protesting unfair treatment, unjust actions, and deceit on the part of government, institutions, and big business. These kids picked up the antiestablishment values that were bombarding them through the media and people they came in contact with. They developed an incredible mistrust of the status quo. This caused a large number of them to question and then reject many of the values of their parents, which led to much misunderstanding and tension in families. The values they clashed over included such things as hair and clothing style, music preference, attitudes toward money and materialism, morality, sexual freedom, war, drugs, religion, the government, the environment, health food, and authority. There seemed to be few topics that parents and their kids agreed on. The concept of the generation gap was quite real and strongly felt. It encouraged strong identification with their peer group, who understood and shared similar values (or at least similar questions).

A Portrait of the '60s

Demographics in 1960
Population: 177,830,000
Farmers: 8.7%
Life expectancy:
Men: 66.6 years
Women: 73.1 years

Money Matters in 1960
GNP: $503.7 billion
Federal budget: 92.3 billion
National debt: $286.3 billion
Prime interest rate: 3.9%
Average annual salary: $4,743

Cost of Living in 1960
Eggs: 58¢ (doz.)
Milk: 26¢ (qt.)
Bread: 20¢ (loaf)
Coffee: 75¢ (lb.)
Round steak: $1.06 (lb.)

Key Events

1960	John F. Kennedy elected president
1960	70,000 blacks and whites hold sit-ins in more than 100 cities in civil rights demonstrations
1961	Alan Shepard is first American in space
1961	Roger Maris hits 61 home runs, setting new record
1962	Bay of Pigs invasion of Cuba
1962	Cuban missile crisis
1963	Troops sent to Vietnam as advisors
1963	Civil Rights March on Washington, D.C.; Dr. Martin Luther King's "I Have a Dream" speech
1963	President Kennedy assassinated in Dallas; Lyndon Johnson becomes president
1964	Lyndon Johnson reelected president
1964	U.S. bombing of Vietnam begins
1964	Beatles arrive in the U.S.
1965	First combat troops sent to Vietnam
1965	Watts riots in L.A.
1966	Astronauts walk in space
1967	Blacks riot in Newark, N.J., and Detroit
1968	Martin Luther King Jr. assassinated
1968	Robert Kennedy assassinated
1968	Richard Nixon elected president
1969	Neil Armstrong, of *Apollo XI*, is the first man to walk on the moon
1969	Second manned lunar landing in *Apollo XII*

Fads and Trends
Ken and Barbie dolls, troll dolls
Comedy records (e.g., Bob Newhart)
Folksinging in coffee shops
Artificial tanning creams
"T.P.ing" (toilet-papering friends' homes)
Surfing, skateboarding
Yo-yos, Superballs, science kits, model planes, trains,
    and cars
Mickey Mouse watches
Dances: the twist, the pony, the swim, the jerk, the
    mashed potato
Hootenannies—folk concerts with audience participation
Beatlemania
Go-go girls
Ouija boards, astrology, tarot cards
Jogging, health food
Psychedelic art, lava lamps
Underground newspapers

New Inventions/Technology
The Pill, oral contraceptive
Aluminum cans for food and beverages
Lasers
Digital display for pocket calculators and watches
First communications and weather satellites
Mariner II, first space probe, declares Venus inhospitable
Telstar is launched; first transatlantic TV broadcast
Diet Rite and Tab introduced (first diet sodas)
First human lung, heart, liver, and pancreas transplants
Valium tranquilizer
Stereo cassette decks
German measles and rubella vaccines made available
Integrated circuits for electronics and computers
Mariner IV transmits photos of Mars

Popular TV Shows

1960	Kennedy-Nixon debate; *Route 66; The Flintstones*
1961	*Dr. Kildare; The Dick Van Dyke Show*
1962	*Beverly Hillbillies; Bonanza; The Tonight Show* (Carson)
1963	*Candid Camera; My Favorite Martian*
1964	*Bewitched; Peyton Place; Jeopardy*
1965	*Batman; Hogan's Heroes; Red Skelton Hour*
1966	*Mission Impossible; Get Smart; Dating Game*
1967	*A Family Affair; Ironside; The Phil Donahue Show*
1968	*Rowan & Martin's Laugh-In; 60 Minutes; The Mod Squad*
1969	*Marcus Welby, MD; The Brady Bunch; Sesame Street*

Hit Songs

1960	"Are You Lonesome Tonight?"; "Chain Gang"
1961	"Big Bad John"; "Moon River"; "Wimoweh"
1962	"I Left My Heart in San Francisco"; "Go Away, Little Girl"
1963	"Wipe Out"; "If I Had a Hammer"; "Puff the Magic Dragon"
1964	"I Get Around"; "I Want to Hold Your Hand"; "People"
1965	"Help!"; "Like a Rolling Stone"; "The Look of Love"
1966	"Ballad of the Green Beret"; "Sounds of Silence"; "Michelle"
1967	"The Beat Goes On"; "Lucy in the Sky with Diamonds"; "Windy"
1968	"Lady Madonna"; "Stoned Soul Picnic"; "Love Is Blue"
1969	"Good Morning, Starshine"; "Hair"; "Wichita Lineman"

Fashions

The Jackie Kennedy look, pillbox hats
The Barbra Streisand look
Hot pants, bell-bottoms, hip huggers
The mod look
Secondhand clothing, fringe, patches
Boots, sandals
Bright colors, wild patterns, tie-dye T-shirts
Platform shoes

Pantsuits, turtlenecks, tights
Nehru jackets
Love beads (men and women), headbands
Men: long hair, big sideburns, mustaches
Women: long straight hair (ironed)

Publications
1960 *Hawaii; To Kill a Mockingbird; Advice and Consent*
1961 *Catch-22; The Agony and the Ecstasy; Carpetbaggers*
1962 *Silent Spring; Ship of Fools; Dearly Beloved*
1963 *Feminine Mystique; Happiness Is a Warm Puppy*
1964 *The Spy Who Came in from the Cold; Games People Play*
1965 *The Source; Up the Down Staircase; World Aflame*
1966 *Valley of the Dolls; The Fixer; Human Sexual Response*
1967 *Rosemary's Baby; Christy; The Naked Ape*
1968 *Soul on Ice; Listen to the Warm; Myra Breckenridge*
1969 *Andromeda Strain; The Peter Principle; On Death and Dying*

Movies
Movie attendance = 40 million weekly
1960 *Psycho; Spartacus; The Magnificent Seven*
1961 *West Side Story; The Hustler; The Guns
       of Navarrone*
1962 *Lawrence of Arabia; The Miracle Worker; Dr. No*
1963 *Cleopatra; How the West Was Won; The Birds*
1964 *My Fair Lady; Dr. Strangelove; Mary Poppins*
1965 *The Sound of Music; Cat Ballou; Dr. Zhivago*
1966 *A Man for All Seasons; Who's Afraid of
       Virginia Woolf?*
1967 *The Graduate; In the Heat of the Night; Dirty
       Dozen*
1968 *Funny Girl; Oliver; 2001: A Space Odyssey*
1969 *Midnight Cowboy; True Grit; Hello, Dolly;
       Easy Rider*

Heroes

Johnny Unitas	Roger Maris
Willie Mays	Sandy Koufax
Don Drysdale	Bart Starr
Wilt Chamberlain	Jerry West
Elvis Presley	The Beatles
The Rolling Stones	John F. Kennedy
Dr. Martin Luther King, Jr.	Malcolm X
Neil Armstrong	Betty Friedan
Jackie Kennedy	Abbie Hoffman

Chapter 11

The '70s
"Bridge Over
Troubled Waters"

The '70s were a time of real transition from the quest for political and social change of the '60s to the search for personal fulfillment and enlightenment that continued into the '80s. As the Baby Boomers grew to adulthood, a new group began to form its values in the turbulent society that had developed.

Dave, now in his mid-30s, was one of the first to be born in the generation after the baby boom. He and his younger brother, Mike, have a tradition of bringing their families together for an annual vacation. Today they're down at the lake, watching the kids while their wives have their customary "Mom's day out," shopping at the cute little shops in the nearby resort town. Watching the kids play reminds them of their own childhood together and gets them talking about the past.

"Remember those family vacations we used to have at the beach, before Mom and Dad got divorced?" asked Mike, as he rubbed suntan lotion onto his daughter's back, trying not to rub sand on her already-pink skin. "Mom would cover us with lotion, and then we'd bury each other in the sand, and it would stick all over us."

"We didn't seem to care about being sandy, but Mom would send us down to the water to rinse off. The hardest part was trying to wash out the sand that was inside our trunks," laughed Dave. "Those were fun times. It's my great memories of those days that made me suggest having our families' vacation

149

together. It's too bad Mom couldn't afford to continue those kinds of vacations after Dad left."

"Yeah, things definitely got tighter when they split up. I don't think I missed the money as much as I missed having Mom home. Moving to an apartment wasn't so bad. At least we didn't have to mow the lawn anymore, and we had a pool. But waiting for Mom to come home from work was kind of a drag, and she always had so much to do. I got really tired of those Crock-Pot meals, and she hardly ever had the time or energy to bake her great chocolate chip cookies. But Mom would still try to do special things for us when she could afford it, like those trips to Disneyland," remembered Mike.

"But a day at Disneyland is not the same as a week at a house on the beach for making memories." Dave smiled as he watched his sons, Christopher and Michael, trying to skip rocks on the lake with their cousin Jason. "Remember when we used to do that when we were their age?"

"What do you mean, 'when we were their age'? If I remember correctly, we were doing it last night after dinner, and I got the most skips," laughed Mike. "I always was better at it than you. Some things never change."

"But I was always better at fishing," Dave reminded him.

"Only because Dad took you fishing more than he took me," complained Mike.

"That's because you couldn't sit still very long, and you scared the fish away with all the commotion you made. It used to drive Dad nuts."

"Still, I was really bummed out when he'd pick you up to go fishing on the weekend and didn't take me. I felt really left out," admitted Mike. "Mom would try and make me feel better by taking me to the movies, but I just kept thinking that you were getting to be with Dad and I wasn't. I guess I was afraid he liked you better than he liked me."

"I never knew you felt like that! You were always bragging about the movie that you got to see that I didn't. I thought you were glad you didn't have to go fishing because you didn't like it." Dave was amazed at this revelation. "Why didn't you say something? You could have come. We could have done something else. I know Dad didn't mean to hurt you. I'm sure he had no idea you felt that way. I certainly didn't."

"I don't think I really understood it myself. I wouldn't have been able to put it into words. When I went to that counselor, when Susan and I were going through our divorce, a lot of these kinds of feelings that I never really admitted to myself came out. That counseling couldn't save our marriage; Susan was too determined to get out. But I really benefited from the insight it gave me about myself, and it helped me to let go of some things and forgive people I had been holding grudges against, like Dad and Susan. Just being able understand them better, to see things from their point of view, helped me a lot."

"Sometimes I wonder if Mom and Dad could have worked things out if he'd been willing to go to counseling with her. But he was so turned off by all her self-help stuff—the TM and EST and whatever else she was into—that I don't think he would have gone," remarked Dave. They were quiet for a few moments, each thinking his own thoughts, when Mike's daughter, Jessica, came running back to them. "Daddy, the boys say I can't skip rocks with them. They say it's a boy's game."

"They're probably just afraid you'll show them up. I happen to know you're a great rock skipper. After all, I taught you myself." Turning toward the boys at the water's edge, Mike yelled, "Hey, guys! Let Jessica play. This is an equal-opportunity vacation."

"Thanks, Daddy," she called over her shoulder as she ran to find a good, smooth stone.

"How are Jessica and Jason handling the whole divorce, joint custody, and remarriage thing? They look like they're doing fine," remarked Dave.

"Yeah, they seem to be," agreed Mike. "They come and spend every other weekend with us, and they have their own rooms with their stuff in them, so I think they're okay with it. Sometimes they don't seem to have the right thing at the right house, or they leave something they need for school, and that's a hassle, but for the most part it works. They seem to really like Karen and get along well with her kids. I think it helps that her kids are a little younger, so there's not really much competition between them. In fact, I think Jessica likes mothering them."

"You know, you would have been welcome to bring them along on this trip. I hope Karen realized that."

"Oh, she knew that," assured Mike. "Their father really wanted them with him this week. They have a family wedding or something like that. Actually, I'm kind of glad it worked out this way. It makes it more like the other years we've done it. There will be plenty of other times when my stepkids will be with us. They're good kids. I guess my one regret about them not coming is that you're not getting a chance to know them better. But that will come."

"So, changing the subject, how are things going for you at work? You still liking your job?" asked Dave as he twisted the cap off a bottle of spring water.

"Yeah, it's going pretty good. The VPs are starting to realize what I can do on the computer, and they're starting to come to me for some of the things they can't figure out or don't want to take the time to learn. I guess that puts me in a good situation. I was beginning to think I would never get anywhere in that company. It's full of overcommitted boomers who have no intention of retiring in the near future and don't mind working overtime. I just can't see doing that to my family. I'd rather put in my eight hours a day and then have a real life. At my last evaluation, my supervisor thought I wasn't showing enough initiative or motivation because I wasn't willing to stay late or come in on the weekends, even for time-and-a-half. He just doesn't understand that my identity doesn't come from my job like his seems to. It's a good thing, with the kinds of jobs people our age have to settle for. It seemed like every company was downsizing when we got out of school."

"Sometimes it seems like we were born in the wrong era," said Dave, shaking his head. "Do you ever stop and think about what was going on when we grew up? Older people wonder why we're not more patriotic, or why we're so skeptical about institutions and can't trust the government. But think about it! The war in Vietnam was still going on, but as some of the vets came home—and when those secret Pentagon papers were published—we found out that the government had been lying to us about what was really going on over there. Remember the picture of those Vietnamese children running down the street after the napalm attack on their village? Everyone was so shocked that American forces had done this. It really impressed me when even the returning vets were protesting the war and throwing their medals on the steps of the Capitol. They couldn't be proud of what they had been a part of. And then in the end, after all those years and all those people died, we ended up losing the war anyway."

"And then there was the whole Watergate scandal, with Nixon resigning. And even before that, his vice president, Agnew, had resigned because he got caught cheating on his taxes or something," added Mike.

"Remember how the Watergate investigation seemed to be on TV forever? And remember how shocked everyone was when the transcripts of the president's tapes were released, and the words 'expletive deleted' showed up all over the pages?" asked Dave. "It showed a side of Nixon that the public had never seen. I remember how disappointed Mom was. She had really respected him up to that point. I remember her saying, 'It's a sad thing when you have to tell your children not to follow the example of the president, but boys, using that kind of language is not acceptable.'"

"It's 'déjà vu all over again' with Clinton, only the revelations of his private actions were a lot more shocking than using four-letter words," interjected Mike. "Talk about kids losing respect for their president!"

"Let's not get started on that topic," groaned Dave. "We've heard enough about that to last a hundred lifetimes! We were talking about all the things that happened in the '70s that messed us up. We can talk about what is messing up our kids another time."

"Okay, okay. There was the war, the lies and corruption in the government. What else scarred us for life?" asked Mike.

"How about the insecurity of realizing that things we took for granted, like gas and electricity, were not limitless and there might not be enough to go around? Remember when we could only buy gas every other day, and we had to wait in long lines at the gas station and hope it wouldn't run out before we got our turn?"

"Oh, yeah," remembered Mike. "And didn't we have to turn our thermostats down to 68 degrees, and they wanted everyone to carpool? It was even considered unpatriotic to put Christmas lights on your house during that time because it wasted energy."

"And they kept talking about how polluted the air and rivers were getting and that we needed to start protecting certain animals or they would disappear from the face of the earth. Then we started finding out about toxic wastes poisoning whole neighborhoods of people, and the ozone layer was being destroyed. And do you remember Three Mile Island? The partial meltdown at the power plant could have become the nuclear disaster many had been predicting."

"And they wonder why our generation is less than optimistic about the future? It's a wonder we didn't all lose hope and commit suicide. I'm getting depressed just thinking about it," said Mike, but only half joking. "Speaking of suicide, remember that weird Jim Jones cult, the People's Temple? I still remember seeing the pictures of rows and rows of bodies lying next to each other after they drank poisoned Kool-Aid in Jonestown, Guyana. I remember wondering, *Why would they do that? How could one man have such power over so many people that he could convince them all to kill themselves?* It was something like a thousand people, wasn't it?"

"Yeah. That was weird," agreed Dave. "There were lots of cults becoming popular then. Remember the family that lived in our apartment complex, the one whose son quit college and ran off to become a Moonie? He wouldn't have anything to do with his family, and his family was convinced he had been brainwashed. They hired a guy to go 'rescue' him by kidnapping him and deprogramming him." Dave was thoughtful for a moment. "I think there was so much uncertainty and so many shattered beliefs that people were just looking for something or someone to believe in. When someone came along offering 'absolute truth,' people were hungry for it. I remember feeling that way. There didn't seem to be any leaders in the country that could be trusted. We were in the process of destroying our environment, so the future was uncertain. The economy was in trouble, so we couldn't count on working hard and achieving the good life, like previous generations. I'm just glad I didn't end up following the wrong leader, like so many others did. I really found hope and direction when I was born again in Christ."

"You really got into that whole Jesus movement thing," remarked Mike. "Mom was concerned at first, because most of the Jesus freaks looked like hippies, and she was afraid they were into smoking marijuana and all that. But when you were so into studying the Bible and going to church, she figured it was okay. That was probably why she started going back to church herself and listening to those TV evangelists all the time. And you about drove me crazy listening to all that Maranatha music!"

Dave hesitated a moment, then looked at Mike and said, "She and I have always hoped and prayed that you'd come to know Christ personally someday. It wasn't just a passing fad, you know. He's still the source of peace and purpose in our lives today, and if you haven't noticed, the world hasn't gotten any better than it was in the '70s."

Mike laughed a little as he turned his head to watch the kids working on a sand fort. "You know, it's been several years since you've preached to me, Dave. And I appreciate you giving me my space on this." He paused for a moment, and then continued, "Actually, I've been doing a little soul-searching since my divorce, and I might actually be closer to taking that step than you might think."

Just then they were attacked by a troop of hungry kids who were yelling, "When are we going to have lunch? We're starving!"

"There are peanut-butter-and-jelly sandwiches in the cooler and chips in the bag," said Dave, as he pointed toward the cabana.

"Who made the sandwiches?" asked his son Michael.

"I did," said Dave with a smile.

"Yeah! Dad made the sandwiches!" Michael and Christopher yelled simultaneously as they ran toward the cooler.

Dave looked at his brother and grinned. "I use more jelly than their mom does."

A Closer Look

The kids of the '70s had a lot to deal with. Let's take a look at some of the major events and trends that helped to shape their values.

■ ■ ■

In 1972, Congress approved the Equal Rights Amendment (ERA) and sent it to the states to be ratified. It failed to be ratified by the necessary three-fourths of the states and eventually died in 1982.[1] However, the feminist movement was probably the most influential social movement of the decade, leaving few institutions and traditional norms unchallenged, if not changed. It impacted the workplace, churches, government, and especially the family. The '70s saw the first female commercial pilot, astronaut trainee, president of a coed university, and two female generals. In 1972, women increased their representation in state legislatures by 28 percent, the proportion of women entering law schools increased 500 percent, and 40 percent of those entering classes in medical schools were women.[2] Little girls were given the right to play on Little League baseball teams in the '70s, and the title *Ms.* was accepted by federal agencies instead of *Mrs.* or *Miss.*

■ ■ ■

In a 1976 revision of his book *The Common Sense Book of Baby and Child Care*, Dr. Benjamin Spock redefined the sex roles by writing, "The father's responsibility is as great as the mother's."[3]

■ ■ ■

In 1970, the Census Bureau reported that 143,000 unmarried couples lived together, compared to 17,000 in 1960. A *New York Times* survey estimated that there were 2,000 communes in the U.S. in 1970.[4]

■ ■ ■

A Yankelovich poll taken in 1971 showed that 34 percent of the general population believed that marriage was obsolete, up from 24 percent in 1969.[5]

■ ■ ■

In 1973, it was estimated that one out of three meals was eaten someplace other than home. In 1965 it was one in eight.[6] By 1977, one dollar out of every three spent on food went to restaurants and fast-food businesses.[7]

■ ■ ■

A survey of upper-class women at a major eastern college indicated that only 18 percent would stop working if they became mothers, compared to 59 percent in 1943.[8]

■ ■ ■

Day care became an increasing trend of the '70s as the number of working mothers (single and married) increased. By 1976, one-half of all mothers were employed.[9] The number of children in preschool programs rose from 27 percent in 1966 to 55 percent in 1986.[10]

■ ■ ■

In 1976, one out of five children lived in a one-parent home, and three out of five marriages ended in divorce.[11] By 1979, the divorce rate had increased 69 percent since 1968, the median duration of a marriage being 6.6 years. Forty percent of the children born during the decade spent some time in a single-parent household, 90 percent headed by the mother.[12]

■ ■ ■

In 1960, married couples with children comprised 44.2 percent of American households; by 1980, the percentage had dropped to 30.9. The number of men living alone rose from 4.3 percent to 8.6 percent. Women living alone changed from 8.7 percent to 14 percent. The percentage of the population that never married increased from 17.3 to 22.5.[13] The concept of "singles communities" developed in the '70s.

■ ■ ■

In 1979, a *New York Times* poll indicated that 55 percent of the population saw nothing wrong with premarital sex, more than double the percentage in 1969.[14] Surveys taken during the '70s reported that by age 19, four-fifths of all males and two-thirds of all females had had sex.[15]

■ ■ ■

In 1977, over 400,000 abortions were performed on teenagers, a third of the total abortions in the United States; 21 percent of the pregnant unmarried teens gave birth, and 87 percent of these kept their children.[16]

■ ■ ■

Housing costs increased tremendously in the '70s. The median-priced single-family home in 1970 cost $23,000 at an average interest rate of 8.5 percent, and payments represented 17 percent of the homeowner's annual income. By 1979, the same house cost $55,700 at 10.9 percent interest, with payments equaling 25 percent of the owner's income.[17]

■ ■ ■

The American people's faith in the government (what little survived the '60s) took several blows in the '70s, with the killing of four students by National Guards at the Kent State University antiwar protest; the resignation of Vice President Agnew due to a conviction for tax evasion; the resignation of President Nixon over the Watergate scandal; President Ford's pardon of Nixon; the exposure of the CIA's illegal spying on domestic dissidents and assassination attempts against foreign leaders; and the revelation that the FBI had been violating the civil rights of U.S. citizens in many of its operations.[18]

■ ■ ■

A national opinion poll in 1975 indicated that 69 percent of the population believed that "over the last 10 years, this country's leaders have consistently lied to the people"; public confidence in physicians dropped from 73 percent (1966) to 42 percent; faith in big business plummeted from 55 percent to 16 percent.[19]

■ ■ ■

The decade started with increased protesting against the Vietnam War, especially after the revelation of the My Lai massacre in 1969, in which U.S. soldiers murdered hundreds of innocent Vietnamese civilians. The publishing of the *Pentagon Papers* in 1971 informed the nation that the government had been lying to them about its motives and conduct in Vietnam. Nixon started withdrawing American troops while trying to reinforce the South Vietnamese (called "Vietnamization"), but by 1972 it was obvious that South Vietnam could not hold up against the communists, and hope for an honorable withdrawal vanished. By the end of the war, over 540,000 Americans had participated and more than 57,000 had died.[20]

■ ■ ■

In Vietnam, troops steadily became demoralized. A number

of returning GIs began protesting the war based on what they had seen or even participated in. Some started organizations like the Vietnam Veterans Against the War.[21] In 1971, 2,000 Vietnam veterans protested the war by throwing their war medals on the steps of the Capitol.[22]

■ ■ ■

Terrorism increased in the '70s in the form of airplane hijackings, which led to the use of x-ray machines in airports. At the end of the decade, student revolutionaries in Iran seized the U.S. embassy in Tehran and took 63 Americans hostage, demanding the return of the shah for trial in his country. The hostages' captivity lasted 444 days, with update reports watched nightly on ABC's program called *America Held Hostage*, hosted by Ted Koppel. Americans watched their nation humiliated on TV, as their leaders seemed powerless against this small country's actions.

■ ■ ■

The civil rights protests of the '60s led to changes in education in the '70s that emphasized equal opportunity for those who had previously been restricted in the educational process: African-Americans, immigrants, individuals with handicapping conditions, and, to some extent, women. There was also a greater emphasis on helping underachievers, which resulted in lower achievement overall. In 1977, SAT scores of entering freshmen were the lowest in the 51 years of the test's existence.[23] There were also reports that 13 percent of high school graduates were functionally illiterate, leading to a back-to-basics trend in many school districts.[24]

■ ■ ■

A big issue for education in the '70s was integration through the forced busing of kids to schools in other neighborhoods. A series of Supreme Court rulings, protests, boycotts, and enforcement by police, marshals, and the National Guard resulted. By the end of the decade, busing was curbed in response to public protest, and the controversy diminished.

■ ■ ■

New Age environmentalism, the belief that people could attain an increased level of awareness by communing with nature, became popular during this time. This resulted in many moving from urban to rural areas, starting New Age farms using organic methods and rejecting the urban capitalist industrial society.

■ ■ ■

Even the government became concerned about the environment in the '70s. In 1970, President Nixon signed the National Environmental Policy Act, which required government agencies to assess the impact of public projects on the environment and protect endangered species. Other '70s legislation included the Clean Air Act (1970), the Clean Water Act (1972), and the Pesticide Control Act (1972). Fluorocarbons, harmful to the ozone layer, were banned in 1977.

■ ■ ■

The energy crisis, which was brought to public attention by OPEC's (the Organization of Petroleum Exporting Countries) oil embargo from October 1973 to March 1974, caused President Nixon to impose emergency energy conservation measures. He ordered thermostats lowered to 68 degrees in winter and reduced air travel and highway speed limits. He licensed more nuclear power plants, relaxed environmental regulations, and approved daylight savings time in winter. Carpools and public transportation increased, while gas stations closed or limited sales. Business and school schedules were shortened to conserve fuel. Smaller, more fuel-efficient cars became popular.[25]

■ ■ ■

In the later '70s, people became more interested in health.

In 1978, 47 percent of the adult population exercised daily or "almost daily" (up from 24 percent in 1961); one person in nine ran for exercise.[26] Health food sales in 1979 reached $1.6 billion, as compared to $140 million in 1970.[27]

■ ■ ■

The '70s brought about greater awareness of homosexuals and demands for their rights. In 1973, the American Psychiatric Association ruled that homosexuality was not a mental disorder. In 1979, 100,000 people marched in Washington, D.C., in support of gay liberation.[28] The election of several gay candidates into public office during this decade showed a new mood of tolerance and acceptance by some. But in 1978, opposition to the gay rights movement began in what was called the New Right. Leaders like Anita Bryant and the Reverend Jerry Falwell, as well as other evangelical groups, worked to repeal civil rights laws prohibiting discrimination on the basis of sexual orientation and were successful in some states.[29]

■ ■ ■

Drug use, especially marijuana use, became common in the '70s. In 1975, the National Institute on Drug Abuse found that 45 percent of high school seniors reported they had used some illegal drugs in the past year. This figure increased to 54 percent by 1979. Among the 18- to 25-year-olds in 1979, the number who reported illicit drug use was 69.9 percent. Eleven percent of teens reported they smoked marijuana every day; two-thirds reported they smoked the drug at least three times a week.[30]

■ ■ ■

The purpose of drug use changed from a search for increased spirituality and meaning in life in the '60s to an escape from reality in the '70s. Suppliers changed from counter-cultural hippies to organized crime; users became addicts instead of hippies. Drug addiction became a serious problem in the late '70s and was closely connected to an increase in urban crime. By the end of the decade, half of all crimes were committed by kids between the ages of 10 and 17, many of whom were addicted to drugs.[31]

■ ■ ■

Mainstream society began to embrace many of the elements of the counter-culture of the '60s: music, styles, attitudes, art, drug use, and so on. TV shows like *The Partridge Family* and *The Brady Bunch* combined traditional family values and counter-culture fashions and attitudes. Men let their hair grow and bought suits with bell-bottom pants. At the same time, the counter-cultural rebels began to join the mainstream as hippie capitalists, creating livelihoods by marketing things like alternative medicine, therapeutic massage, rock music, and waterbeds. By the end of the decade, most communes had failed, student activists became college professors, feminists became politicians, and antiwar protesters became lawyers and stockbrokers.

■ ■ ■

African-Americans reclaimed their African heritage in the '70s, wearing the Afro hairstyle and West African cotton prints. Sitcoms showing African-Americans in a positive light, like *Sanford and Son, Good Times,* and *The Jeffersons* became popular. The miniseries *Roots* contributed to growing pride in their ethnic and racial origins.

■ ■ ■

In 1973, the cities of Atlanta, Los Angeles, and Detroit each elected their first African-American mayors. Frank Robinson became the first African-American manager of a major-league baseball team, the Cleveland Indians.[32] In addition, the decade also saw the first black general in the marines and the first black astronauts.

■ ■ ■

The '70s were a time of preoccupation with self-awareness,

self-improvement, and self-fulfillment. It also seemed to be a time of spiritual crisis, as many looked to nontraditional sources of spiritual enlightenment. Cults like Hare Krishna, Hindu Mysticism, Zen Buddhism, the Children of God, and Rev. Sun Myung Moon's Unification Church were growing. Transcendental Meditation, EST, primal-scream therapy, humanistic psychology, Silva mind control, Rolfing, and Scientology were popular therapeutic techniques. The public was shocked into increased scrutiny of cults after the mass suicide and murder of over 900 members of Jim Jones's cult, the People's Temple, in Jonestown, Guyana, in 1978.

■ ■ ■

The '70s also brought an increased interest in the occult. Films like *The Exorcist* (1974) and *The Omen* (1976) were popular. Many experimented with I Ching, tarot cards, and astrology. Parapsychology interested many as they sought to understand ESP, telekinesis, and out-of-body experiences.

■ ■ ■

Many in this decade found answers to their spiritual crisis by turning to the Jesus movement and joining fundamental and evangelical churches as born-again Christians. Protestant churches, especially in the South and West, saw an increase in membership in the '70s. In a 1970 Gallup poll, only 4 percent said that religion was influential in their lives. By 1976, 44 percent acknowledged its importance, and 65 percent had more confidence in the church than in any other institution.[33]

■ ■ ■

Televangelists like Billy Graham, Oral Roberts, and Jerry Falwell had an estimated audience of 24 million weekly viewers. Pat Robertson founded the Christian Broadcasting Network in 1960 and was the host of the popular conservative television talk show *The 700 Club* from 1968 to 1986. In 1979, Jerry Falwell organized the Moral Majority as a force to lobby for laws reflecting conservative Christian values, such as prayer in schools and the teaching of biblical creationism. They opposed abortion, homosexuality, pornography, and the Equal Rights Amendment.[34]

■ ■ ■

New Christian music emerged in the '70s. Maranatha! Music, established in 1972 in Costa Mesa, California, was the beginning of a whole new type of Christian music associated with the Jesus movement.

■ ■ ■

The music of the decade went in several directions. The Beatles broke up, and Elvis died. There was "easy listening," like the Carpenters, "Glam-rock," by singers like David Bowie, and Jamaican reggae led by Bob Marley. One of the most popular styles in the '70s was disco music, made popular by the movie *Saturday Night Fever*. Punk rockers with safety-pin-pierced noses and spiked hair arrived from Britain to bring rebellion back to rock music.

The '70s have been described by some as the "non-decade." The first half was really the wrapping-up of the movements of the '60s. The last half seemed to be the introduction of the attitudes and trends of the '80s. Although significant events occurred, like the ending of the Vietnam War and the resignation of President Nixon, many of these events contributed to the questioning and reevaluation of many long-held beliefs about things like the role of the U.S. in the world, the validity of the American Dream, and the trustworthiness of the government. Those raised in the '70s developed a mistrust and disrespect for authority, especially for the government, but also for adults in general.

These kids were made quite aware of the limitations and exploitation of our natural resources. Rather than a booming economy, they experienced an economy plagued by inflation and rising unemployment. Unlike kids of previous decades, they did not believe that if you worked hard enough, you could expect to be better off than your parents were. They were just hoping their parents would leave enough jobs and resources for them to survive on.

The changing makeup of the American family and the effects of feminism on the roles and attitudes of women also contributed to the complexity, diversity, and confusion that seemed to dominate this time and affect those growing up in it. Because so many mothers were going to work, becoming more independent and concentrating on their own needs, millions of latchkey kids were left to raise themselves. Media and peers had more impact on them than previous generations. With the rise of violence and sex in the media, these kids soaked it all in and developed values that were reflected back in their attitudes and behaviors.

Another influence of the women's lib movement was that these individuals have developed more of a "50/50 marriage" concept, where husbands and wives more equally contribute to income, housework, child care, and decision-making in the home. Fathers are more likely to file for custody of their children in divorce cases.

Because these kids were left on their own so much, they reacted by growing up with a higher commitment to people and personal relationships than their parents had. They reject the workaholic lifestyle in favor of a more family-friendly work schedule.

A Portrait of the '70s

Demographics in 1970
Population: 204,879,000
Farmers: 4.8%
Life Expectancy:
Men: 67.1 years
Women: 74.8 years

Money Matters in 1970
GNP: $977.1 billion
Federal budget: $197.2 billion
National debt: $382 billion
Prime interest rate: 7.7%
Average annual salary: $7,564

Cost of Living in 1970
Eggs: 61¢ (doz.)
Milk: 33¢ (qt.)
Bread: 24¢ (loaf)
Coffee: 91¢ (lb.)
Round steak: $1.30 (lb.)

Key Events

1970 First Earth Day celebration; four college students killed by National Guard at Kent State University protest; Manson family murders

1971 Voting age lowered to 18; *Pentagon Papers* published; Supreme Court mandates busing for school desegregation

1972 Last U.S. combat troops leave Vietnam; bombings of North Vietnam continue; sixth and last lunar landing

1972 Watergate break-in occurs and is connected to the Committee to Reelect the President; Nixon is reelected by a landslide

1973 Nixon admits responsibility for Watergate as "man at the top"; secret taping system is revealed, and he refuses to give tapes

1973 Vice President Agnew resigns due to tax evasion charges; Gerald Ford is appointed vice president

1974 Patty Hearst is kidnapped by Symbionese Liberation Army; Nixon makes transcripts of tapes available; 55 mph speed limit enacted

1974 Nixon resigns from the presidency to avoid impeachment trial; Gerald Ford becomes president and pardons Nixon

1975 President Ford officially ends the American involvement in Vietnam; Patty Hearst is arrested by FBI

1976 Vietnam is reunified; *Viking I* lands and sends photos from Mars; Jimmy Carter is elected president

1977 President Carter grants amnesty to Vietnam draft dodgers; Son of Sam serial killer arrested; Elvis Presley dies

1978   100,000 march in Washington, D.C., in support of the
        ERA; more than 900 cult members commit mass suicide in
        Jonestown, Guyana
1979   Accident at nuclear plant at Three Mile Island, Pennsylvania;
        62 Americans are taken hostage in Iran
1979   Gay Liberation March on Washington, D.C.; gas rationing
        begins in many states, leading to long gas lines

Fads and Trends

The Jesus movement, Jesus freaks
Health food, food processors, bottled water
Acupuncture, biorhythms, self-awareness
TM, EST
Pinball, backgammon, smiley faces
Martial arts, jogging
Skateboarding, hang gliding
CB radios, mood rings, pet rocks, POW bracelets
Disco music, dances: the hustle, the bump, and robot
Streaking (running naked through public places)
Dune buggies, director's chairs
Farrah Fawcett-Majors posters
Roller disco, mopeds
College toga parties
Hacky-sacks, Rubik's cubes
Nostalgia
Atari, video arcade games
Singles' communities

New Inventions/Technology

Floppy disks, microprocessor "computer on a chip"
Robotics
Space probes, colored pictures from space
Genetic engineering
Pocket calculators
Betamax videocassette recorder

First videotape film rentals (Sears)
CAT scanners
Manned skylabs for medical experiments in space
Mini TVs
First personal computers for home use
First test-tube baby
Holograms
Concorde, Boeing 747s
Minicams, slow-motion replay
Walkman cassette players

Popular TV Shows

1970   *The Mary Tyler Moore Show; Flip Wilson;*
        Monday Night Football
1971   *All in the Family; Sonny and Cher; Columbo*
1972   *M*A*S*H; The Waltons; Sanford and Son; Kung Fu*
1973   *Kojak; The Six-Million-Dollar Man; The Young and the Restless*
1974   *Good Times; Chico and the Man; Happy Days*
1975   *Saturday Night Live; The Jeffersons; One Day at a Time*
1976   *Laverne and Shirley; Charlie's Angels; The Bionic Woman*
1977   *Three's Company; Love Boat; Lou Grant; Roots* (special)
1978   *Mork and Mindy; Taxi; Dallas; The Incredible Hulk; 20/20*
1979   *The Dukes of Hazard; Benson;* Nickelodeon (CATV)

Hit Songs

1970   "Bridge over Troubled Water"; "Let It Be"; "I'll Be There"
1971   "You've Got a Friend"; "Jesus Christ Superstar"
1972   "I'd Like to Teach the World to Sing"; "I Am Woman"
1973   "Tie a Yellow Ribbon"; "You're So Vain"; "Crocodile Rock"
1974   "I Honestly Love You"; "Way We Were"; "Cat's in the Cradle"
1975   "Thank God I'm a Country Boy"; "Fame"; "The Hustle"
1976   "I Write the Songs"; "50 Ways to Leave Your Lover"
1977   "You Light Up My Life"; "Handyman"; "Hotel California"
1978   "Stayin' Alive"; "Just the Way You Are"; "Three Times a Lady"
1979   "What a Fool Believes"; "YMCA"; "I Will Survive"; "Bad Girls"

Fashions

Freedom in fashion—skirts all lengths, pants for all occasions
The eclectic look (from thrift shops)
Hot pants with hip boots, platform shoes
Jeans with patches, tie-dye
Designer jeans, T-shirts with messages
Ethnic looks, caftans, big Afro hairstyle
Khaki clothes with pseudo-military badges
Jogging suits, Dorothy Hamill haircut, the shag haircut
The layered look
The Annie Hall look (derby hats, tweed jackets,
    neckties, baggy pants, and skirts)
Men: Leisure suits, long hair (styled)
Hip-hugger pants, knit turtlenecks with flared slacks
The Great Gatsby look
Bow ties, wide ties, print shirts

Publications

1970   *Everything You Wanted to Know About Sex but Were Afraid to Ask; Love Story*

1971   *The Exorcist; I'm O.K., You're O.K.; Passions of the Mind*

1972   *Jonathan Livingston Seagull; Two From Galilee; The Living Bible*

1973   *The Joy of Sex; Dr. Atkins' Diet Revolution; The Odessa File*

1974   *All the President's Men; Total Woman; Jaws; Centennial*

1975   *Shogun; Angels: God's Secret Agents; TM; Ragtime*

1976   *Born Again; Passages; Your Erroneous Zones; Roots*

1977   *Looking Out for #1; Age of Uncertainty; Silmarillion*

1978   *The Complete Book of Running; Mommie Dearest; Chesapeake*

1979   *The Complete Scarsdale Medical Diet; Pritikin Program for Diet & Exercise*

Movies

Movie attendance =18 million weekly

1970	*Patton; Love Story; M*A*S*H; Woodstock; Ryan's Daughter*
1971	*The French Connection; Dirty Harry; A Clockwork Orange; Shaft*
1972	*The Godfather; Cabaret; The Poseidon Adventure; The Candidate; Sleuth*
1973	*The Sting; American Graffiti; The Exorcist; The Way We Were; Serpico*
1974	*The Godfather, Part II; Young Frankenstein; The Great Gatsby*
1975	*One Flew over the Cuckoo's Nest; Jaws; Tommy; Shampoo*
1976	*Rocky; Network; A Star Is Born; The Omen; Marathon Man*
1977	*Annie Hall; Saturday Night Fever; Star Wars; Close Encounters of the Third Kind*
1978	*The Deer Hunter; Coming Home; Grease; Superman; Foul Play*
1979	*Kramer vs. Kramer; Apocalypse Now; Star Trek; Norma Rae*

Heroes

O.J. Simpson	"Dr. J" Julius Erving
Kareem Abdul-Jabbar	Muhammed Ali
Jack Nicklaus	Mark Spitz
Hank Aaron	Billie Jean King
Gloria Steinem	Farrah Fawcett-Majors
Dorothy Hamill	

Chapter 12

The '80s
"We Are the
World"

The '80s, in some ways, continued what had been happening at the end of the '70s. Many of the same issues were still being debated, such as feminism, abortion, and gay rights. The deterioration of the traditional family continued, homelessness increased, and drug use continued to be a growing problem. But the '80s also brought some new trends and issues that greatly impacted the youth who were trying to make sense of it all as their values were being formed.

Jennifer, Lisa, and Kim are all in their late 20s and are roommates in an apartment on the outskirts of Boston. They met in college and are now struggling to make a living and pay off their school loans. Kim, with her degree in sociology, has ended up working in a retail clothing store and has recently been promoted to manager. Lisa, with her degree in education, is working for a temporary agency and does some substitute teaching when she can. Jennifer, not knowing what to do with her humanities degree, opted to go to graduate school until she can figure it out and get a job to pay off her growing student loan debt. They have furnished their modest apartment with an intriguing assortment of hand-me-down furniture from their parents, enhanced with great finds from garage sales and discount stores. Their neighbors often speculate about how many people actually live there, since there seems to be a steady stream of young adults coming and going and just hanging out.

"Okay, I'm going to order the pizza now. What do we want, and how many?" Jennifer asked the group that was sprawled around the TV. "Are you all going to stay and eat? Who's taking off?"

"Make one a vegetarian for me," called Lisa from her bedroom, where she and Matt were playing an Internet trivia game called You Don't Know Jack on her computer. "Oh, oh! I know that. Let me do it, Matt."

"I've gotta go. I'm meeting some of the guys from work, and we're gonna hang out at that new coffeehouse downtown," explained Jeff as he pulled himself out of the beanbag chair and grabbed his jacket. "I may come by later if you guys are still up."

"I hear that place is totally cool," said Kevin as he moved from the floor to the vacated beanbag. "Let us know if it's someplace we should check out."

"See ya, Jeff," Kim called as Jeff headed for the door. "Mushroom and pepperoni sounds good to me, Jen. Better order plenty; I think Heather and Amy might come over. I saw them at the video store and told them we were having a movie night."

"Where's your cell phone, Kim?" asked Jennifer. "I can't use our phone because Matt and Lisa are on-line."

"Sorry, the battery's dead. I just put it on to charge," apologized Kim. "They've been on-line long enough. Tell them to get off."

"Hey you two cyber dweebs need to get off so we can order the pizzas," yelled Jennifer through the doorway. "We're starving out here!"

"Hold on a sec. We have one more question left, and I'm hot!" Matt yelled back.

A few minutes later, as they emerged from the bedroom, Lisa was shaking her head. "I am so not into the sports questions. I'm more into the TV trivia stuff. I totally lived my childhood in front of the TV set."

"Didn't we all," remarked Kevin, looking up from the rerun of *Family Ties* on TV. "What else was there to do while we waited for our parents to come home from work? We weren't allowed outside because some stranger would come along and coax us into his car. The next thing you know, our faces would be on a milk carton on the breakfast table!"

"Exactly," agreed Kim. "Didn't it kind of freak you out that we were always being told to be careful and not trust anyone? My mom bought me a coloring book about 'stranger danger,' and there were those commercials between cartoons on Saturday mornings. But then there were so many reports about child abuse in families and child care centers, too. And they wonder why we're such an untrusting generation! Who were we supposed to trust?"

"Not the government! Even though our parents seemed to think Reagan would be able to fix everything, at least that's what my parents believed." Lisa settled onto the couch next to Matt. "In fact, that's one of the few things I remember them agreeing on before the divorce. When Iran let the hostages go just hours after his inauguration, they thought that was, you know, a good sign. They expected Reagan would, like, bring back world respect for the U.S. and everything."

"Well, he did help get the economy straightened out eventually. A lot of people were better off at the end of the '80s, after the recession and with interest rates going down and all," defended Matt, who was known for his conservative, Republican leanings.

"Yeah, if you were a yuppie, it was great!" countered Kevin. "But what about all the homeless people? They were everywhere because Reagan closed all the VA hospitals. Reaganomics didn't do much for them! And then the whole Iran-Contra thing messed up his credibility."

"It wasn't just the government that screwed up," interjected Jennifer. "There was other scary stuff, too. How about AIDS? At first we thought it was just the gay community, but then other people got infected. Like that Ryan White kid, who wasn't allowed to go to school because he had AIDS."

"Yeah, everyone went condom crazy. They were passing them out at school, and some parents were really freaked out about it," remarked Kevin.

"Hey, did I ever tell you what I told my mom last summer when she found out that Jeff was living here for a while?" Kim asked. "I told her he was between jobs and needed a place to stay. She was all uptight just 'cause he's a guy, and she can't believe that guys and girls can spend the night in the same apartment and not have sex!"

"Didn't you tell her that Jeff is gay?" laughed Kevin.

"Oh, yeah. Like that would make her feel better about him!" exclaimed Kim. "No, I totally freaked her out by saying, 'It's okay, Mom. We have a supply of condoms in every room, just in case.'"

"No way! What did she say?" asked Lisa in amazement.

"At first she was so totally shocked she didn't say anything. But then she realized I was kidding and kinda laughed. It took the edge off the conversation, and I assured her it was cool, and he was just a good friend needing some help. I still don't think she was too happy about it, but what could she do?" asked Kim, shrugging her shoulders. "It's hard for her to accept that her old rules don't apply in our world."

"Totally!" agreed Lisa. "It's like they grew up in *Happy Days,* when the world was simpler and their problems were things like getting pimples and who liked who. We grew up with Chernobyl and the Challenger space shuttle blowing up."

"And major oil spills and pollution destroying the environment," added Kevin.

"Hey, this is getting depressing," interrupted Matt. "There must have been something positive. How about the Vietnam War Memorial that finally honored the soldiers who were killed? Oh, yeah! And what about the Berlin wall coming down? That was a big deal."

"That was so cool!" agreed Lisa. "And the fact that the Cold War was over, and we didn't have to always be worrying about Russia being the big enemy and everything."

"Yeah, and then there were those Live Aid concerts to raise money for the famine in Ethiopia," reminded Jennifer, who had just rejoined the group after ordering the pizzas. The group broke into a spontaneous chorus of "We Are the World," swaying and taking turns mimicking the solos of the recording artists who had come together for that famous recording session.

"That was awesome. I love that song," remarked Lisa.

"Hey, it's Friday night. We should have that radio station on that plays all '80s music on Fridays," said Kevin. "I'd love to hear some Michael Jackson or Madonna. I bet Matt was into country music."

"My parents were really into country," said Matt, ignoring the gibe. "They'd go line-dancing and two-stepping a lot. I like Michael, but I'm also a Springsteen fan."

"Okay, now that we're in this nostalgia mode, what were your favorite '80s TV shows?" asked Kim.

"*Cheers*," said Lisa, "'cause everybody knows your name."

"MTV," added Kevin.

"*The Cosby Show*. I always wished I had a dad as understanding, wise, and fun as him," explained Jennifer almost wistfully.

"*Family Ties*," said Matt. "I always thought Alex was so cool."

"You *are* Alex," teased Kim. "Hey, here's a trivia question from the *Family Ties* web site. Which actress from the show *Friends* played one of Alex's girlfriends?"

"That's easy—Courtney Cox. Now here's one for you," Matt smiled mischievously. "Which two *Family Ties* cast members were born on the same day?"

Kim looked perplexed, so Matt looked around at the others for the answer. They all shrugged. "Michael Gross and Meredith Baxter-Birney," Matt stated triumphantly.

It was Lisa's turn to jump in with a question. "What were Alex's parting words as he left home in the final episode?"

"I love you guys!" they all said in unison and then laughed.

"So has TV had an impact on our lives, or what?" asked Jennifer, still laughing.

"Probably more than we realize," admitted Kevin. "Our family even watched TV evangelists instead of going to church. It was mostly my mom, but she would make us sit with her sometimes and watch Jimmy Swaggart. It was pretty entertaining at times, and sometimes it even made sense. But when that scandal about him and the prostitute came out, it really turned me off. And also that Bakker couple who took a bunch of people's money, and he had an affair with a secretary or something. It made me pretty skeptical about the whole church scene. I believe in God in my own way and stuff, but organized religion is not for me."

"Yeah, I know what you mean. They make everything so black and white. I just don't see it that way. I mean, most of the time lying is bad, but there are times when it just seems like the best way. You just gotta look at every situation and decide what's best at the time. That's my philosophy," stated Kim.

Just then the doorbell rang. "That would be the pizza," announced Jennifer. "Who has some money to pitch in?"

"I spent my last dollar at the video store renting *Princess Bride,*" admitted Kim.

" 'That's inconceivable,' " quoted Kevin.

" 'I do not think that word means what you think it means,' " retorted Matt in a bad Spanish accent as he handed Jennifer some cash.

A Closer Look

This group of kids grew up in a very different world than their parents did. Let's take a closer look at what they experienced and try to understand it from their viewpoint and see how it affected them.

■ ■ ■

At the beginning of the decade, the economy was in decline. There was double-digit inflation, with CDs at 18 percent and mortgage rates over 20 percent.[1] As the decade progressed, "Reagonomics" improved the economy for the "haves," allowing them to experience affluence and luxury. But his trickle-down theory (if the rich get richer, then they will invest in the economy, and the financial benefit will trickle down to all economic levels) didn't seem to make it to the "have-nots." The homeless population grew by an estimated 25 percent per year. In 1986, the homeless population was estimated to be 40,000 in New York City, 38,000 in Los Angeles, 25,000 in Chicago, 20,000 in St. Louis, and 10,000 each in Boston and Washington.[2] The Hands Across America human chain of more than 5 million people from Long Beach, California to New York City raised $100 million for the poor and homeless in 1986.[3]

■ ■ ■

During the recession (1979–1982), unemployment rose to 10.8 percent (more than 12 million Americans out of work). Business bankruptcies rose 50 percent from 1981 to 1982. In June 1982, 584 businesses failed, which came close to the Depression record of 612 in one month in 1932.[4]

■ ■ ■

Because of inflation, overall prices rose 142 percent during the decade.[5]

■ ■ ■

The price of housing skyrocketed. A typical San Francisco house that cost $87,000 in 1977 cost $385,000 in 1984; the cost of an eight-room co-op on Fifth Avenue in New York, rose from $150,000 to $800,000.[6]

■ ■ ■

In 1988, the average family income (before taxes) was $46,848, compared to $29,627 in 1980. When adjusted for inflation, the increase only amounted to $3,700.[7]

■ ■ ■

The family continued to deteriorate. In 1980, the divorce rate had grown from one in three (1970) to one in two;

one-parent families had increased 50 percent; unmarried couples living together were up 300 percent; one million teenagers became pregnant, two-thirds of them unmarried.[8] In 1988, two-parent families made up only 27 percent of the population, compared to 49 percent in 1970. Since 1980, the number of singles was up 20 percent; unmarried couples, 63 percent.[9]

■ ■ ■

The problem of child abuse came to public attention during the '80s. Highly publicized cases, like the McMartin preschool sexual abuse case, raised the public's concern and awareness. Charges against Boy Scout leaders and priests created concern for parents. One result of these concerns was books, games, coloring books, and public service announcements during children's shows warning them about strangers and instructing them on what to do if someone does something inappropriate to you. Unfortunately, many of the millions of cases of abuse reported were actually of children abused in their own homes.

■ ■ ■

The problem of the abduction of children also became highly publicized as the pictures of missing children began showing up on milk cartons in the mid-'80s. (That had to have an effect on the children who saw them every morning as they ate their cereal.) In 1985, more than one million children were reported missing; 6,000 of them were abducted by strangers.[10]

■ ■ ■

By 1980, the focus of college students was shifting. A survey by UCLA and the American Council on Education showed that college freshmen were more interested in power, money, and status than at any time during the previous 15 years (62.5 percent vs. 50 percent); business and management were the most popular majors.[11] In 1984, the

American Council on Education reported a narrowing of
the generation gap in college students, who began to
espouse the more traditional career, marriage, and financial goals of their parents.[12]

■ ■ ■

In 1982, the College Board reported that SAT scores for
college-bound seniors rose for the first time in 19 years.
The average verbal score was 425 (compared to 478 when
the decline began in 1963); the average math score was
467 (compared to 502).[13]

■ ■ ■

An Education Department survey of 15,000 kids taken in
1983 revealed that children of working mothers scored
lower on reading and math tests than those whose mothers stayed home.[14]

■ ■ ■

In the annual Gallup poll of education in 1986, parents,
for the first time, listed drugs as the number-one problem
in schools. For several years, the most serious problem in
the parents' opinion had been discipline.[15]

■ ■ ■

In 1987, microwave ovens were in 60 percent of kitchens,
and 40 percent of the money spent on food was used for
eating out.[16]

■ ■ ■

VCR sales increased 72 percent from 1980 to 1981, totaling an estimated 34 million in use.[17]

■ ■ ■

Prices for computers dropped, making them more affordable.
- In 1982, there were 1.5 million computers in
  homes, five times the number in 1980.[18]
- Between 1984 and 1988, 39.4 million computers
  were shipped.

- In 1984, Americans bought $37.6 million worth of software; two-thirds of it was for computer games.
- At the end of 1982, 250 different computer games were available.
- In 1981, there were 180,000 modems in American homes; by 1988, there were 10.9 million.[19]

■ ■ ■

Women continued to pursue careers. In 1988, women accounted for nearly half of all graduating accountants, one-third of MBAs, and one-fourth of lawyers and physicians (up 300 percent in 10 years).[20]

■ ■ ■

Many other women had to work out of necessity, being single mothers who were supporting their children. Even mothers with infants were working. One report found that over half of all new mothers were employed in 1988, compared to less than one-third in 1976.[21]

■ ■ ■

A study by the University of Minnesota in 1986 found that 80 percent of latchkey children liked being at home alone, and that almost 30 percent of kids in kindergarten through third grade went home to a situation with no adult supervision.[22]

■ ■ ■

Since so many kids were, in effect, raising themselves while their parents worked, media had a tremendous influence on this group. Increasing sex and violence on TV greatly shaped their values. MTV started and grew in popularity throughout the decade.

■ ■ ■

As more women postponed childbirth to pursue education and careers, first births for women between the ages of 30 and 39 increased more than 400 percent by the end of the decade.[23]

■ ■ ■

Prisons became overcrowded as the United States had a higher percentage of incarcerated persons than any other western country: in 1984, one out of every 529.[24]

■ ■ ■

In 1986, the government started random drug testing of federal workers in "sensitive" tasks after a presidential commission estimated that 20 million people per month used marijuana, 5 million used cocaine, and 500,000 used heroin.[25]

■ ■ ■

In 1989, cocaine addiction (including the new form, crack) was up 35 percent since 1985. One percent of sixth graders were regular users.[26]

■ ■ ■

Gang violence became a major problem in urban areas. By 1989, metal detectors were common in many urban schools, and a survey by the American Federation of Teachers reported that 66 percent of teachers feared violence from their students.[27]

■ ■ ■

AIDS was discovered and became a well-publicized epidemic during the '80s. Fear of AIDS led more people to consider monogamy and abstinence as part of a safe lifestyle. Condom and clean needle distribution were considered ways of limiting spread of the disease. "Safe sex" became a common term in American society. The number of reported cases of AIDS in the United States grew from 225 in 1981 to 4,000 in 1987.[28]

■ ■ ■

In 1987, after the surgeon general's directive on passive smoking (inhaling secondhand smoke), 40 states and hundreds of cities restricted smoking in public buildings, restaurants, and schools.[29]

■ ■ ■

Research by the Youth Suicide Center in 1985 said that

11 percent of the nation's high school seniors had made a suicide attempt sometime in their lives.[30]

■ ■ ■

The Republican Party, which was dominant through the '80s, became much more conservative because of the rise of the religious right. Groups like the Moral Majority, led by Jerry Falwell, were vocal and influential during this decade, particularly on issues such as abortion, prayer in schools, and the ERA.

■ ■ ■

The '80s marked the third consecutive decade of declining membership for the more liberal, mainline religious denominations. The conservative evangelical churches, however, continued to grow. By 1986, Gallup polls reported that 31 percent of Americans felt comfortable referring to themselves as evangelicals or born-again Christians. It was estimated that evangelicals numbered somewhere between 40 and 60 million.[31]

■ ■ ■

Evangelical preachers expanded their ministries and influence through the increasing use of television. The most popular televangelists included Jerry Falwell, Pat Robertson, Robert Schuller, Jim and Tammy Faye Bakker, Oral Roberts, and Jimmy Swaggart. Unfortunately (especially for the youth, who were already skeptical of authority figures), the public moral failures of the Bakkers and Jimmy Swaggart during this decade affected the credibility of the others in many people's minds.

■ ■ ■

The New Age movement found its way into the mainstream of society in the mid-'80s. Included in its tenets were beliefs in reincarnation, spiritual healing, out-of-body experiences, meditation, yoga, astrology, and the supernatural or extraterrestrial. New Age music, speakers, and books became widely available. In 1988, there were more than 2,500 New Age bookstores, 25,000 titles in print, and annual sales amounting to $1 billion.[32]

■ ■ ■

Patriotism was revived during the '80s. In July 1981, *Newsweek* reported that enlistments in the military were increasing, flag sales were on the rise, and people were singing "The Star Spangled Banner" with enthusiasm. A Gallup poll found that 81 percent of teenagers surveyed were very proud to be Americans.[33]

The '80s were a rough time for kids to grow up. Their parents tended to be self-absorbed and distracted by things like making a living and finding their own fulfillment. There were many broken homes with single-parent families struggling to survive financially. A lot of kids were left to fend for themselves emotionally, if not physically. Latchkey kids (those who came home from school to an empty house) were common. Because of this, TV and movies (especially with the invention of the VCR) become an ever-increasing source of values input. Older kids looked to peers, even gangs, for a sense of belonging or for role models that were missing in their homes.

Political and environmental issues and events left these young people with the sense that the adults were ruining their futures, giving them a sense of hopelessness and cynicism. Moral failures of public figures, including parents, convinced them that people, especially older ones in established institutions, could probably not be trusted. Many of the children of the '80s have an ingrained skepticism about life.

The difficult financial times they experienced growing up, plus the challenge of finding jobs, even after they earned college degrees, has caused this group to be careful with their resources and to have lower expectations about their financial future than their parents had.

The lack of a nurturing environment many experienced as children has led this group to value relationships. Once they get past the difficulty of trusting, they tend to be loyal to those they allow into their lives. Growing up in a society that emphasized the rights of various minority groups, they tend to be more tolerant and accepting of individuals of various backgrounds and lifestyles. Their exposure to so many different beliefs and philosophies, plus their commitment to tolerance, has made it difficult for them to believe that there are any absolute truths in life to live by.

A Portrait of the '80s

Demographics in 1980
Population: 226,546,000
Farmers: 2.7%
Life expectancy:
Men: 69.9 years
Women: 77.6 years

Money Matters in 1980
GNP: $2.633 trillion
Federal budget: $579.6 billion
National debt: $914 billion
Prime interest rate: 21.5%
Average annual salary: $15,757

Cost of Living in 1980
Eggs: 84¢ (doz.)
Milk: $1.04 (qt.)
Bread: 51¢ (loaf)
Coffee: $2.98 (lb.)
Round steak: $2.37 (lb.)

Key Events
1980   Failed attempt to rescue hostages in Iran; Mt. Saint Helens erupts; U.S. boycotts Moscow Olympics

1980   ABSCAM scandal; Ronald Reagan elected president; John Lennon killed

1981   Iran releases U.S. hostages; first female Supreme Court justice; wedding of Prince Charles and Lady Diana

1981   President Reagan shot in assassination attempt; striking air traffic controllers fired by president; first space shuttle

1982   ERA defeated; seven people die from poisoned Tylenol leading to tamper-proof packaging

1983   First female astronaut; bombings at U.S. embassy and marine headquarters in Beirut; U.S. troops invade Grenada

1984   Settlement for Vietnam vets who were exposed to Agent Orange; President Reagan reelected

1984   Russia boycotts Olympics in Los Angeles

1985   TWA Flight 847 is hijacked by Shiite terrorists; American hostages dispersed in Beirut and later released

1986   *Challenger* shuttle explodes; accident at nuclear plant in Chernobyl, USSR; Iran-Contra scandal revealed

1987   Iran-Contra hearings; "Black Monday" on October 19 (Dow drops 508 points, the worst fall in history)

1988   First launch of space shuttle *Discovery*

1988   George Bush is elected president; Pan Am Flight 103 explodes over Scotland

1989   Exxon *Valdez* tanker spills 11 million barrels of oil off Alaskan coast; Oliver North convicted in Iran-Contra affair

1989   San Francisco earthquake; East Germany opens Berlin Wall

1989   Tiananmen Square demonstration; U.S. invades Panama

Fads and Trend

Country-western music, mechanical bulls
Rap music, hip-hop, break dancing
"Moon walking," music videos, MTV
Baby on Board signs, Jelly Bellies
Suction Garfield cats on car windows
Cabbage Patch dolls, My Pet Monster
Smurfs, ET, Teenage Mutant Ninja Turtles
Trivial Pursuit, Rubik's Cube, Nintendo video games
Sony Walkman, state lotteries
Valley girls, "Where's the beef?" commercial, patriotism
USA Today, Jane Fonda fitness videos

Aerobics, oat bran, gourmet foods, salad bars
Photos of missing children on milk cartons
Codependency groups, "safe sex"
Yuppies (young urban professionals)

New Inventions/Technology
Compact discs, video Walkman
Fax machines
Space shuttles, B-2 stealth bombers
Computerized car features, airbags
Cell phones
Microwave ovens
Digital clocks
Cordless phones
ATMs
Synthesizers
Laptop computers
Megabit memory chips
Genetic fingerprinting
Cloning
Chicken pox vaccine, Rogaine

Popular TV Shows
1980   *Magnum, P.I.; Nightline; Too Close for Comfort*
1981   *Dynasty; Private Benjamin; Hill Street Blues; MTV*
1982   *Cheers; Cagney and Lacey; The David Letterman Show; St. Elsewhere*
1983   *The A-Team; Wheel of Fortune; Webster; Night Court*
1984   *The Cosby Show; Miami Vice; Murder, She Wrote*
1985   *Golden Girls; The Oprah Winfrey Show; The Equalizer*
1986   *L.A. Law; Alf; Matlock; Perfect Strangers*
1987   *Beauty and the Beast; Different World; Thirtysomething*
1988   *Roseanne; Wonder Years; Murphy Brown; Dear John*
1989   *Life Goes On; Anything But Love; Amazing Teddy Z*

Hit Songs

1980	"Sailing"; "The Rose"; "Magic"; "Coward of the County"
1981	"Bette Davis Eyes"; "Lady"; "9 to 5"; "Endless Love"
1982	"Always on My Mind"; "Physical"; "Ebony and Ivory"
1983	"Every Breath You Take"; "Beat It"; "All Night Long"
1984	"What's Love Got to Do with It?"; "God Bless the USA"
1985	"We Are the World"; "Like a Virgin"; "Crazy for You"
1986	"Graceland"; "That's What Friends Are For"
1987	"Somewhere out There"; "La Bamba"; "Here I Go Again"
1988	"Don't Worry, Be Happy"; "So Emotional"; "One More Try"
1989	"Wind Beneath My Wings"; "Better Man"; "Cold-Hearted"

Fashions

Preppy look: navy blazer, kilt or skirt, cardigan sweaters
Designer jeans, polo shirts
Baggy shorts and shirts, backward caps (rappers)
Cowboy and Native American dress, fringe
Cornrows (hairstyle)
Nancy Reagan and Princess Di bring back opulent styles:
Billowing skirts, capes, tent-like dresses, ruffles
Androgynous fashions: pinstriped, double-breasted suits
   with ankle-length skirts, oversized coats over tailored and
   cuffed pants
Large shirts, sweaters, and jackets with stirrup pants or leggings
Denim
Safari-style clothes, "dressing for success"
Miniskirt returns, as well as long skirts, bike shorts

Publications

1980	*The Covenant; Beloved; The Third Wave*
1981	*Rabbit Is Rich; A Light in the Attic; Cujo*
1982	*The Color Purple; Space; Jane Fonda's Workout Book*
1983	*In Search of Excellence; Megatrends; Poland*
1984	*Talisman; Bright Lights, Big City; Iacocca*
1985	*Less Than Zero; Lake Wobegon Days; Texas*

1986   *Fatherhood; Red Storm Rising; I'll Take Manhattan*
1987   *Closing of the American Mind; Patriot Games*
1988   *Bonfire of the Vanities; Cardinal of the Kremlin; Alaska*
1989   *All I Really Need to Know I Learned in Kindergarten*

Movies
Movie attendance = 20 million weekly
1980   *Ordinary People; The Empire Strikes Back; Urban Cowboy*
1981   *Chariots of Fire; On Golden Pond; Raiders of the Lost Ark*
1982   *Gandhi; ET, The Extra-Terrestrial; Tootsie; Victor/Victoria*
1983   *Terms of Endearment; Flashdance; Return of the Jedi*
1984   *Amadeus; Ghostbusters; Indiana Jones and the Temple of Doom*
1985   *Out of Africa; The Color Purple; Back to the Future; Witness*
1986   *Platoon; Top Gun; Alien; Crocodile Dundee; The Color of Money*
1987   *The Last Emperor; Fatal Attraction; Baby Boom; Three Men and a Baby*
1988   *Rain Man; Who Framed Roger Rabbit?; Gorillas in the Mist*
1989   *Driving Miss Daisy; Field of Dreams; Batman; The Little Mermaid*

Heroes

Michael Jordan	Larry Byrd
Magic Johnson	Martina Navratilova
Joe Montana	Florence Griffith Joyner
Reverend Jesse Jackson	President Ronald Reagan
Tom Cruise	Lee Iacocca
Michael Jackson	Madonna

Chapter 13

The '90s "Candle in the Wind"

As we come to look at the '90s, we don't have quite the same perspective as with previous decades. The future effects of the events of this decade are yet to be seen. The kids whose values are affected are still in process. Let's take a look at some of the issues that make up their world as we eavesdrop on a high school classroom in an Atlanta suburb.

"Class, we have extended homeroom today, so y'all just socialize among yourselves until the bell rings," Ms. Young announced. The group of students in the room made various comments and started moving around the room to find someone to talk to. The room was filled with kids of all kinds—punks, hicks, preps, and others.

"Good," Jesse said as he put his head down. His metal ball chain necklace hit the desk, and he had to shift to make sure he wasn't lying on his eyebrow ring. His hair used to be dyed, but now it was bleached and a couple inches long at the top. His roots showed that his true hair color was brown. "I need a chance to sleep."

"Why are you so tired, Jesse?" Sarah asked. She walked over to sit by him, smoothing out her khaki skirt. She checked her shoulder-length hair in the mirror on the wall as she walked by and adjusted her silver necklace. "What did you do this weekend?"

"Get another tattoo?" Steven said with a drawl as he sauntered over. He had a large belt buckle, tight jeans, and a shaved head.

"No, I haven't decided what I want to get yet," Jesse stated.

"So what did you do?" Sarah asked.

"I went to this concert. It was great. I was moshing and crowd surfing—but then they dropped me, and I hit the floor. There was this explosion, and I thought that a bomb went off or something, but it was just the band's amp."

"That would have freaked me out! With all the bombings going on, it could happen." Sarah seemed disturbed.

"Yeah," Steven agreed. "There was the Oklahoma bombin', and that abortion clinic, and the World Trade Center."

Just then, two students walked in the door. The girl looked like a model from *YM* magazine with her long hair, capri pants, and perfect makeup. The guy was wearing a Hawaiian shirt and surfer-style board shorts. He had a hemp necklace, and his hair was spiked. "You're late," Ms. Young scolded.

"I know, I'm sorry," the guy apologized.

"My locker was stuck, and Mike helped me get it open," the girl smiled at him as she said the words. The two took seats by the others and joined the conversation.

"You're lookin' nice, Heather," Steven told her.

"Thanks. What are y'all talking about?" she asked.

"Oh, we were just talking about all the bombings that have been going on," Sarah informed her.

"Remember when someone set off those firecrackers in the hallway?" Heather asked.

"Yeah, that was my first week here, and it stinkin' scared me to death. I heard this noise that sounded like gunshots and then everyone was running for the doors and hitting the floor. I thought someone had opened fire on the school. That morning I was listening to a news report about some kid who killed his classmates doing that, and it was still fresh in my mind. What kind of jerk would do something like that?" Mike paused a moment and then said, "How did we get started on this conversation anyway?"

"Jesse was tellin' us about the concert he went to where the amp blew." Steven didn't seem all that impressed.

"Really? What kind of concert was it?" Mike asked with interest.

"Hardcore."

"Cool. I like hardcore, but I like ska and swing better. Some punk, too. And then you mix ska and punk and swing together, and—"

"That's great, Mike," Sarah interrupted. "I prefer alternative myself."

"Country is the best kind of music," Steven stated.

"Maybe for you, but everyone's entitled to their own opinion. I listen to rap." Heather shocked everyone.

"You listen to rap?" Mike asked in disbelief.

"Yes, I do. What? Is there something wrong with that?"

"No. Like you said, everyone does what he wants. It just surprised me." Mike didn't want to look like he was judging her.

"Lots of people are different than what you expect," Sarah seemed to preach. "Take Jesse, for example. You might look at him and think that he was some kind of juvenile delinquent. But in reality, he's a part of the Key Club."

"Isn't that the club that picks up trash on the side of the road and visits nursin' homes? You're in that, Jesse?" Steven asked.

"Yeah, I like helping people. It makes me feel good. Did you see those people in front of the school this morning?"

"You mean for the 'See You at the Pole' thing? What made you think of that?" Sarah asked.

"I saw a lot of the people from the Key Club there. What were they doing?"

"They were praying. On September 16th, the Christians at schools all around the country get together to pray for their schools, country, families, and stuff like that," Mike offered.

"Hey, man, didn't I see you out there?" Jesse wanted to know.

"Yeah, I'm a Christian. I was there," Mike said.

"That's cool." Heather quit doodling on her paper and looked up. "Religion is getting kind of popular. One of my friends started getting into meditation. She says it really helps to relax her and get rid of her stress. I was thinking about trying it."

"So, Heather, what did you do this weekend?" Sarah got up to throw something away and then came back and sat down.

"I went to my mom's house. When I got there, she was crying. I asked her what was wrong, but she wouldn't answer me. Then I looked at the TV and saw that she had been watching Princess Di's funeral again. She taped it and watches it all the time. And every time, she ends up crying. She was so into Diana and watched every special that came on about her."

"Princess Diana was so nice," Sarah said. "She gave to so many people. She was the 'Queen of Hearts.' She's really an inspiration, especially now that she's dead."

"What about Mother Teresa?" Mike asked. "She died right after Diana, but nobody really paid attention. I think she was more of an inspiration than Di was. She gave up her life to help others. If you want someone to look up to, it should be her."

"I look up to Bill Clinton," Steven interjected.

"How can you? He lied to the whole country!" Sarah said in amazement.

"Yeah, but look at all he's done for the country. Who cares if he lied. We all lie every day."

"I don't know," Mike said. "I think we need a leader who we can look up to. I just don't think that's Clinton."

"What I don't understand is what Monica was thinking," Heather said. "I would never go for a guy who looked like that, and he's so much older than she is. I wish everyone would just get over this whole thing so that we can get on with our lives. It's so boring!"

"What do you think, Jesse?" Sarah looked over and found him asleep at his desk.

"See? This whole thing put him to sleep. What is it with all the long trials?" Heather seemed to be getting impatient.

"What trials are you talkin' about?" Steven asked.

"You know, Tonya Harding, O.J. Simpson—those trials."

"Oh, yeah, O.J. My parents said that the chase in the white Bronco was one of those events where everyone remembers where they were when it happened." Sarah looked only partially interested.

"Well, do you remember where you were?" asked Mike.

"Yeah, I was at my neighbor's house. We were outside playing, and we came inside and saw it on TV. O.J. Simpson—another person lying to a jury."

"I don't think he lied," Mike said in defense. "After all, the glove didn't fit."

"Whatever. I can make anything not fit if I try," Heather said with a flip of her hair.

"Oh, dude! Remember the bomb at the Olympics!" Jesse lifted his head from the desk.

"That was so 20 minutes ago. We're on a new subject now." Heather gave Jesse a strange look.

"What went on in your world this weekend, Steven?"

"My dad got remarried."

"Really? Wow. Do you like your new stepmom?" Sarah questioned.

"Yeah, she's pretty nice. She has this daughter named Julie. I'm fixin' to go crazy with her around. But overall, I guess they're okay. It's nice to have a woman around the house. My mama left us so long ago that we haven't had any good cookin' in a long time. My dad mostly fixes microwave dinners, or we go out to eat sometimes. I'm lookin' forward to some good, homemade grits."

"It's totally opposite in my situation. My mom usually doesn't have time to cook because she's working, so we usually go out when I'm with her. But my dad always takes time to fix a special meal for us. It's kind of weird having two different homes.

It can get confusing, too." Heather didn't seem to like the conversation, so she changed the subject. "So Mike, what did you do this weekend?"

"Not much. I spent most of my time on the Internet E-mailing my friends in California. Then this guy E-mailed me, and it turned out he was the drummer of one of my favorite bands! It was so stinkin' awesome! We were like joking around and talking about all kinds of stuff. Next time I see them in concert, I'm going to go up to him and be like, 'Hey, man! I talked to you on-line!' It'll be so sweet! I also found this great board shop on-line! They have surfboards, snowboards, skateboards—you name it, they've got it. I was in heaven!"

"That sounds great. Maybe sometime you could teach me how to surf." Heather smiled at him.

"Um, yeah. Let me know when you find a beach around here. Hey, Jesse, did you finish that health project?"

"No." Jesse just looked at him.

"Have you even started it?"

"I'm not sure."

"What project are you talking about?" Sarah asked.

"We have to think of the best way to prevent AIDS and present our solution to the class. My answer is abstinence," Mike said firmly.

"I think that's the best answer, too," Sarah agreed.

"What are you talking about? As long as you're careful, you won't get AIDS," Heather practically yelled.

"Really. If you use a condom, then you're safe," Steven agreed.

"You never know. They fail sometimes." Mike looked at his friend with a worried expression.

"You know what I think?" Jesse was cut off by the bell. He tried to finish his sentence, but his friends quickly gathered their stuff and left the room for their next classes. "I think I'll go to class," he said to himself as he watched them head out the door.

A Closer Look

As with each decade before it, this one had its own unique set of events helping to shape the values of the kids. Although we've all experienced this period and these events together, let's review them to understand how they might have affected developing values.

■ ■ ■

In 1991, the number of single parents was up 41 percent from 1980. There was also an 80 percent increase in unmarried couples living together. Twenty-six percent of all babies were born to single women.[1]

■ ■ ■

In 1990, 51 percent of mothers with children under one year old worked; 56 percent with children under six; and 73 percent with children between six and 17.[2]

■ ■ ■

The 1990 census included new questions that took into consideration the changing nature of family groups, including gay households. For the first time, an attempt was made to count the homeless population. It was found that only 26 percent of households with children under 18 included a married couple. One in four Americans was a member of a minority group. The fastest growing group was made up of Asians and Pacific Islanders—2.9 percent of the population. Hispanics made up 9 percent, and African-Americans 12.1 percent.[3]

■ ■ ■

The '90s were a time when many minorities spoke up for their rights. In addition to African-Americans, Hispanics, and feminists, Native Americans, gays, people with disabilities, and environmental activists all found their voices. These groups demonstrated and lobbied for legislation on their behalf and worked for better understanding and acceptance in American society.

■ ■ ■

The quest for better awareness and sensitivity toward minority groups led to political correctness in American speech and writing. Terms like "differently abled" for "disabled," "Native American" for "Indian," and "hearing impaired" for "deaf" came into common usage.

■ ■ ■

School violence escalated in this decade. Metal detectors were installed in many schools. Twenty-five percent of whites and 20 percent of blacks said they feared attack at school.[4] In the late '90s, several incidents of teens bringing guns to school and shooting teachers and fellow classmates occurred.

■ ■ ■

The wars of this decade (Desert Storm, Bosnia, Desert Fox, and NATO's bombing of Serbia) were comparatively short, with relatively low impact on the people in the United States. They were viewed on TV as an event but didn't require emotional support and national participation in the war effort like WW I and WW II. These kids were not threatened by the draft like their parents were during the Vietnam War. Many were unaware or unconcerned about the wars that were taking place. In our own survey of high school kids, when asked, "What word or phrase best describes your feelings, attitudes or involvement with current wars in the world?" 26 percent of the responses were either "I don't know" or "I don't care." Another 54 percent gave negative responses like "They are stupid" or "I'd rather we didn't get involved."

■ ■ ■

The introduction and rapid growth of the Internet during the '90s has virtually created a different world for this new generation. It has changed the ways they communicate with each other, do research, entertain themselves, create projects for school, work at school, and relate to their parents (as they often teach their parents how to use it).

■ ■ ■

Politically, the '90s presented a new global dynamic as the Cold War ended, the USSR split apart, and the United States' role as defender of the free world was over. The reduction of nuclear arms in the late '80s eased the pressure and fear of nuclear disaster that had hung over previous decades. The Russians became people to help and cooperate with rather than being the ultimate enemy.

■ ■ ■

The '90s started out with economic problems left over from the '80s. This affected many areas, such as homelessness, health care, and education. Public education and achievement scores continued to fall, as they had in the '70s and '80s. According to a January 1988 report from the Educational Testing Service, American students scored near the bottom in an international comparison of math and science skills.[5] By 1993, 47 percent of 21- to 25-year-olds couldn't use a calculator to figure a price discount. Neither could they write a letter explaining an error on a credit card bill. Their literacy rate was 11 to 14 percent lower than those tested in 1985.[6]

■ ■ ■

In 1990, housing values plummeted, and personal bankruptcies rose 60 percent.[7]

■ ■ ■

Although the '90s started out rough economically, with a recession in 1991, the economy turned around during the decade. Unemployment, which peaked at almost 8 percent in 1992, declined to almost 4 percent by 1999.[8] Analysts described it as a "booming" economy, and the stock market saw unprecedented increases. In 1998, the inflation rate was only 1.5 percent, and for the first time in 30 years the U.S. federal budget experienced a surplus.

■ ■ ■

The health care situation was becoming critical. By 1991,

14.1 percent of all Americans and 28.9 percent of the poor did not have health insurance.[9] The cost of medical care was rapidly increasing. Other related issues included controversy over the right to die, the right to receive the latest medical procedures (in spite of expense), and the right to have an abortion.

■ ■ ■

The abortion issue continued to divide the country throughout the decade. Demonstrations, counter-demonstrations, lobbying, legislation, and court rulings between the pro-life and pro-choice groups were ongoing. The issue was taken to an illogical extreme when "pro-life" advocates murdered doctors who performed abortions.

■ ■ ■

A patient's right to die and doctor-assisted suicide became a hot topic. In 1991, a best-selling book by Derek Humphry, the director of the Hemlock Society, gave instructions on how to kill oneself with a combination of prescription drugs. Dr. Jack Kevorkian became well known as the doctor who, by the spring of 1998, had assisted 100 people in committing suicide, in spite of laws making it illegal.[10] On November 22, 1998, *60 Minutes* aired a videotape of Dr. Kevorkian assisting in a suicide. The audience was esti-mated to include 15.6 million households.

■ ■ ■

A change in mental health policy that caused the release of patients from hospitals, increased joblessness, a scarcity of affordable housing, and an increase in substance abuse—all these combined to cause a huge homeless population. It was believed that 250,000 Vietnam vets were homeless. An estimated 20,000 people in Chicago were homeless, and 90,000 in Los Angeles. At the end of 1993, the per-centage of homeless that were members of families with children increased to 43 percent, from 33 percent at the end of 1992.[11]

■ ■ ■

The issue of sexual harassment was brought to public attention through the Clarence Thomas senate hearings in 1991. After being nominated as the next justice of the Supreme Court, Judge Thomas was accused by Anita Hill, a former coworker, of sexual harassment on the job. The televised hearings were of great interest to the American public and led to increased sensitivity to and awareness of the problem. The issue gained national attention again in 1992, when charges were brought by 26 women against the Navy and Marines for sexual molestation they suffered during the 1991 Tailhook Convention. One hundred forty airmen were accused of indecent exposure, assault, and lying under oath. Eventually three admirals were censured and administrative action was taken against 30 senior officers for their participation.[12]

■ ■ ■

Women's issues gained more prominence, and women gained more power in the '90s. In the 1992 election, the number of women in the Senate increased from two to six, and the number of congresswomen in the House of Representatives swelled from 29 to 48. The election of Bill Clinton to the presidency placed his wife, Hillary Rodham Clinton, in the national headlines. She became the most politically active First Lady to date. This decade also witnessed the appointment of a second woman, Ruth Bader Ginsburg, to the Supreme Court, and of Madeline Albright as secretary of state and Janet Reno as attorney general.

■ ■ ■

One example of victory in the women's rights movement was Clinton's approval in 1993 of legislation that lifted the ban on women serving on combat vessels. Within a year, more than 400 women were placed on warships.[13]

■ ■ ■

Equal opportunity for disabled Americans made progress, as equal access laws were enacted and enforced. The movement to make all public buildings accessible to the handicapped has created highly visible facilities (ramps, handicapped parking, etc.) promoting the acceptance of people with disabilities into the mainstream of life. Education laws and national funding for public schools required school districts to provide equal education for virtually all forms of handicap: emotional, mental, and physical.

■ ■ ■

Civil rights for African-Americans continued to be a passionate issue. One notable example was the biggest riot of the century, which occurred in Los Angeles in April 1992, after the acquittal of the police officers who beat Rodney King. Fires broke out, stores were looted, and motorists were pulled from their cars and brutally beaten. In three days of rioting, 54 people were killed and more than $900 million worth of property was destroyed.[14]

■ ■ ■

In 1995, Louis Farrakhan led the Million Man March on Washington. Controversial, because it excluded both women and whites, thus appearing to promote separatism, the stated goal of the event was to address the image of the black American male and character issues such as repeutance and self-reliance. Due to previous intolerant pronouncements by Farrakhan, however, the march provoked a mixed reaction from the general public.

■ ■ ■

The fight against AIDS, other sexually transmitted diseases, and teenage pregnancy brought about the free distribution of condoms to junior high and high school students. Sex education in schools was expanded to cover topics such as alternative lifestyles (homosexuality and bisexuality), prevention of STDs, and methods of birth control. Many promoted abstinence, while others believed that teenage sex was inevitable and teaching them to protect themselves was preferable. Making abortions available to teenage girls without parental consent was also a big issue. A program called "True Love Waits," promoting abstinence and involving public, group commitments of teens vowing to remain virgins until marriage, became popular among Christian youth groups.

■ ■ ■

"Alternative lifestyle" became a term to promote acceptance of homosexual relationships. Issues of same-sex marriage, employment benefits for same-sex partners, adoption rights for same-sex partners, and equal employment were all hotly disputed. The issue of gays in the military came to a head in 1993 when the policy of "don't ask, don't tell, don't pursue" was issued.

■ ■ ■

Sports heroes fell off their pedestals throughout the decade as their private lives were exposed to the world. Some of the most memorable were Magic Johnson's announcement that he was HIV-positive; Greg Louganis admitting to having AIDS; Mike Tyson receiving a six-year prison sentence for rape; and O.J. Simpson's murder trial.

■ ■ ■

Political figures' moral failings were continually investigated and exposed. The most historic, of course, being the investigations of President Clinton in several areas: the Whitewater scandal, questionable campaign funding, and sexual misconduct, which caused Bill Clinton to become the second president in U.S. history to be impeached. The charges were perjury and obstruction of justice.

■ ■ ■

Bizarre and violent stories dominated the news throughout the decade: Jeffrey Dahmer convicted of 16 murders and

cannibalism; the Unabomber's final discovery and conviction; Heaven's Gate cult mass suicide to enable the
followers to join the mother spaceship that would take
them to heaven; Susan Smith's admission that she had
drowned her two sons after claiming they had been kidnapped; Nancy Kerrigan attacked by competing figure
skater Tonya Harding's ex-boyfriend; standoff at the
Branch Davidian compound in Waco, Texas, ending in
the fiery deaths of 84 loyal cult followers.

■ ■ ■

Terrorism was big news, both from international terrorists,
such as the bombing of the World Trade Center, and from
American citizens, as was the case in the Oklahoma City
bombing of the Murrah Federal Building.

■ ■ ■

Several interdenominational movements began among
evangelical Christians in the '90s:
  • The Promise Keepers movement saw more than 2
    million men participate in their stadium confer-
    ences. In October of 1997, hundreds of thousands
    of men from all denominations, races, and socio-
    economic groups met in Washington, D.C., for
    the "Stand in the Gap Sacred Assembly of Men," a
    day of personal repentance and prayer for the
    nation.[15]
  • March for Jesus, a worldwide movement, which
    started in 1980 in England, began in the United
    States in 1990 with a march in Austin, Texas. The
    first march, with 1,500 participants, was followed
    nine months later with 15,000 in Austin and 7,000
    in Houston. By 1993, U.S. participation had grown
    to 800,000 in 350 cities (1.7 million worldwide). It
    peaked in 1994 with 1.5 million participants in the
    U.S. (10 million worldwide in 178 nations) and
    continued throughout the decade. Marchers carried

signs praising Jesus and sang worship songs through the streets of their cities.[16]

- "See You at the Pole" became an annual event for Christian students all around the nation who met at their schools' flagpoles before school on a Wednesday in September to pray as a group.

■ ■ ■

Science continued to make great strides, but often with moral issues attached. Some of these achievements include cloning, genetic altering, new methods of creating babies for infertile couples, and life-support systems.

■ ■ ■

The Internet was embraced as the new medium that would change the way we live. Phenomenal growth occurred and increasing applications were developed for use in the workplace, in education, and in homes.

■ ■ ■

Video games were big business and continued to grow in popularity throughout this decade. In 1990, sales of electronic games were just under $3.5 billion. In 1997, sales had risen to over $5.5 billion.[17]

■ ■ ■

The space program continued with the Hubble telescope giving unprecedented views of outer space. The spacecraft *Galileo* was sent to orbit Jupiter. The United States and Russia began to cooperate, and in 1995, the U.S. shuttle *Atlantis* docked with Russian space station *Mir* in preparation for building an international space station. By the end of 1998, occupancy of the *Mir* space station by U.S. astronauts amounted to 1,000 days, involving numerous experiments.[18] In 1998, the space program recaptured the attention of the American people when John Glenn returned to outer space for research related to the aging process.

The full impact of the '90s on these future adults is yet to be seen, but some effects are already beginning to show. Here are a few trends to give you a taste of what they are.

Because these kids grew up in the age of "political correctness" and have been surrounded by various groups that demand to be recognized, accepted, and given rights, these young people seem to be more tolerant of different lifestyles and more willing to "live and let live." Many have nontraditional family settings, so their expectations of family life are not the same as those in previous decades. They seem to accept the miscellaneous assortment of blended and fractured families with the odd arrangements of relationships better than might be expected. Their tolerance of differences and their nonjudgmental attitudes make them more accepting of others but also mean they are less likely to believe in absolutes (right and wrong, good and bad, truth, etc.).

Being raised with the Internet, they are comfortable with the new technology and have greater access to knowledge than any group of people before them. This creates a sense of confidence and competence for them. That, plus the booming economy that the nation experienced in the second half of the decade, tends to give them a positive outlook on the future.

In spite of the breakdown of the traditional family, parents, through increased awareness of the effects of poor parenting in the past, have made their relationships more of a priority and seem to have more impact on these kids than parents in the last few decades.

This group loves diversity. The clothing styles of the '90s borrow from many decades, are very eclectic, and are very individual. These kids enjoy a variety of music—everything from swing to rock 'n' roll to alternative to ska to heavy metal. In a survey asking for music preferences, everything imaginable was listed (and several types we'd never heard of). Most listed several styles, and many said "everything but" and listed only one kind of music they didn't like.

Public figures have not provided positive role models for

these kids. When asked who their heroes are, many respond that they don't have any. An amazing number list their parents, other family members, or influential people in their lives, such as teachers.[19]

We have found the study of this group to be very interesting, and believe that you will, too. They are definitely unique, and we need to understand them as the new group in our homes, our organizations, and our workplaces. We will explore the place of each group as we move from the study of individual decades to the defining and comparison of the four generations that interact (and often clash) in the course of our daily lives.

A Portrait of the '90s

Demographics in 1990
Population: 248,700,000
Farmers: 1.8%
Life Expectancy:
Men: 72 years
Women: 78.8 years

Money Matters in 1990
GNP: $5,465.1 billion
Federal budget: $1,251.8 billion
National debt: $3,233.3 billion
Prime interest rate: 10.0%
Average annual salary: $23,602

Cost of Living in 1990
Eggs: $1.00 (doz.)
Milk: 71¢ (qt.)
Bread: 76¢ (loaf)
Coffee: $2.94 (lb.)
Round steak: $3.42 (lb.)

Key Events
1990   U.S. economy slumps; savings & loan bailout; East and West Germany reunite; Iraq invades Kuwait
1991   Cold War ends; nuclear arms reduction; Clarence Thomas hearings; Persian Gulf War, Desert Storm

1992   Bill Clinton elected president; U.S. economy in recession; Los Angeles riots after acquittals in Rodney King trial

1992   Hurricane Andrew devastates parts of Florida and Louisiana; *Roe vs. Wade* upheld by Supreme Court

1993   Midwest flooding; siege on Davidian compound in Waco; World Trade Center bombing; NAFTA

1994   O.J. Simpson chase and arrest; Nancy Kerrigan/Tonya Harding scandal; Northridge, California earthquake

1995   Bombing of federal building in Oklahoma City; O.J. Simpson verdict

1996   President Clinton reelected; U.S. economy booms; Atlanta Olympic Games (and bombing)

1996   Unabomber arrested; TWA crash; Valujet crash; blizzard hits Northeast

1997   Death of Princess Diana; death of Mother Teresa; conviction of Timothy McVeigh for Oklahoma City bombing

1998   Monica Lewinski scandal; impeachment of President Clinton; bombing of Iraq; John Glenn back in space

1999   Trial and acquittal of President Clinton; Dow Jones stock index hits record highs; 14 people are killed at Columbine High School in Colorado; Kosovo crisis

Fads/Trends

Barney, the purple dinosaur; Winnie the Pooh

Super Nintendo, video arcades, Sony Playstation

Batman, the Simpsons, and Teenage Mutant Ninja Turtles merchandise

Beanie Babies, Tickle-Me-Elmo dolls

Pogs, WWJD bracelets and merchandise

Rollerblading, skateboarding, snowboarding

Body piercing, tattoos

Shaved heads and spiked, bleached, and colored hair

Dances: swing, skanking, country line dancing

Teen raves, clubbing

E-mail, chat rooms, Web pages

New Inventions/Technology

Internet gained in popularity and usage

Caller ID developed

Heart surgery performed on a fetus in the womb

"Smart bombs" with laser guidance systems

Virtual reality invented

Nicotine patches developed

Intel 486 chip developed

Cloning a living creature becomes reality

Genetic engineering creates cows with disease-fighting milk

CD-ROM, CD-Rewritable

DVD-ROM

Intel Pentium III chip

Popular TV Shows

1990	*The Simpsons; America's Funniest Home Videos; Seinfeld*
1991	*Home Improvement; Step by Step; 911; Commish*
1992	*The Tonight Show with Jay Leno; Picket Fences*
1993	*Grace Under Fire; NYPD Blue; The X-Files; Frasier; Sea Quest*
1994	*E.R.; TV Nation; Friends; Touched by an Angel*
1995	*Naked Truth; Caroline in the City; Sliders; JAG*
1996	*Sabrina, the Teenage Witch; 3rd Rock From the Sun*
1997	*Dharma and Greg; Veronica's Closet; Ally McBeal*
1998	*Dawson's Creek; The Magnificent Seven; Felicity*
1999	*The PJs; Turks; Providence; Zoe, Duncan, Jack and Jane*

Hit Songs

1990	"Oh"; "Pretty Woman"; "Unanswered Prayers"
1991	"Unforgettable"; "The First Time"; "Someday"
1992	"I Will Always Love You"; "Jump"
1993	"Dreamlover"; "Have I Told You Lately"; "River of Dreams"
1994	"All I Wanna Do"; "Can You Feel the Love Tonight?"
1995	"Exhale"; "Fantasy"; "Take a Bow, Baby"
1996	"Macarena"; "Sittin' up in My Room"; "Because You Loved Me"

1997   "How Do I Live?"; "You Make Me Wanna"; "Butterfly Kisses"

1998   "You're Still the One"; "The Boy is Mine"; "Titanic"

1999   "From This Moment On"; "Angel"; "Written in the Stars"

Fashion

High-priced athletic sneakers

'60s revival: hot pants, miniskirts, psychedelic and op art prints

Black becomes a popular fashion color for all ages and occasions

Youth: bicycle shorts and T-shirts, baseball hats worn backward

Evening wear that looks like lingerie (Madonna-style)

Plaids (both outerwear and underwear), animal prints

Revival of '40s, '50s, and '70s styles, resulting in the eclectic look

Tapered pant legs (narrow as leggings)

Bulky platform shoes, flared jeans, capri pants

"Dress-down Fridays" at businesses

Young men: the "grunge look" (slashed and tattered clothing)

Oversized, baggy pants; tattoos; body piercing

Makeup with glitter

Publications

1990   *Clear and Present Danger; Megatrends 2000*

1991   *The Firm; Star Wars: Heir to the Empire*

1992   *Pelican Brief; It Doesn't Take a Hero; Silent Passages*

1993   *Bridges of Madison County; Without Remorse*

1994   *Men Are from Mars, Women Are from Venus; Op-Center*

1995   *Road Ahead; Politically Correct Bedtime Stories*

1996   *Rainmaker; Primary Colors; The Horse Whisperer; Zone*

1997   *Ghost; Midnight in the Garden of Good and Evil*

1998   *The Century; The Partner*

1999   *Greatest Generation; The Street Lawyer; Message in a Bottle*

Movies

Movie attendance = 20 million weekly

1990   *Pretty Woman; Dances With Wolves; Home Alone*
1991   *Silence of the Lambs; Terminator 2; Beauty and the Beast*
1992   *Basic Instinct; Wayne's World; Sister Act; Aladdin*
1993   *Jurassic Park; The Fugitive; Sleepless in Seattle; The Firm*
1994   *Pulp Fiction; Schindler's List; The Lion King; Forrest Gump*
1995   *Toy Story; Batman Forever; Apollo 13; Pocahontas*
1996   *Independence Day; Twister; 101 Dalmatians*
1997   *Titanic; Men in Black; Air Force One; The Lost World*
1998   *Armageddon; Saving Private Ryan; The Truman Show; Antz*
1999   *The Matrix; Star Wars, the Phantom Menace; The Wild, Wild West*

Heroes

Michael Jordan	Magic Johnson
General Colin Powell	Hillary Clinton
President Bill Clinton	Mark McGwire
Sammy Sosa	Leonardo Di Caprio
John Glenn	Christopher Reeves
Tiger Woods	Brad Pitt
Princess Diana	Nelson Mandela

DEFINING THE GENERATIONS

Chapter 14

The Tidal Wave of Negative Values

One day while channel surfing, I came upon a story about a tidal wave that caught my interest and actually caused me to pause for a while. I settled into the couch to watch the story unfold and ended up watching the entire documentary.

It started on a small, Pacific island with a warning to the people that a tidal wave was coming. The scene then shifted to a place out in the Pacific, hundreds of miles away, where an earthquake had taken place in the ocean floor. At that spot, there was a disruption on the surface of the ocean—just a little ripple that started hundreds of miles away from the island. The scene then shifted back to that island, where scientists were warning the inhabitants that this small wave was building and would hit in a few days. There were some on the island who took it quite seriously and began to pack and move to higher ground. Others had lived through such things before and didn't seem to be too concerned. They went about their business, saying that these things seldom materialized and showing very little concern about the warnings from the scientists.

Meanwhile, out in the Pacific Ocean, that little ripple had turned into a wave and was getting larger and larger. Nothing in its way could divert it. Ships in its way were overturned. By the time it approached the island, it had become enormous. The breakwaters couldn't stop it. The outlying peninsula of the island couldn't stop it. Finally it hit shore, devastating everything in its path. This tidal wave unleashed its power on the tiny island, and nothing was the same when it left. Everything in its path—including trees, buildings, cars, and people—was all swept away. The only ones who survived that incredible tidal wave were those who heeded the warnings of the scientists and took the advice to flee to higher ground.

We see the same kind of situation taking place with values in our country today. We have been warned in the past that values are changing. They started with just a few changes—a little ripple. Over time, those small differences have been growing.

Reading about all the changes from 1920 through the 1990s can be a bit overwhelming, and the meaning of it all is hard to grasp. In the next few pages, we'll condense it to give you a better understanding of the importance of each decade. We'll discuss which events in each decade led to which values. Looking at any one decade by itself may be interesting, but it doesn't give us a clear comprehension of how each decade fits into the big picture. For that we need to compare it with other decades.

As we observe how various factors or events changed from one decade to another, we'll see how those modifications affected the behavior of that decade. Things like involvement in or attitude toward war, the financial health of the nation, technological advancements, attitudes toward sex and marriage, and the role of women in society are just some of the issues and circumstances that have greatly influenced American values and behaviors over the years.

The Decade Values Developed

To gain a perspective of all that happened from 1920 to 1999 as it affects our values, we have created a chart, "The Decade Values Developed," that summarizes some of the major events and trends of each decade. This review and condensation of what we have described in previous chapters helps us to see the significance of each decade and the progression that value development has taken.[1]

The Decade Values Developed

'20s	'30s	'40s	'50s	'60s	'70s	'80s	'90s
Aftermath of World War I	Wall Street Crash	World War II	Korean War	Vietnam War	Vietnam Impact	Diminished World Respect/Hostages	Desert Storm Desert Fox
Close Family	The Great Depression	The War Effort	Cold War	Civil Rights	Watergate	High-tech Society	Cold War Ends
Mother/Housewife	Government Involvement	Working Women	Affluence	Kennedy Shot	Hypocrisy	AIDS	Domestic Terrorism
Radio Developed	The New Deal	Kindergartens Flourish	Indulged Kids	Space Program	"Me" Generation	Drugs	Politically Correct
Model T	Very Security Oriented	Mobility	Television	Generation Gap	Gay Liberation	Personal Computers	Internet
Prohibition		GI Bill	Rock 'n' Roll	Sexual Revolution (The Pill)	Equal Rights Amendment	Yuppies	Generation Lap
Flapper		The Good Life	Suburbs	Feminists	Environmentalists		Booming Economy
			Beatniks	Hippies			Clinton Scandals
							Tolerance
Commander Richard Byrd	FDR	General Eisenhower	Gen. Douglas MacArthur	John F. Kennedy	OJ Simpson	Ronald Reagan	Bill Clinton
Babe Ruth	Jesse Owens	Rosie the Riveter	Dr. Spock	Dr. Martin Luther King	Muhammad Ali	Lee Iacocca	McGwire and Sosa
Charles Lindbergh	Shirley Temple	Frank Sinatra	Elvis Presley	Neil Armstrong	Mary Tyler Moore	Magic Johnson	Michael Jordan
				The Beatles			

'20s   As you look at the chart, it's clear to see that in the '20s, values were more wholesome, more patriotic, and more family-oriented.

'30s   The key event of the '30s was the Great Depression started by the Wall Street crash of 1929. Although these tough times created a group of people who were very security-oriented, they also led to patriotism as the government stepped in and pulled the country out of its disaster and despair.

'40s   The dominant factor of this decade was World War II and the effect it had on society and the family. People pulled together for the common cause of the war effort. Women began to work, and kindergartens began to flourish. After the war, increased mobility accompanied the changes in technology, and the good life was finally here.

'50s   In the '50s, the postwar economy created a rather affluent society that moved in great numbers toward the suburbs. Parents overindulged their kids to make up for the sacrifices of the war years and in reaction to the deprivation of their own childhood. Dr. Spock's baby book was widely read and his principles applied (or misapplied). One of the key value-development factors—for this decade and all future ones—was the invention of television. It became a national pastime, greatly influencing values then and now. The development of rock 'n' roll and the ability of TV to create instant fads joined with other factors to produce a group of teenagers more distinct from their parents than ever before. One of the few shadows hanging over the '50s was the Cold War: the fear of communism and the potential of a nuclear attack on our country by the USSR.

'60s   We see the space program starting off with a bang during this decade, but the public seemed to lose interest after the lunar landing. Civil rights protests gained widespread attention, partially because they were seen on TV. Widespread use of the Pill helped both the women's rights movement and the sexual revolution. The Vietnam War had a significant impact on youth, many of whom questioned and protested the government's motives and actions.

'70s Mistrust of government continued into the '70s and was further reinforced by the Watergate scandal, which forced President Nixon out of office because of illegal actions. The overall lack of faith in any form of establishment (government, military, industry, school administrations, parents) left over from the '60s led to the belief that there was no one to trust but oneself. This focus on self—self-fulfillment, self-improvement, self-acceptance, self-enlightenment, self-help—earned this group the title of the "me" generation.

'80s In the 1980s, the world's attitude toward the United States was changing. The Iran hostage situation showed that even a small country, one that most had never heard of, could create a problem we couldn't solve. We began to see the impact of the personal computer and other inventions that ushered us into a high-tech society. One of the negative factors was the discovery and epidemic spread of AIDS. Drug use increased significantly, causing the president to appoint a drug czar to wage a war on drugs.

'90s This decade brought us more negative influences on value development, but also some factors that had a more positive impact. Domestic terrorism became more common. Not only were terrorists threatening Americans abroad, but our own citizens were attacking each other, bombing federal buildings and firing on people in public places.

On a positive note, the Berlin Wall came down, the Soviet Union broke up, and the Cold War came to an end. The politically correct movement also began to take a foothold in the '90s, affecting the way we look at and describe people and things. The Internet came on the scene, which began a whole new way of relating and doing business around the country and around the world (which we will discuss more extensively when we look at the Net Generation). One of the real benefits of the '90s was the booming economy. Remember the principle that we tend to take for granted and expect what we grow up with? These children will assume that the economy will always be good and that they can get all the "things" that they need (as opposed to the security-minded people influenced by the Depression or the pessimistic kids of the '70s and '80s who don't expect to have a lot). What this generation seems to be striving for is family security and close relationships with loyalty.

One of the final influences of the '90s impacting those who are growing up is tolerance. Now tolerance, in and of itself, is a great concept as people are gracious and accepting of others who are different than they are. But tolerance may be going too far when it leads to the approval of virtually anything people want to do in any lifestyle. The downside of extreme tolerance is that there are no standards or convictions to live by, and everyone is doing what is right in his own eyes, even if it has negative ramifications for the individual, the community, or the nation.

As we look from the '20s to the '90s, we see how life changed in the United States from a relatively simple, family-oriented society with traditional standards to one of political and relational turmoil, accelerated pace, advanced technology, and a lack of absolute standards.

However, there is more to understanding these decades

than just looking at specific occurrences. As events shaped values, values shaped behavior and trends changed over time. Let's take a step back and look at some of the trends that evolved over the course of the decades and see how they shaped our society.

Then and Now

I (Rick) grew up in Southern California, where the weather is generally warm. The schools I attended were relatively close, so I could usually walk; and if not, I could ride the bus. If I dared to complain, I heard from my parents and grandparents, as many of you have, the stories of how hard it was for them to get to school. They reportedly had to walk five miles to school . . . in a blizzard, barefoot, and backward. These stories of the past were told, apparently, to make us feel guilty and to help us understand just how difficult it was to do some of the normal day-to-day things. I guess they wanted us to appreciate what we had in comparison. But after a while, the stories were sloughed off as hyperbole.

But now it's the Boomers' turn to say, "When I was your age . . ." and to try and communicate to the younger generations what it was like before they arrived. After all, times *have* changed.

Remember when...

- A computer was something on TV from a science fiction show?
- An application was for employment, and a program was a TV show?
- A cursor used profanity, and a keyboard was a musical instrument?
- Memory was something that you lost with age, and a CD was a bank account?
- "Log on" was adding wood to the fire, and a hard drive was a long trip on the road?
- A mouse pad was where a mouse lived, and back up happened to your commode?

- Cut you did with a pocketknife, and paste you did with glue?
- A web was a spider's home, and a virus was the flu?
Now they all mean different things, and that really *megabites!*
                                        (multiple Internet sources)

As we compare trends, attitudes, and behaviors to show how life in the United States has changed over the decades, it doesn't take long to see that we're up against a tidal wave of negative values. Like the ripple in the middle of the ocean that eventually became a devastating tidal wave, the changes were gradual, slowly building over time until they became a powerful force, altering the values within our society. For many, this force is influencing values in a direction very different from the standards we want to live by or that we want to teach our children.

In the chart called "Tidal Wave of Negative Values" on the next page, we can see that, in the 1920s, values in the United States were, by and large, Judeo-Christian values. As we move along the time continuum, the closer we get to the '90s, the farther we get from Judeo-Christian values.

In the '20s and '30s, our values were quite traditional as they related to family, political perspective, and our views as a country about God. Then as we move through the decades, with the onslaught of World War II, the family structure itself began to change. As many men left the country to fight, more women were left to be responsible for family income and child care. Even after the men came home from the war, the trend toward more women, even mothers, joining the workforce continued to grow throughout the decades, especially when the feminist movement began to take hold. As the divorce rate rose, what used to be considered a traditional family—a mom and dad and 2.5 children—became less common. With fewer fathers in the home, more mothers were working and child rearing was abdicated to caregivers and preschools, and older children were increasingly left on their own as "latch-key" kids.

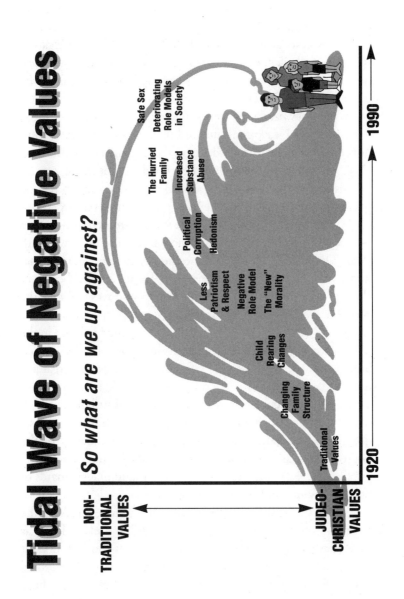

Tidal Wave of Negative Values

So what are we up against?

As we move on, this tidal wave begins to pick up speed. We can see our country beginning to question the government with serious protests again the Vietnam War. The higher education system was challenged by college students, who began to question and mistrust anyone and anything associated with "the establishment." Rejection of traditional values led to the emergence of a "new morality" which included the sexual revolution.

As the tidal wave continues to build, we see political corruption, even as high as the presidency of the United States in the early '70s. Since government couldn't be trusted, and other big organizations and institutions were also suspect, this generation had no one to turn to or trust, and the "me" generation developed.

As we move into the '80s, there were no military skirmishes to shape values, but the family almost seemed to be at war with itself. The hurried family became the norm. Fewer families sat down and had their meals together. Family values began to change. The divorce rate was up, drug abuse was up, and the good life seemed to be slipping away.

As the tidal wave of negative values continued to build in the '90s, its strength was reinforced with the threat of AIDS, which brought on the battle cry of "safe sex." Public service organizations and schools sent the message that sex would be okay as long as you had protection. Condoms were freely distributed at high schools, in spite of parental protests. We continued to have deteriorating role models, again as high as the presidency of the United States, and the reaction of much of the public and many public officials sent the message that the traditional standards of right and wrong didn't apply anymore.

What started off as a ripple of value changes back in the beginning of this century has been building and building as time goes along. It has reached the point that those who want to raise their family with Judeo-Christian ethics, or traditional values, are up against a tidal wave of negative values. We have progressed (or regressed) over the decades from mandatory Bible reading and prayer in schools to banning these activities, including the traditional celebrations of holidays. People who lack moral character become celebrities instead of bearing the shame and consequences of their misdeeds, as they would have in earlier decades. Children, who used to be shielded from exposure to adult sexual acts and violence, are now repeatedly exposed to vivid portrayals in the media. We have moved from a society built upon the tenets of the Christian faith and the principles of right and wrong to a society where many live by situational ethics, with a lack of moral direction for their lives, leading to confusion and destructive choices. While this might sound like the voice of a pessimist or alarmist, it's important to realize that changes like these have a tremendous impact. A society doesn't change its core values, its basic beliefs, without it affecting the day-to-day realities of that society.

In an article in *The Wall Street Journal* in 1993, William Bennett compared various social trends of that year with what was happening in 1966. According to Bennett, between 1966 and 1993, violent crime in the United States increased by 560 percent, illegitimate births increased 419 percent, divorce rates quadrupled, the percentage of children living in single-parent homes tripled, the teenage suicide rate increased more than 300 percent, and SAT scores dropped almost 80 points. Rapes, murders, and gang violence became common occurrences.[2]

The Washington, D.C.-based Children's Defense Fund reported that every day in the United States:

- 2,781 teenage girls get pregnant (500 percent more than in 1966)
- 1,115 teenage girls have abortions (about 1,100 percent more than in 1966)
- 1,295 teenage girls give birth
- 2,556 children are born out of wedlock
- 4,219 teenagers contract a sexually transmitted disease (about 335 percent more than in 1966)
- 5,314 teenagers are arrested
- 135,000 children come to school with a gun.[3]

These statistics leave little doubt that the changes in our country's values over the years have resulted in an increase in negative consequences in our society. But in some areas a glimmer of hope is beginning. When things get really bad, it forces people to look for causes and solutions. We are starting to see Boomer and Gen-Xer parents reconsider their values and the consequences to their children. There is a trend for them to make families more of a priority and return to the more traditional values of their childhood, when life was simpler and more child-friendly. According to Smith and Clurman in *Rocking the Ages: The Yankelovich Report on Generational Marketing:*

"The importance of home and family for women is on the rise. In just the last few years, women are increasingly likely to cite home and family as a priority. For example, since 1993 the percentage of women agreeing that 'most working mothers would rather stay home and be with their children full-time' has risen from 57 percent to 66 percent, and this increase is true of both working and nonworking women. Along with this is an increasing interest in returning to more traditional styles of homemaking."[4]

This tidal wave of negative values threatening our growing families has caused a reaction that Faith Popcorn, a trend analyst and the author of *Clicking,* has called "cocooning." This refers to a pattern among today's families to want to protect themselves from "the harsh, unpredictable realities of the outside world. Studies show that there has been a three-year tripling in the popularity of 'staying home with the family.'"[5]

I was at a conference sharing this concept of the tidal wave of negative values when someone approached and gave me some handwritten notes from a sermon her pastor had recently given. These words give an interesting view of the relationship of circumstances, values, attitudes, and behavior and the progression (or regression) that takes place over time.

History shows that the average age of the world's greatest civilizations has been 200 years. These nations passed through 10 stages:

From bondage to spiritual faith
From spiritual faith to great courage
From great courage to liberty
From liberty to abundance
From abundance to selfishness
From selfishness to complacency
From complacency to apathy
From apathy to moral decay
From moral decay to dependence
From dependence back to bondage

Take a look at that list. Where you think America is today may depend on what decade you were raised in. Those who were not raised with traditional moral standards, and who question whether there are any absolute truths to live by (as we will see is true of the younger generations today), may not think we are as far along in the process as members of our older generations would. But if there is any truth to this theory, our future could be in jeopardy.

Up until this point, we've been comparing our values decade by decade. But to take it one step further, we can group a few decades together and define those who were raised during that period of time as a generation, whose experiences and values set them apart from other generations. In the next chapter, we'll identify the four generations that currently exist in our society. Then, as we look at the typical characteristics of each group, we'll be able to identify some of the clashes that each generation may have with the others.

Chapter 15

The Builder Generation

Defining the Generations

Now we're ready to divide ourselves into generations. In this chapter we're going to name and define by years of birth each of the four generations that make up our American society today. Then we'll concentrate on the first and most "chronologically gifted" of the four groups.

As we look at these generations, it's not easy to come up with names for them. For those born before 1946, a lot of names have been suggested to capture the significance of this generation. They have been referred to as Traditionalists because of the traditional values they maintained. Others have called them Matures because of their age. The name GI Generation has been given to them because so many fought in World War I and World War II. The title Survivor Generation was granted them because they, in fact, survived the Great Depression, World War I, and World War II.

This generation includes two groups of individuals. First came the GIs, who fought the wars for us and "made the world safe for democracy." The second group, coming after them, has been referred to as either the Silent Generation or the Swing Generation. Some even label the latter part of this generation the In-betweeners, since they are in between the GI Generation and the Baby Boomers.

For the purpose of this book, we are going to refer to this

generation, as others have, as the Builder Generation. We believe this title best encompasses all the other concepts. They returned from World War I and began to build a new society. They survived the Great Depression and began to rebuild society. Then they made it through World War II and returned to build the economy, cities, highways, railways, and the airline systems of this country. Not only did they build material things, the Builders also were the architects of our traditional, family-oriented value system.

Next came the Baby Boomers, between 1946 and 1964. They are the only generation that has a clearly defining name. For decades, the birthrate was relatively level, until the end of World War II. Within nine months, in 1946, the population took off and there was a boom in the number of births, which continued for 18 years (until 1964). The birth of these 76 million Americans gave them impressive power as a generation and allowed them to have perhaps the most significant impact of any generation since the founding of this nation. Needing a name for easy reference, Baby Boom became their title.

The next generation is considerably more difficult to label. This is the group of individuals who were born between 1965 and 1976. We have heard several names suggested, such as Generation 13, Echo Boomers, and Baby Busters. But the name that we hear used most often to refer to this group is Generation X or, as we refer to them, Xers. This is not necessarily a becoming title and not one that all from this generation accept, but it does seem to be the title that is most commonly used.

The final generation of this century, and the one leading us into the next century, is very young—born between 1977 and 1997. However, it has already acquired a number of names. Some have referred to them as the Millennials or the Bridgers because they will lead us into the next millennium. Others have called them Generation Next or the Y Generation (because they follow Generation X). But the name that seems to make the most sense to me comes from Don Tapscott's book *Growing Up Digital—The*

Rise of the Net Generation. I believe the Net Generation, or N-Gen, is a descriptive and accurate title for this emerging group. They are the first generation to grow up with access to the Internet, and, as we will see later in this section, this is a defining factor for this generation and will have great significance—not only for them, but for the other three generations in our society today as well.

It is important to keep in mind that we are looking at generations and not simply age. For example, what a teenager is going through today is not what teenagers were going through 20 or 30 years ago at the same age. Even the Builder Generation is not dealing with the same types of issues that their parents or grandparents were dealing with at their age. A great book that describes this concept further is *The Age Wave,* by Ken Dychtwald and Joe Flower (Tarcher, Inc., 1989). Gail Sheehy, in her book *New Passages: Mapping Your Life Across Time* (Random House, 1995), also explains this concept quite clearly. In her research comparing the generations today, she has discovered that there seems to have been a revolution in the way we grow up. In the space of one generation, the whole process has basically changed. Today, people leave childhood much sooner, but they take more time to grow up and, ultimately, live quite a bit longer. It used to be that midlife started around age 40. Now Sheehy, in her research, indicates that midlife starts around age 50, with a much more active lifestyle from the 50s into the 60s and 70s. So simply comparing generations at certain ages doesn't give a clear understanding of what is happening. One must look at the generation one has been raised in, see what is taking place as that generation moves through time, and understand what the changing trends are.

If you've read other articles or books on generations, you've probably noticed that demographers sometimes use different dates to define the various groups. Strauss and Howe, in their classic book, *Generations,* determined that a generation is approximately a 20-year period. Others see it differently—in fact, many see it in such a variety of different ways that it is difficult to come up with one definition. Diane Crispell, in an article in *American*

Total Number of Births in the USA

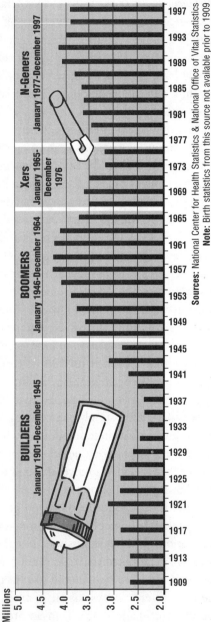

Sources: National Center for Health Statistics & National Office of Vital Statistics
Note: Birth statistics from this source not available prior to 1909

Demographics, states, "None of these generations is carved in stone."[1]

The method we have chosen to divide these groups into a generation is determined by looking at population increase and decrease.

As the chart on page 232 shows, the Builder Generation's birthrate was relatively flat, with the number of births staying about the same for many years. Then, in 1946, we see a dramatic increase in births, which was the beginning of the Baby Boom. This ended in 1964 with a major decline in births. The following group, Gen-X, started in 1965 and had a general decline until 1977, when we had what some refer to as a second baby boom. The birthrate begins to increase and grow until 1997, where it levels off, thus defining the Net Generation.

Those who study demographics have referred to the Baby Boom as a pig in a python. The demographics simply looked like a flat snake that swallowed a whole pig: a big bulge with flatness before and after. But I'd submit that these days, with the increase in the birthrate of the N-Geners, it's more like a camel in a cobra—with a double hump!

These population increases are more than just numbers on a chart. Having this many people in a generation has some very significant ramifications. It's well documented that much of the marketing world caters to the Baby Boomers because of their sheer numbers. We also see the results of what they were able to accomplish when they decided to challenge and change the status quo. On the other hand, the Gen-X crowd doesn't have nearly the size and will not have as significant an impact on society. Now we're seeing this emerging generation, the N-Geners, having the potential to equal the significance of the Baby Boomers, since they have a total population that's even larger.

It's one thing to look at these generations on the chart, but it's more important to look deeper and find out what makes them unique and, in fact, where they may clash with one another. In this and the next few chapters, we'll focus on these

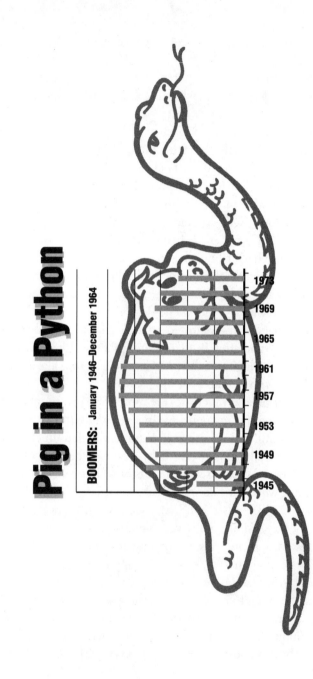

Pig in a Python

BOOMERS: January 1946–December 1964

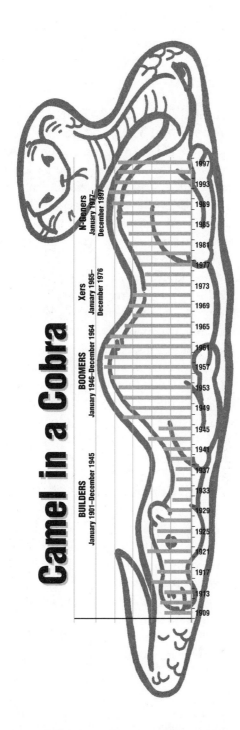

Camel in a Cobra

four generations, further defining who they are and how each distinguishes itself from the others. We start off our exploration by looking at the first generation, the Builders.

THE BUILDER GENERATION
Born between 1901 and 1945

As we take a look at the oldest living generation in America today, we need to tell you that it's actually two generations in one. As you can see, the time span we are referring to is over 40 years instead of the more typical 20-year period. The reason we're treating them as one generation in our study is that, although there are some differences, their values are basically the same. Both groups (although different ages at the time) experienced the Depression and World War II in ways that greatly affected their values. Remember we mentioned that the Depression was a Significant Emotional Event that affected everyone who lived through it, no matter what his or her age? That would be true of World War II also. Plus, before television, the changes in our society's values occurred much more gradually, so the changes from 1910 to 1940 were not as dramatic as those from 1950 to 1970. Therefore, for the purpose of our comparisons, we will treat those born from 1901 to 1945 as one generation, called the Builders. But before we lump them together, let's look at some of the distinctive features of each group.

GI Generation

The GI Builders, born from 1901 to 1924, set the tone and direction for this generation, and in fact, the whole country for decades to come. The list of who the GI Builders are and the things that they have done for our country is absolutely overwhelming. Certainly this society was in need of being built or rebuilt. The men and women of this generation took on the challenge and succeeded in ways far beyond their own expectations.

This generation includes people like Walt Disney, Bob Hope, Katherine Hepburn, William Levitt (who built Levittown, the first suburb development), Jimmy Stewart, William Westmoreland, Ann Landers, Robert McNamara, Walter Cronkite, Billy Graham, and Lee Iacocca. These people were willing to be servants and meet the needs of society. At the same time they were prepared to take bold new steps to be the first to bring in new ideas and accomplishments to our country—from Charles Lindbergh, the first to fly across the Atlantic, to Neil Armstrong, the first to set foot on the moon.

The accomplishments that this generation brought forth bear testimony to their discipline, their courage, and their commitment to their country. From surviving the Great Depression to bringing our enemies to surrender in World War II, they spread out in different fields and different disciplines to claim a variety of victories. They built the major bridges and dams and the interstate highway system we use today. The Civilian Conservation Corps planted trees all across the country and helped to establish the national park system as we know it today. They developed medicine and serums that would heal disease, not only in this country but all around the world. The airline industry was developed and became one of the major systems of transportation around the world. And this was just the beginning.

Members of this generation felt a responsibility to offer up the leadership skills they had. GI Builders provided presidents for the United States from the early '60s through the early '90s, starting with John F. Kennedy, including Lyndon Johnson, Richard Nixon, Gerald Ford, Jimmy Carter, Ronald Reagan, and ending with George Bush. It is clear that the GI wave of leadership in the Builder Generation had a special relationship with and dependency on the U.S. government.

According to Strauss and Howe:

> The GI life cycle has shown an extraordinary association with the growth of modern government activity, much of it directed toward whatever phase of life they occupied. When GIs were young, government protected them

from people and things that could hurt them. When they were coming of age, government gave them jobs. When they were rising adults, government provided them with numerous preferential advantages in education, employment, and family formation. When they were in midlife, they benefited from tax cuts and an economy run full throttle. When they reached elderhood, many received newly generous pensions and subsidized medical care—and gained more than others from deficit-laden financing schemes that pushed cost far into the future. Not surprisingly, GIs have always regarded government as their benefactor, almost like a buddy who has grown up right alongside them. They have been what historian Joseph Goulden describes as "a generation content to put its trust in government and authority."[2]

As a result of surviving the Great Depression and coming through World War II victorious, in the late '40s, the GI Builders were in a position to attain a goal that people in this country have been trying to reach since its inception: the good life. Strauss and Howe, in *Generations,* comment on the way this group saw themselves. Six out of seven reported having fared better financially than their parents. This is the highest proportion ever recorded. In 1940, approximately 46 percent of Americans owned their own homes. By 1960, a mere 20 years later, that number had risen to 64 percent. This increase is understandable when you see the prices they were dealing with back in the '50s. With the average wage for a 35-year-old being $3,000 per year and a new home selling for $7,000, a mortgage with a 4 percent interest rate would require approximately $350 down and about $30 per month.[3] (You'd have difficulty buying a new car for that today!)

The character of this group was at the heart of its success and longevity. Discipline, self-sacrifice, teamwork, and pitching in for the common good defined the mutual understanding of how people lived out their lives. During World War II, the Navy Seabees had a motto that describes this group's attitude: "The difficult we do at once; the impossible takes a bit longer."[4]

Even though teamwork and unity were goals to strive for, this generation was not afraid to step out and try things in a different way. Again, during World War II, when many of the men were called into military service, women were needed to supply the labor force for the factories. For the first time in our history, Rosie the Riveter and her coworkers constituted an industrial workforce that was predominantly female. This wasn't the way things had been done in the past, and it wasn't what seemed normal, but it was needed for the sake of the country, and they did it. The desire of this generation was not to be unique, not to stand out, but to fit in with the crowd and accomplish things together. George Gallup defined the "average man" at that time in society as more eager to celebrate sameness than differences among people.[5]

The Silent Generation

As the early GI Builders were moving on in life, climbing the corporate ladders and taking their positions as government leaders, the Silent Builders fell into place directly behind. This was the generation born from about the mid-'20s to the mid-'40s, during the Depression and previous to, or during, World War II. They didn't suffer as much as the GI Builders did, but they learned their lessons from those who had lived through these difficult times. This group found themselves sandwiched between the GI Builders and the Baby Boomers. They grew up observing the GIs and identifying with those values. But when the Baby Boomers came along and they saw all of the freedom that this new generation was experiencing, they felt (and in many cases, still feel) caught in between. They just weren't sure which generation they belonged in. They certainly grew up understanding responsibility, but as they got a bit older and entered adulthood, they also began to identify with the younger generation.

This was the group that helped to nurture, teach, and even produce some of the radical thoughts of the Baby Boom Generation. People like Bob Dylan, Abbie Hoffman, and the Chicago Seven were from this group. There were also movie stars and recording artists that Baby Boomers grew up listening to, like Shirley Temple, Jerry Lewis, James Dean, Elvis Presley, Woody Allen, Jack Nicholson, and Barbra Streisand. This generation was like a support group for the GIs. They had no presidents in their number, but provided a number of presidential aides, such as John Sununu for George Bush, James Baker III for Ronald Reagan, Stuart Eizenstat for Jimmy Carter, Dick Cheney for Gerald Ford, John Ehrlichman for Richard Nixon, Bill Moyers for Lyndon Johnson, and Pierre Salinger for John Kennedy. They weren't old enough to fight in World War II but took on a war of their own and joined the Peace Corps.

Strauss and Howe noted that "16 percent of Harvard's Class of '64 joined the Peace Corps, Harvard's top postgraduate destination for that year, whereas the next year's graduates began criticizing the Peace Corps amid the early stirrings of the Boom's antiestablishment rebellion."[6]

This was not their only avenue for trying to address social concerns of the day. As a matter of fact, the Silent Builders hold within their ranks virtually every major figure in our country's modern civil rights movement. From Russell Means, who started the Native American movement, to Cesar Chavez, who developed the Farm Workers Union, to Malcolm X and Martin Luther King, Jr. As the early GI Builders are retiring, or are quickly moving in that direction, the Silent Builders have taken key leadership positions all across the country.

Now that we've acknowledged the differences between the GI Builders and the Silent Builders, let's see how they're similar and why we can consider them to be one group as we compare them to the other three generations. The success that both the GI Builders and Silent Builders have experienced in governmental and industrial leadership roles has to do with their character and personal discipline. Both groups believe that if you are going to take on a big job or a task, you have to put your own personal interests aside. Discipline means postponing immediate gratification for future good, and many of these Builders lived that out. As young families, they learned to save their money to buy their first house and forgo personal pleasures and pursuits so that they might provide "things" for their young children, that emerging generation known as the Baby Boomers.

Chapter 16

The Baby Boom Generation

Nine months after World War II ended, the maternity wards filled up and didn't empty out for 19 years. From 1946 to 1964, approximately 76 million American babies were born. The population growth went "boom." When the Pill was introduced in the '60s, it helped to turn the tide on this baby boom by giving families more control over the number of children they would have and when they would have them.

The Baby Book

As we mentioned in previous chapters, Dr. Benjamin Spock's classic book on raising children focuses on some good and, at the time, relatively new concepts in raising children. Rather than the sterile, emotionally cold, and highly structured methods of child rearing that had previously been promoted, Spock encouraged parents to view their children as little people with real needs that should be met. These parents, having survived the Depression and World War II, wanted their kids to have better and happier childhoods than they had, so they embraced Dr. Spock's new ideas with enthusiasm. But when it came to discipline, whether it was the application or misapplication of his principles, there was a great effect on both the parents and the children. "Boomers grew up spoiled and pampered. Spock helped create the most permissive parents in history."[1]

The influence of this permissiveness helped to create a very different generation. Unlike the Builders, these young Boomers grew up focusing more on themselves and their own needs versus the needs of the country. They inherited a sense of privilege and uniqueness. With this generation, the motto shifted from "Good things come to those who wait" (a Builder sentiment) to "Get it now." That's one of the characteristics that Madison Avenue helped to create in the Baby Boom culture. The advertising focused on the newest thing children could get, whether it was a hula hoop, a Slinky, or an Etch-a-Sketch. The advertisers would end by saying, "Don't wait. *Get yours today!*"

The Builders, as children, didn't have a lot of toys as they were living through the Depression. They weren't able to spend a lot of money on themselves as they were fighting World War II. The "right" thing to do was sacrifice and ration for the good of all. But now that all that was over, they wanted their children to have it better than they did. In the process they neglected to teach an important character quality that children had been taught for ages—the discipline of delayed gratification.

Television

One of the most significant influences on the young Boomer Generation was the rise of television. This generation was the first raised with this new influence. As the Boomers grew, so did the young broadcast industry. *The Howdy Doody Show* was the first children's show and ran from 1947 to 1960. It was action-packed, fun, exciting, and always lots of laughs. So innocent compared to programming today. But, whether it was designed to or not, it certainly did have an impact on society, according to Steven Stark's insightful book, *Glued to the Set:*

"*Howdy Doody* systematically alienated the establishment—which, by and large, meant parents—while becoming the darling of their children, which meant baby boomers. . . . ABC analyst Jeff Greenfield would later credit the show for the rise of the sixties counterculture and generational war, calling Clarabell the original Yippie and likening Mayor Bluster to a puppet version of then-president Dwight Eisenhower."[2]

Watching the show as children, we had no idea there would be any kind of counterculture effects, any kind of input in our lives that would help to determine how we, or the generation we were growing up in, would behave. But the simple, seemingly innocent show did have its effect on society.

From the beginning, the TV industry knew that it would have an impact on children, although it was packaged as a positive influence by ads such as "Tomorrow's children, through the great new medium of television, will be enrolled in a world university before they leave their cradles."[3]

Most of us Baby Boomers were well into our viewing patterns and addicted to television before we had any clue that it would have an effect on us. TV watching became an ingrained part of our American culture and shaped our beliefs, attitudes, and actions. Advertisers could create instant fads through national advertisement campaigns. The country's attitudes and sensibilities could be greatly influenced through widespread coverage of protests or abuses suffered by minority groups. Comparatively small groups, like hippies, could greatly influence behavior, styles, and attitudes of people who never met them but saw them regularly in their living rooms through the magic of TV.

And it wasn't just advertisers and news coverage that was shaping our values. As networks competed with each other for the interest of viewers, programs needed to be increasingly more exciting, which somehow seemed to translate into more sex and more violence. Flirting with the taboos of society seemed to be an irresistible element to many viewers, so over the years the standards of acceptability have increasingly been changed, and our values along with them. Remember when Lucy and Ricky Ricardo had to have twin beds because it was unacceptable to show a husband and wife in bed together? Compare that to what we are seeing on TV today and realize how far the standards have changed. And we have changed with them.

Studies have revealed very tangible and devastating effects of television viewing on any generation that is consumed by it (and from the Boomers on, they all have been). A revealing study on the effects of television by Brandon Centerwall, MD, MPH, reported in the *Journal of the American Medical Association* in 1992, compared the rates of homicides committed by whites in the United States and Canada with those of South African whites over a 42-year period. The South African government did not allow television broadcasting in that country until 1975, so this allowed for an enlightening study of its effects on the violent behavior of viewers. In the United States and Canada, the rates of homicides doubled from 1950 to 1975, as these TV-raised children became adults.

Without television, the homicide rate in South Africa during those same years remained fairly stable. After the introduction of television in 1975, the homicide rate increased 130 percent in 12 years as South Africa's first TV-raised children grew up, mirroring the results of TV viewing observed in the United States and Canada. In comparison, the already TV-saturated societies of the United States and Canada saw their homicide rates level off where they had peaked in 1974. As a result of this study, Dr. Centerwall estimated that television is responsible for 10,000 homicides, 70,000 rapes, and 700,000 violent assaults per year in the United States alone.[4]

From the very beginning of television to the most current studies, television obviously has had a very significant impact on our beliefs and behavior. Even our expectations concerning problem solving have been influenced. No matter what major problem occurred in a TV show, large or small, it was always solved by the time the program was over. In 60, or even 30, minutes, some of the most difficult problems in life could be dealt with (and that included several commercial breaks to help viewers see what products they needed for the good life). Those raised on TV are less likely to patiently endure or accept life's challenges or consider long-term solutions. They want answers, solutions, change—and they want it now!

Antiestablishment

As the Boomers were growing up and observing the adults in their world, they found many reasons to mistrust them. On their televisions (and in their own neighborhoods), they saw government officials, who were supposed to protect citizens and uphold laws, actually attacking those who were claiming their legal civil rights. They became aware of hypocrisy and double standards in their homes, their churches, their schools, and their government. They found that industries supposedly providing the good life were, in many cases, destroying the environment in the process. The more they learned about the government, the more reason they had to mistrust it. Whenever the truth ultimately came out, like in the *Pentagon Papers* and the Watergate investigation, it confirmed what the Boomers had already come to believe—that there was always an inside story, the true story, behind what the public was initially being told.

Many of the movies released in recent years have an underlying plot that the government is not telling the whole truth. In some cases, not even part of the truth! Some plots have the government hiding information about UFOs or using computers in elaborate conspiracies that endanger citizens who end up knowing too much. A number of recent movies focus on the White House and cover-up plots to hide sexual misconduct, murders, and political deal making that is not in the best interest of the country. Many of the writers, directors, and producers of these movies are the "don't-trust-the-establishment" Baby Boomers. The fact that some of the plots they are creating actually parallel real-life situations today doesn't help with the credibility gap that continues in the minds of Boomers (and for that matter, the generations following them) today.

Generation Gap

One of the common phrases of the '60s and '70s was "the generation gap." There was, in fact, a gap between the values, attitudes, and actions of Baby Boomers and those of their parents. While this gap was created partially because of changes in child-rearing techniques, courtesy of Dr. Spock, and the influence of television, perhaps the greatest cause of the conflicts between the two generations was the difference between the education level of the Baby Boomers and their parents.

In her exhaustive study, *American Generations: Who They Are, How They Live, What They Think,* Susan Mitchell mapped out the differences between the groups, from the Builder Generation to the Net Generation, looking at behaviors, trends, statistics, and sociological differences. She feels that the generation gap between the Baby Boomers and their parents can be greatly attributed to the Boomers' intellectual outlook.

"Education influences a person's attitudes, lifestyle, and consumer behavior. The striking generational differences in educational attainment are one of the most important causes of the generation gap between older and younger Americans. . . . Because education influences attitudes, the gap creates many differences of opinion.[5]

In a research project, the Builders were asked to choose between learning a skill at a job or going to college for an education as the best way for self-improvement. Overwhelmingly the Builder Generation chose learning a skill, which is certainly a reflection of their value of hard work, one-step-at-a-time achievement, and on-the-job training. When that same question was posed to a group of Baby Boomers (who were approximately the same age as the Builders were when they were first asked that question), the Boomers overwhelmingly chose going to college,[6] consistent with their view of education, learning, and advancing themselves in their intellectual pursuits.

The generation gap seemed to center on differing attitudes toward money, sex, religion, drugs, and war. Whether these attitudes helped to create the generation gap or were a reflection of it, the differences between the Builders and the Boomers led to conflict, mistrust, and a major clash of gut-level values.

The New Morality

As the Baby Boomers grew up, they began to develop a sense that rules were not made for them but were made to be broken. These Baby Boomers realized that they were the best-educated generation in history, which led to the attitude that they had a better perspective than their parents did. They believed they had a clearer picture of what was going on, and if they needed to alter rules to get to where they wanted to be, that was okay. We can see how this was lived out when these Baby Boomers went to college and felt that their needs weren't being met by the system. They decided to challenge the established educational system of that time and actually won, bringing about significant changes in the way colleges and universities were run, and even the type of curriculum that was offered.

As Boomers questioned anything connected with the establishment, the traditional organized church denominations were rejected by many as being irrelevant or hypocritical. This seemed to free them to also reject the teachings they were based on, and many began looking for new or enlightened truth in other places, such as Eastern religions, mysticism, and psychedelic drug use.

This group's questioning and rejection of many of the values and actions of the previous generation also extended into the area of morality. Many embraced a new morality. Love-ins and sex with no responsibility or commitment were seen by some as a new form of freedom from their parents' traditional views. Couples living together without being married became acceptable to many in this generation. Even some of those who did decide to get married didn't have the commitment level of their parents, and their focus on their own needs and self-fulfillment led to a climbing divorce rate. Illegal use of drugs was acceptable to many as a way of seeking enlightenment. Illegal actions, such as burning draft cards or lying to the government to avoid the draft, were justified in their minds because of their belief that the war was wrong and immoral.

As the Baby Boomers emerged into the marketplace, we also saw radical rule-breaking in the form of insider trading, banking problems, and corruption in industry. Those who got caught in these violations often gave excuses that they didn't feel they were hurting anyone. They believed that they didn't do anything wrong—that they were just doing what was best for themselves as individuals.

The Times Are Changing

As the Boomer generation got older, they kept true to some of their core values, which had to do with meeting their own personal needs, believing themselves to be very special, and not needing to play by the rules of the previous generation. But a big change in how they lived their lives began in the late '70s and '80s. As they matured, most abandoned their protesting and began joining the adult world. Even one of their role models, Jerry Ruben—who was an active member of the Chicago Seven and violently protested against the government and the status quo—emerged in the '80s as a true capitalist, declaring to Wall Street that he was coming in to make millions of dollars.

From the beginning, these Boomers were consumers raised on having the good life now. This shift in their attention, from trying to solve the nation's problems to concentrating on their own financial desires, was one that caught many by surprise but wasn't totally untrue to the Boomer character. Their attention continued to be centered on themselves—what they believed to be right, what they wanted, what was good for them. As they aged, the old battle cry of "Don't trust anyone over 30" ceased to be heard. Now, even the youngest Boomers are older than 30 and the battle cry might be changed to "Don't trust anyone under 30."

In more recent years there has been another shift in Boomer lifestyles as they seem to be yearning for the simplicity and traditional values of their childhoods. Nostalgia is popular, and there is a growing conservative movement in our society today. After seeing the negative effects of early Boomers neglecting their Gen-Xer children, later Boomers have become much more attentive parents, looking for self-fulfillment in successful parent-child relationships with their younger, N-Gen children. To protect their children (and themselves), Boomers have again taken to fighting social ills, such as smoking, drug abuse, child abuse, and activities that would lead to exposure to AIDS.

The Baby Boomers illustrate well that as time moves along, generations do change, but generally speaking, their core values stay with them.

Who They Are

Some well-known Baby Boomers include the first Boomer president, Bill Clinton, as well as Steven Spielberg and Bill Gates. Other recognizable names are Kareem Abdul-Jabbar, David Letterman, Oprah Winfrey, Steven Jobs, Roseanne, and Michael Jordan. Some of the early Boomers are O.J. Simpson, Stephen King, Andrew Lloyd Webber, James Taylor, Whoopi Goldberg, Rush Limbaugh, Sting, and Robin Williams. Those with birthdays near the end of the Boomer era include Madonna, John Elway, Amy Grant, Dennis Rodman, Jim Carrey, Tom Cruise, and Demi Moore.

Chapter 17

Generation X

I (Rick) grew up in California in the John Wooden era of college basketball. This was one of the most significant collegiate sports dynasties ever. Wooden coached from 1946 to 1975. His UCLA teams won 10 NCAA basketball championships in 12 years, including seven straight titles from 1967 to 1973. Some of the great college basketball stars of all time played in this era, such as Kareem Abdul-Jabbar, Gail Goodrich, and Bill Walton, just to name a few. It was exciting to watch that dynasty: the momentum, the dominance, the results. But it didn't last forever. After John Wooden left, the UCLA basketball program was out of the spotlight for some time. The dynasty was over. Who would ever be able to experience that kind of success again? His was a hard act to follow.

The next generation that we're going to look at suffered a similar fate. It's been difficult being the group that followed the Baby Boomers, who were called the Weathervane Generation. Some have said that if you know what's going on in the Baby Boomers' lives, you know what's going on in the nation. Many social and buying trends in this country can be traced to the Baby Boom Generation. If you knew what the Baby Boomers were up to, you had your thumb on the pulse of American society.

Then enters Generation X. Born between 1965 and 1976, they don't have the size, power, or influence that the Baby Boomers have. They are not a precedent-setting generation, but don't sell them short. They're not going to roll over and play dead.

The Gen-Xers, like the Silent Builders, are sandwiched right between what could be considered two generational dynasties. In front of the Xers are the Baby Boomers, over 76 million strong. Behind them is the emerging Net Generation, numbering over 80 million. Like the Silents, the Xers will make their mark on our society. They're just going to have to work harder at it because, at about 44 million, there are far fewer of them to accomplish the task.

It's difficult to define this generation because they haven't taken their full place in adult society yet. This isn't because of a lack of desire on their part. They're not getting jobs at the level they feel they deserve, nor are they being offered the positions of responsibility they would like. (Basically, the Boomers have the good jobs and are not making room for the Xers.) Often they're given a bad rap by the older generations. They're the new kids on the block and need to prove themselves, but they're not getting the chance to do so. To older generations, their values seem to be negative, not just different. They don't do things the way Boomers or Builders did, and, therefore, they must be wrong. It's this type of thinking that leads to serious generational tension. The Xer Generation has even been given names like the Cry-Baby Generation.

Have I mentioned that the Gen-Xers are not just going to roll over and play dead? They're a group of tough individuals. They grew up in difficult financial times. They were being raised when the traditional family in America was deteriorating, but they held on, and they are ready to fight for their future.

George Barna, in his book *Baby Busters* (as he calls this generation), reports the following findings of surveys conducted by the Barna Research Group about the prevailing views of the Gen-Xers:

1. **Busters Are Disillusioned.** They are skeptical because of the deception and superficiality they have experienced. They

lack heroes, causes, vision, and an abiding confidence in the goodness of their future (unlike Boomers, who assumed they would have the good life).

2. **Busters Feel Abandoned.** Not only do the Busters feel they are being cheated out of the wealth that would traditionally have been theirs, but they are also losing out on the other resources and commitments that could have provided them a nurturing and worthwhile existence. They resent having been emotionally neglected by their parents and the older generations (latchkey kids, working mothers, workaholic parents).

3. **Busters Want a High Quality of Life.** They don't want to settle for what's left over. They want it all, and they want it now. The fact that they are unlikely to exceed the quality of life set by their parents has created resentment in many of them. Quality of life, for them, means a high "fun" quotient without sacrifice.

4. **Busters Are Independent.** They think and act according to their instincts. They behave as individuals. They may listen to counsel, but they make their own decisions and generally reject demands made on them without opportunity to debate.

5. **Busters Are Defensive.** Raised in an age of materialism and prosperity, they expected more than they are apparently going to receive. They are protective of what they possess and determined to achieve whatever they can. They have learned that people may mean well but generally cannot be trusted since it's a competitive world.

6. **Busters Are Comfortable with Change.** They grew up in the midst of chaos, and they know nothing else. They are used to the fast pace and lack of stability. They are not concerned about traditions or what honors the past or provides emotional security. They embrace change because it enables them to reject the Boomer mind-set and culture.

7. **Busters Are More Sensitive to People.** Although Busters

want good salaries, they are less career-driven and less impersonal about life than Boomers. They have a desire to build lasting relationships and to exhibit sensitivity to people. Although they have a hard time trusting, they still have a strong desire to work in cooperation with others who have common interests. They do not commit easily or quickly, but their commitments are more meaningful than those of the Boomers.

8. **Busters Are Pluralists.** They have no problem accepting competing points of view or allowing seemingly contradictory perspectives or actions to coexist. They will accept divergent approaches to religion, politics, relationships, and so on.

9. **Busters Are Flexible.** They have few absolutes or immovable standards in their lives. They are ready to handle rapid change, take advantage of unforeseen opportunities, or consider unique strategies. They are influenced by what works rather that what "ought" to be.

10. **Busters Are Pragmatic.** They seem to lack a sense of mission or a worldview; thus they cope on a situational basis. Denying the existence of absolute truths, they handle each situation on its own merit and potential, responding the best that they can given the available input.[1]

Different Strokes

There is clearly tension between the Boomers' values and views and those of Generation X. As we've pointed out in previous chapters, it's helpful to understand the circumstances and environment people grew up in when trying to understand their view of themselves and life. Let's consider the differences encountered by the Boomers and Gen-Xers as they were each growing up and see how they were affected by them.

BOOMERS grew up in an era when traditional family values were still cherished by adults.

GEN-XERS grew up in the shadow of their rebellious parents, being more likely to experience an unconventional lifestyle.

BOOMERS were idealistic, believing that people were basically good and that the world was worth saving and improving.

GEN-XERS are not confident in people and institutions. They are not sure it is possible to save the world, but are trying to do so in order to survive. For example, they grew up with recycling and consider it normal behavior.

BOOMERS believed that the future was waiting to be created. There were optimistic and willing to experiment without fear of failure.

GEN-XERS are world-class skeptics, cynical about mankind and pessimistic about the future.

BOOMERS felt they were a very special people and were entitled to the best the world had to offer.

GEN-XERS feel as if they have been forgotten if not intentionally limited. They would like to have the best, but realistically have lower expectations.

BOOMERS grew up accepting the possibility of change yet balanced it with a desire for stability.

GEN-XERS have grown up knowing only change. They desire to have influence over the changes around them.

BOOMERS matured in a period when information was highly valued but a difficult commodity to obtain.

GEN-XERS have grown up during the information explosion.

BOOMERS were rebellious, but they remained convinced of the value of education.

GEN-XERS view education as something that has to be endured.

BOOMERS have seen work as an end in itself. A significant portion of their identity comes from their status and performance on the job.

GEN-XERS view work as a means to an end. They are not as willing to work long hours to climb the corporate ladder.

BOOMERS have experienced unparalleled economic expansion.

GEN-XERS expect to experience economic parity or decline in comparison with their parents.

BOOMERS defined economic success as achieving greater wealth and prosperity than any prior generation had ever experienced.

GEN-XERS define economic success as achieving levels of wealth commensurate with that reached by their parents.

BOOMERS have remained an abundantly self-indulgent, bold, and aggressive lot.

GEN-XERS have always felt inferior. Although also selfish and unyielding on principles, their principles are different.

BOOMERS valued relationships but built them in new ways. They were the original networkers, a concept that fit well with their utilitarian view of life and people.

GEN-XERS have outright rejected the impersonal, short-term, fluid relational character of their parents.[2]

Some Builders and Boomers have serious concerns about what contributions Generation X will make as they get older and take a more productive role in our society. Certain Gen-X behaviors could lead to real difficulties in the future. Other behaviors displayed by this generation create optimism and provide hope that they will break new ground and bring worthwhile ideas to our society.

Areas of Concern

MTV first aired as Generation X was entering adolescence. This very different type of TV led to a very different way of looking at life, elevating feeling and sensation over thought. The subject matter of the continuous-play rock videos created concern in parents, as violence, sex, and bizarre behavior became commonplace. MTV epitomized (if not influenced) this group's need for fast-paced, exciting, and sensual entertainment.

The types of sports some of them enjoy are unique, as seen in the advent of the X Games and extreme sports. These are not just soccer, basketball, or baseball. They're not the traditional team sports that develop a sense of teamwork. Extreme sports are more active, more individualistic, and, in fact, involve more extreme danger. They appeal to Xers' love of diversity and fast-paced action and their desire to do things differently from previous generations. These include events such as aggressive in-line skating, bicycle stunt riding, big-air snowboarding, ice climbing, and sky surfing. Some also enjoy street luge—hurtling down mountain roads on sleds in excess of 70 miles per hour a half-inch above the ground with no brakes. Others like barefoot jumping—waterskiing barefoot around obstacles, doing tricks, and then skiing up a ramp to try and land the longest jump.

When it comes to participating in society, we see that this generation has the lowest voting percentage of any of the adult generations. The Gen-Xers are more educated than any generation previous to them, but they seem to come out of college with fewer tangible skills. Certainly a share of the blame has to go to the public school system, which seems to be less proficient at accomplishing the educational goals that generations in the past have reached.

Suicide among Gen-Xers is also very alarming. "America has never experienced a suicide rate as high among any previous generation. More than 5,000 Busters (or Gen-Xers) commit suicide each year. The suicide rate has more than doubled since Boomers were in their teens and early 20s."[3] Among this group, suicide is viewed as one of many viable choices available to a healthy, functional young person. Many Xers see it as a rational choice in which the alternatives are less attractive. Today, the decision to reject suicide is a conscious statement of priorities and values. In essence, this is the first generation who are intentionally making a choice between life (a decision that was initially made for them) and death (a decision that they may now control).[4]

Life is difficult. There are plenty of problems facing these Gen-Xers, and suicide, apparently, is an option they have seen as a way out. Their choice to take their own lives when they don't seem to have the ability or the support systems to deal with life issues is a very real problem. We'll also see this as a continuing trend with the Net Generation.

Another difficulty for Gen-Xers is how they are viewed in the workplace. The Gen-Xers don't find their primary identity in the office (which can certainly be a good thing). Therefore, they are less committed to their employers and less willing to spend long hours at work than previous generations were. Rather than being motivated by work, they consider it to be more of a necessary evil. The concept of starting at the bottom and working your way up seems to be foreign to this generation. They are not driven to excel in their career. They are likely to change careers more often than other generations. They find the concept of working an eight-hour day every day of the workweek on a year-round basis very unappealing. They have ambitions, but these are personal (e.g., they're committed to community and family), not corporate. Loyalty to the company is a foreign concept. Being nonconformists, they are not as interested in teamwork and, at times, don't respond well to authority, preferring to make their own decisions.

Because of all this, Builder and Boomer employers are not enthusiastic about hiring Gen-Xers. "Their commitments are short-term. Their skills are limited. Attitudinally, they are hard to comprehend. They are often seen as flakes and ingrates. They are difficult to manage because they operate with a different set of core values and perspectives."[5]

These differences in values and perspectives often make Gen-Xers unpredictable and confusing to Builders and Boomers who work with them. When I worked at a conference center, one perk I enjoyed was the opportunity to travel, all expenses paid, to interview college students for our summer staff. I loved the flying, staying in hotels, meeting people, connecting with old friends at the colleges where we interviewed—the whole thing. Jack, a member of Generation X, was working for me and had been married for only a few years and had a young child. Thinking I was offering him a welcome opportunity, I asked him to accompany me on a 10-day recruiting trip. He turned me down! His response stunned me for two reasons. First, I was surprised that he refused my offer. Second, I was amazed by his reason. He didn't want to go because it would put too much stress on his wife and child. As his supervisor, I could have interpreted his unwillingness to go as lack of motivation, lack of cooperation, or being unwilling to do what it takes to get the job done for the sake of the company. In Jack's mind, he was making a choice to put his family's needs first, acting out the priority of relationships over work, which is part of his value system.

These differences in perceptions, attitudes, and motivations can lead to great tensions if the reasons for these differences are not understood and allowed for. As the Gen-Xers enter the workforce, they find it difficult to get the types of jobs they would like, even if they have the education and the training, because of these points of tension and misunderstanding (plus the fact that there are still so many Boomers in the workforce).

This difficult job situation is just one more in a series of circumstances that have faced Gen-Xers during their lives. Often their family situations as they were growing up were less than ideal and they were identified as the Latchkey Generation. With so many of their mothers working, they became the first generation to be left on their own for a good part of childhood. They were raised before the current trend toward more intentional, child-centered parenting. (In fact, now that some of these older Xers are parents themselves, they are more focused on the needs of their families than their jobs, because many felt like they were a low priority to their parents.) The economy was the lowest it had been in several decades as they were growing up, which made things difficult financially. As they graduated from college, ready to enter the workforce, they found that there were very few good jobs available, and many of them had to settle for jobs that didn't require college degrees. They found themselves in debt with college loans and very low-paying jobs.

The Other Side of the Coin

Most of the descriptions of the Gen-Xers we have seen so far appear to be negative, condemning, and rather pessimistic. But that's not the only side to Generation X. There are positive characteristics indicating that this generation, when given the chance, will rise to the occasion when it is their turn to become leaders in our society.

One of the most significant characteristics that describes or identifies the Gen-Xers is their commitment to diversity. They grew up in a time when various minority groups were gaining attention and demanding rights. They have been sensitized to the variety of people in our society and taught to recognize them as individuals worthy of respect and an increasing level of tolerance. They were not raised to value conformity, but diversity.

"Diversity is a key fact of life for Xers, the core of the perspective they bring . . . in all its forms—cultural, political, sexual, racial, social—is a hallmark of this generation, a diversity accessible to everyone, that transcends even national borders.

This generation shares in a greatly expanded global network of connections and influences."[6]

The Xers' ability to display that kind of acceptance in a society as diverse as ours is a valuable quality, both socially and in organizational leadership. Gen-Xers began to express their acceptance of diversity and quest for tolerance while they were still on college campuses as they embraced the politically correct movement they encountered there.

"The PC movement has been described by some as the '90s equivalent of radical ideology in the '60s; . . . and by others as the inevitable quest of thinking people to become loving and sensitive to others regardless of heritage, standing, or other false definitions of being."[7]

What appeals to the Gen-Xers about the PC movement is the quest for equality, opportunity, individualism, and justice for those who come from diverse backgrounds. Developing a society where people are not identified by slurs, nicknames, or labels that feature their differences is an admirable goal. But there has been some backlash from members of other generations when it comes to the politically correct movement. Some feel that those in the PC movement are tolerant of everyone except those who don't agree with its tenets, or that in their goal of eliminating negative labels, they are eliminating moral standards, too. Like anything, when taken to extremes, it may do more harm than good. *The Official Politically Correct Dictionary and Handbook*, a collection of real and satirical definitions from the PC movement, shows how some of these names or identifiers can go a bit overboard. For example:

- Instead of referring to someone as *dead*, the suggested phrase would be "terminally inconvenienced."
- Instead of referring to a person as *drunk*, it prefers you refer to them as "sobriety deprived."
- Instead of making reference to a person *failing*, it would be more acceptable to say that they "achieved a deficiency."

- Instead of using the word *pregnant,* a woman could be described as "parasitically oppressed."
- Instead of *prisoner,* a person who is incarcerated should be referred to as a "client of the correctional system."[8]

In spite of the abuses, there have been some helpful results of the PC movement. Development of terms such as "people of color," "African-American," "Native American," and "birth parents" have helped us refer to people in less offensive ways. Whether you agree with the PC movement or not, being more accepting of people who are different from us is a quality that other generations would do well to learn from the Gen-Xers.

Another very significant attribute of the Gen-Xers is their commitment to people and personal relationships. They grew up in a time when strong significant relationships were few and far between. Now, as adults, they see the importance of those relationships and will sacrifice many things to nurture them. They may not show much loyalty to the company they work for, but they tend to be very loyal to individual coworkers, friends, and family, through thick and thin.

One very interesting and enlightening piece of information about Gen-Xers and their relationships is their definition of *family.* Being the generation that has most been affected by divorce and workaholic parents, their concept of family is unique and nontraditional. Most Gen-Xers believe that *family* can include any of several different types of relationships. About one out of every four Gen-Xers describes family in each of the following ways:

- People with whom you have close relationships or deep personal/emotional bonds (28 percent)
- Those individuals with whom you have a mutual personal commitment or love relationship (25 percent)
- Your good friends, those with whom you are compatible, those with whom there is mutual caring (24 percent)

- The people who are there for you to provide help or emotional support, as needed (23 percent)
- People who are related by marriage (21 percent)
- Individuals to whom you are closely related, by marriage or blood (19 percent)[9]

Their concept of family is not so much related to traditional or legal concepts as it is to the level of emotional commitment and support. If their real parents, grandparents, and siblings aren't available for them, they will create a family of relationships with those around them who want to be involved in their lives.

This generation may be criticized for not being as aggressive and focused at work, but they don't get criticized for their intense focus on personal relationships at work. This is something that the generations before them could learn from to be more effective.

Another positive attribute of the Gen-Xers is their familiarity with computers. They grew up with computers as toys. In the early years they were more into Game Boy and Pac-Man than the computer itself. But as access to computers grew, their computer savvy grew. Whereas the Boomers had to learn computers once they were in the workforce as adults, the Gen-Xers became familiar with them while they were growing up. It's a common scenario for a Boomer in leadership who is having problems with a computer program to have to go to a Gen-Xer to get that problem solved. From something as simple as knowing how to use a word processing program to the challenge of retrieving information once the whole system has crashed, Gen-Xers are playing an important role in the increasingly computerized workplace. They're also among the leading Internet entrepreneurs.

Generation X is having a positive impact on the business world in another, more indirect way. Many Builder- or Boomer-led companies have had to train and retrain the incoming Gen-Xers. As they are setting up these training systems, many organizations are finding it quite beneficial to include the older, experienced workers, too. Having effective training for persons of all ages is becoming a significant movement in the workforce now. This training process can be one of the first steps toward one generation identifying how to relate to an emerging generation. This will become even more helpful as we see the Net Generation coming into the workforce in the very early stages of their careers.

Who Are They?

Some of the Gen-Xers we might recognize include Brooke Shields, Mike Tyson, Lisa Bonet, Mary Lou Retton, Sandra Bullock, Shania Twain, Adam Sandler, Julia Roberts, Kirk Cameron, Monica Lewinsky, and Gary Coleman. Others include Andre Agassi, Tracey Gold, Steffi Graf, Christian Slater, Nancy Kerrigan, Sammy Sosa, Drew Barrymore, Tiger Woods, Fred Savage, Alicia Silverstone, Ken Griffey, Jr., Will Smith, and Denzel Washington.

Chapter 18

The Net Generation

The Net Generation is still pretty young. In fact, they are so young that (assuming they were born in 1980):

- They have no meaningful recollection of the Reagan era and do not know he was ever shot.
- They were 11 when the Soviet Union broke apart and do not remember the Cold War.
- They have never feared a nuclear war.
- They have only known one Germany.
- They are too young to remember the space shuttle blowing up, and Tianammen Square means nothing to them.
- Their lifetime has always included AIDS.
- Soda bottle caps have not only always been screw-off, but have always been plastic.
- They have no idea what a pull-top can looks like.
- Atari predates them, as do vinyl record albums.
- *Star Wars* looks very fake and the special effects are pathetic.
- They may have heard of an eight-track tape, but they probably have never actually seen or heard one.
- The compact disc (CD) was introduced when they were one year old.
- They have always had an answering machine.
- There have always been VCRs, but they have no idea what beta is.

- They cannot fathom life without a remote control (neither can I).
- They were born the year the Walkman was introduced by Sony.
- *The Tonight Show* has always been with Jay Leno.
- Popcorn has always been cooked in a microwave.
- They have never seen Larry Bird play basketball, and Kareem Abdul-Jabbar is a football player.
- The Vietnam War is as ancient history to them as World War I, World War II, or even the Civil War.
- They have no idea that Americans were ever held hostage in Iran.
- Most have never seen or used a rotary dial phone.[1]

For the purpose of our study, we'll use Don Tapscott's definition of the Net Generation as those born from 1977 to 1997. Using these years, the Net Generation adds up to over 81 million young people, which is approximately 30 percent of our current population. In case you haven't picked up on this yet, this group is larger than the Baby Boom. This is not just a few kids coming along with some new trends. These N-Geners are bringing a force into our American culture that needs to be reckoned with.

Negative Image

As this generation emerges, little information on them is currently available. What most adults hear about them appears to be somewhat negative. "If you listen to the traditional media, you hear a sad tale. Today's youth are described in ways that make the 'me' generation look like a generation of philanthropists and social activists. They are said to be self-centered and obsessed with short-term gratification."[2]

There are things about this generation that concern the older generations who are observing them: the loud music (not that this is new with this generation), the tattoos, the body piercing, their styles. At first glance they seem to be lack-ing leadership skills. They seem to lack initiative and the moti-vation and commitment to follow through. And then there's the issue of suicide that seems to be running rampant with this generation.

As we saw in Generation X, suicide is considered a rea-sonable alternative to a difficult living situation for youth today. However, because of their young age and the lack of availability of the most recent statistics, it's hard to determine a real trend for this group by itself. Many of the current fig-ures include members of Generation X. It was interesting to note a slight decrease in the suicide rate of 15- to 24-year-olds in 1995 and 1996 as more N-Geners entered that age group (the oldest N-Geners were about 19 in 1996). In a survey conducted by the Centers for Disease Control, a comparison of the results from 1991 to 1997 showed a consistent decrease in the percentage of high school students who seriously con-sidered suicide during the 12 months prior to the survey (from 29.0 in 1991 to 20.5 percent in 1997).[3] Hopefully we'll see this as an increasing trend since, as a whole, N-Geners tend to be more optimistic than Gen-Xers.

In spite of this generation's positive outlook, it's easy to see how adults would develop a negative image of these Net Gen-eration kids. And teenagers today are quite aware that adults don't have a very high opinion of them. In a 1997 study by the Barna Research Group, when teens were asked how adults would describe them, they included responses such as lazy (84 percent), rude (74 percent), sloppy (70 percent), dishonest (65 percent), and violent (57 percent).[4] This isn't helping their relationships with their parents or other adults in their lives. According to the same report, "Without a sense of acceptance and respect, young people are not prone to submitting them-selves to the leadership of people or organizations that have failed to embrace them."[5]

This generation, however, doesn't seem to get its self-image from what others say about them. In spite of what they believe adults think, in the same survey they described themselves as happy (92 percent), responsible (91 percent), self-reliant (86 percent), optimistic about the future (82 percent), trusting of other people (80 percent), very intelligent (79 percent), and physically attractive (74 percent).[6]

The Preferred Lifestyle

Teenagers would like to have more structure provided,
>   BUT without having their independence or their freedom to experiment impeded.

Teenagers want to learn from the experiences and wisdom of their parents,
>   BUT they're not willing to allow their elders the latitude to impart those lessons in a manner that fits parents' needs and styles.

Teenagers struggle with the effects of stress,
>   BUT they continue to book busy schedules.

Teenagers appreciate more time in intimate experiences with their families,
>   BUT they will neither push nor create those opportunities.

Teenagers are frightened by the potential consequences of many risky behaviors,
>   BUT they flirt with those dangers regularly.[7]

It seems like these kids are open to input and help from their parents, but on their own terms. It will take a creative, sensitive approach to make it happen effectively, but the possibilities look good.

Because of the overwhelming size of this generation and their incredible potential, both in the marketplace and the workforce, a lot of consumer-based companies are very interested in knowing how this Net Generation thinks and how they can best use that knowledge for their own good. For example, the Coca-Cola company recently did a survey of

27,000 12- to 19-year-olds from around the world and observed nine general trends that they believe are true of what they call "Generation Y."

1. **Self-reliance**—They believe that becoming successful is up to them, and they are not depending on others for help. Finding a good job is a priority.
2. **Love of family**—In light of all of the troubles in the world in which they live, there seems to be a surprising trend toward relying more on their family as a sanctuary against the difficulties of life.
3. **Global icons**—Brand identification in the consumer market seems to be at an all-time high. It's important to wear the right jeans, wear the right athletic shoes, and drink the right kind of beverage. (I'm assuming the authors of the study would like that to be Coca-Cola.)
4. **Consumerism**—These kids know how to shop. They are not going to be fooled into buying products that don't meet their needs. They are skeptical of slick marketing promotions.
5. **Americentric**—The U.S. culture has always been of interest to kids around the world, but today's international youth seems to be more interested than ever.
6. **Itchy feet**—This generation promises to be one of the most mobile ever. They don't intend to stay at home. They have aspirations to travel, not only around this country, but also around the world. They already travel on the Internet to many places, and now they want to go there in person.
7. **Mediavores**—This generation is addicted to media. It is not uncommon for them to be doing their homework, listening to a CD, watching television, and communicating on-line at the same time. They are giving new definition to *multitasking.*
8. **Unabashed fun seekers**—After all, this generation is still mostly made up of kids. Kids want to have fun, and this generation is no different. They will not be bored, because there are so many options open to them.

9. Hope—This is a significant change from the previous generation. These kids are growing up with hope. They are not pessimistic or cynical. Rather, they are optimistic and expect to be happy adults (adapted from *YoungLife Magazine,* spring 1998).[8]

USA Weekend received 272,400 responses to their 11th Annual Teens and Self-Image Survey in the fall of 1997. The results showed how students, grades 6 to 12, rated themselves on a variety of issues.

When asked, "In general, how do you feel about yourself?" 93 percent responded either "really good" (49 percent) or "kind of good" (44 percent). Only 6 percent responded "not very good," and 1 percent, "bad."

There seems to be a significant shift in how this generation responds to peer pressure. When asked, "How pressured do you feel to do the following?" these figures show how many indicated "Not at all" for the listed activities: drink alcohol—77 percent; smoke—77 percent; take illegal drugs—84 percent; have sex—72 percent. This is far different from some of the images of adolescent life that we see portrayed in the media today.[9]

A poll of the first college graduating class of the new millennium (class of 2001), taken when they were freshmen in 1997 by Northwestern Mutual Life Insurance Company, further describes how this generation see themselves.

	Strongly Agreed	Somewhat Agreed
To me, learning is a lifelong priority.	84%	14%
I am sure that someday I will get to where I want to be in life.	78%	20%
Having close family relationships is a key to happiness.	77%	20%

	Strongly Agreed	Somewhat Agreed
In dating, the important thing is how two people get along, not what race or religion they may be.	77%	18%
Staying physically fit is important to overall well-being.	68%	29%
I have established specific goals for the next five years.	58%	30%
I am satisfied with my physical appearance.	44%	47%
Helping others is more important than helping oneself.	43%	47%
Marriage is a cornerstone of societal values.	37%	51%[10]

Of course, MTV is also very interested in knowing what these kids are all about. Some of the shifts that they are seeing in this new generation (as opposed to Generation X) are that the Net Generation tends to look up to their parents, are very optimistic about their future, and want to work hard to get good jobs. They think saving money is cool and are beginning to dress more like other generations.[11]

How Parents Are Raising Them

Now that we have a better view of how this generation sees themselves, it's important to see how their parents are raising them, which does have a significant influence on them becoming this unique generation. There is a perception today that parents are far too busy with dual-income families, single-parent homes, and all of the other trappings of adult life, causing them not to be as involved with their kids as parents were in the past. This isn't necessarily the case, and research would indicate otherwise.

"The fact is, parents of the 1990s are involved with their children. Study after study proves this point. Mothers today are more likely to attend their children's school events than their own mothers were, according to a survey by the Pew Research Center. Parents today spend just as much time with their children as the parents of the 1960s, according to time-use researcher John P. Robinson of the University of Maryland. And because parents now have fewer children, each child is getting more parental attention."[12]

Not only are the parents more involved, other research indicates that today the relationship between kids and their parents is improving. Gen-Xers' relationships with their parents seem to be characterized by friction, animosity, and even a tendency to mistrust each other. But the Net Generation truly seems to have much more positive relationships with their parents. In a *USA Today* survey involving over a quarter of a million kids, 32 percent responded that they had a conversation with their parents every day that lasted over 15 minutes. An additional 34 percent responded that they did so once a week. Those of us who are parents know that finding time to sit down with our children and have significant conversations is difficult. But the fact that at least 66 percent of the children are having this kind of quality conversation at least every week shows promise for this generation.

The survey goes on to ask, "How much influence does each of the following have in your life?" Parents were indicated as influencing them "a lot" by 70 percent of the teens and "some" by 26 percent. The next strongest influence was religion at 34 percent. When asked, "When was the last time an adult, such as a parent or teacher, said something encouraging or supportive to you?" 37 percent responded "today," and an additional 38 percent responded "in the past week."[13]

In addition to having positive relationships with their parents, this generation thinks that their parents are cool. This doesn't mean that the N-Geners totally accept the lifestyle and all the trappings that come with their parents' generations, but they do seem to genuinely respect and admire their parents. In our own survey of high school students, 26 percent considered one or both of their parents someone they admired or would like to be like. After adding in other relatives mentioned (siblings, grandparents, aunts, uncles, and cousins), the result was 36 percent of the teens who responded to this question (722 teens) listed a family member as a person they admired and wanted to be like.[14] There was no other category even close to this percentage, a result confirmed by other published studies.

A significant reason for this trend comes from the path that the Baby Boomers have taken through their life span. Initially they rebelled against their parents, taking a stand against society. Then as age and maturity came to the Baby Boomers (a little later than previous generations), they settled into a more traditional parenting style. Being aware of all the trappings of their youth, Baby Boomers didn't want to pass these values on to their children. Also, an increased awareness of the damage that has been done to children in the past in various forms of abuse and neglect has made these parents more protective and controlling in their children's lives.

In an article called "Reaching Millennial Kids," Christine Yount comments on this recent focus on children:

> The 1990s became what Mario Cuomo termed the "Decade of the Child." Children's issues—or "family values"—topped the agendas of the last three presidential elections. In June of 1996, hundreds of thousands of people went to Washington, D.C., to lobby for children at the Stand for Children Rally."

A protective wave of adult concern bathes this generation of children. William Strauss and Neil Howe, authors of *The Fourth Turning* and *Generations*, write that although Gen-Xers were viewed as castoffs, N-Geners "have become symbols of an Unraveling-era need to stop the social hemorrhaging before it could damage another new generation."

Boomers are working hard to shield N-Geners from the diet of media sex, violence, and profanity that the generation before them was weaned on.[15]

Because of this, we've seen a real turnaround in how Baby Boomers (and Gen-Xers) relate to their kids and the increased involvement they want to have as their children are growing up. The result has been closer relationships between parents and their N-Gen children.

Comparing the Baby Boom with the Net Generation

As we compare the Baby Boom with the Net Generation, two similarities stand out. First is the sheer size of both generations. The Net Generation, including two more years of births than the Baby Boom Generation, is larger by a few million people. The size of a generation has a great impact on how it will function in society and the influence and control it will have on job and consumer markets. So, in impact by size, the N-Geners are equal to the Baby Boomers. It will be interesting to watch the shift of power from the Baby Boom Generation, which has been the focus of attention all of their lives, to the Net Generation.

The second similarity between these two generations is their education. As the Baby Boomers were growing up, they were much more educated than their parents, many of whom were hindered from going to college because of things like a lack of opportunity, the Depression, and WW II. The N-Geners, it appears, will be as educated, if not more so, than the Baby Boomers. The difference between the Baby Boomers' and their parents' education resulted in what some have identified as a generation gap, as Boomers felt themselves to have a superior perspective on life. There doesn't seem to be that kind of generation gap between the Baby Boomers and the N-Geners. As a matter of fact, as we'll see later on, there appears to be just the opposite effect—what some are calling a "generation lap."

Even though the education level is similar, the Net Generation seems to be going to school for very different reasons. In a study comparing the trends in higher education over the past 30 years, some very interesting things were identified. In the late '60s, over 80 percent of the freshmen indicated that their most important goal was to "develop a meaningful philosophy of life." In comparison, being "very well off financially" rated fifth or sixth on their list, with less than 45 percent of the freshmen endorsing it as a very important goal in life. Now, in the late '90s, those two values have basically flip-flopped. Being "very well off financially" is at the top of the list, with over 74 percent choosing it as a very important goal. "Developing a meaningful philosophy of life" is now in sixth place with just over 42 percent choosing it. The same study reports that the percentage of students who say they are attending college "to be able to make more money" has risen from 49.9 percent in 1971 to 74.7 percent in 1991, and has continued at a similar rate through 1996.[16]

As the Boomers went to college, they had high philosophical goals of what they wanted to obtain, and finances were not a big part of that. But as we see the N-Geners coming into college during a time of less financial certainty, they obviously see economic benefit as their major reason for being there. Perhaps this is a reflection of how Baby Boomers really are today, and they're encouraging their children to pursue their financial futures. We've seen a drastic shift in Boomers, from their philosophical, cause-oriented goals when they were in college, to their much more materialistic goals today. The N-Geners may just be taking their parents' advice.

The differences between these two generations are more significant than the similarities. As we reflect back on the Baby

Boomers, they tend to be a somewhat hedonistic generation, living for themselves. With the N-Geners, we see more of a balance. They're certainly not shy about taking care of themselves or attempting to meet their own needs, but they have mixed this with a concern for others, realizing that in such an at-risk society, their actions do have an effect on other people. They like to be involved in helping others. This is illustrated by the Nickelodeon TV network's annual Big Helpathon, which encourages kids to get involved in their communities. In 1994, over 400,000 children volunteered for the event. In 1997, participation grew to eight million.[17]

There seems to be more sensitivity to others around them, with the acknowledgment that there are diverse ways of accomplishing what one wants in life, and others should be allowed the freedom to accomplish those things in their own ways.

Susan Mitchell believes, "This new generation differs from the baby boom in significant ways. While the boomer generation was a relatively uniform group, the children of the next boom [Net-Geners] differ radically from each other in race, living arrangements, and socioeconomic class. . . . Members of the next baby boom may be more competent, confident, and wary than the original baby boom. If you could sum them up in one word, the word would be diverse."[18]

Generation Lap

A businessman paces back and forth behind the computer, instructing his associate at the keyboard about specifics he wants on a flight that is being booked on-line. All you see is the computer screen and all of the options for the flight. The businessman requests an aisle seat. Then he asks the computer operator to see if a special meal can be ordered. He also wants to find out what movie will be shown. He nervously continues to pace, not sure if he can get everything he wants. He orders the computer operator to check again what the different options are. He's becoming impatient. He knows what he wants. He just doesn't know how to get it from the computer listing. Finally everything is secured to the businessman's liking, and, as the camera angle changes, you see that it's the businessman's 10-year-old son who is sitting at the computer. "Dad, can I go play now?" the son asks, and you laugh, realizing how many times you have had to ask your own kids to help you accomplish something on your computer.

This TV commercial for one of the major airlines helps to make our point. This is a good example of what the generation lap is all about. Our children are lapping us in their knowledge of computers and the digital revolution. They navigate on the Internet almost by instinct, while we struggle to understand how it all works and how to get what we want.

In our society, parents have always been the authority. They have had the answers. They have taught their children and given them the answers when the kids weren't sure what the next step was. For the first time in our society we are seeing children as the authorities in some areas. They often know more about computers than their parents do. Don Tapscott, in his book, *Growing Up Digital*, indicates that this is one of the real defining characteristics of the Net Generation.

"If parents think that their kids are catching on to the new technologies much faster than adults, they're right. It's easier for kids. Because N-Gen children are born with technology, they assimilate it. Adults must accommodate—a different and much more difficult learning process. With assimilation, kids view technology as just another part of their environment, and they soak it up along with everything else. For many kids, using the new technology is as natural as breathing."[19]

This Net Generation is lapping Boomers in their ability to use computers and their level of comfort with them. This is an area that they obviously know more about than many of us. If you're the type of person who's uncomfortable learning from those younger than you, and you dislike depending on them to get things that you need, work and family life may prove to be difficult for you in the future.

A while back I (Rick) spent a weekend with my brother, whom I don't get to see very often. We spent the whole evening catching up on each other's lives, finding out what we each had been up to since we'd last been together. As I was on my way to bed, I noticed my nephew, David, at the computer.

"What have you been doing all evening?" I asked. "Playing a computer game?"

"Not exactly," he said. He explained that he was playing a game, but he was playing an interactive game on-line with three other people. His partner was from New Zealand and they were playing a person from Vietnam and another person from Canada.

"Wow! I didn't know that kind of stuff was possible," I exclaimed.

"It probably isn't possible for you, but it is for me," he replied bluntly but accurately. While I've become fairly comfortable using the Internet, his knowledge and skills are at a level far beyond mine.

There's a whole new technological world out there that many of us don't know much about. That new world is causing our geographical world to shrink. This is a global village that we are living in. We have access to people all around the world anytime we want. This very much changes the way this Net Generation sees things—the way they see other countries and people, the way they see life, and it certainly affects their values. We have a whole new breed of people growing up in our country. Kids who have access to computers for learning, communication or entertainment are going to work quite differently than those of us who grew up with TV as our primary source of media entertainment.

There may be another unexpected result of computer use affecting this generation. Some educational researchers have suggested that the high use of computers from an early age is actually changing the way these young people think. It's having an effect on how they collect, organize, and analyze information.

Some have called this a shift from traditional "linear" style of thinking (moving from point A to point B to point C in succession to reach an organized conclusion) to a more technology-driven "parallel" or "mosaic" mode of thought (moving randomly among a series of points before integrating them into a coherent pattern and drawing a conclusion). This new form of thinking is in line with how computers organize data and how some computer games and software packages lead kids to think. This new style may be beneficial to the emerging generation. Mosaic learning permits faster processing and a greater absorption of information than does a linear pattern.[20]

That's a bit technical and maybe even a little frightening to think about, but it's not all bad. This is saying that kids are learning a new process of thinking, random thinking, which enables them to process things differently and more quickly, and will, perhaps, help them process information in a better way. This could be a factor in the generation lap. They are lapping the older generations in how they think and process information. If understood by educators, this could enhance their educational process. It may also contribute to the skills that they bring into the workforce—and to more misunderstanding and tension between generations.

The Net Generation in the Workforce

As this young generation enters the workforce, it's not going to be business as usual. This group has a strong self-image. They feel confident in the abilities they bring and, in terms of computer skills, often feel better equipped than those older than they are. So, if your expectations are that this generation will come into the workforce and fall into the bureaucratic and autocratic system, you will be in for a rude awakening. When the Baby Boomers entered the workforce, a major adjustment had to take place. There was resistance, but, by their sheer numbers, they were able to impose their self-serving work ethic on the workforce. As we see the Net Generation starting to work, they also have the advantage of large numbers, and they have strong ideas about how they want to work.

In *Growing Up Digital*, Tapscott describes the culture of N-Geners and how it will impact the workforce. Established businesses will need to adjust somewhat if they want the benefit of the skills these N-Geners will be bringing with them, but he believes these changes will benefit the companies who are insightful and flexible enough to make them. Those who don't make room for them in their companies may likely find themselves in direct competition with them, as they create their own style of organization.

One of the N-Gen qualities Tapscott mentions is their inclusiveness, which means they prefer networking, looking for new individuals and new ideas to help accomplish the task. They are the generation that is the most oblivious to gender, race, or other social differences. They judge people according to the contributions they make rather than the positions they hold. They value peer-oriented relationships rather than hierarchies. Meaningful collaboration with others to get the job accomplished is more important to them than competing to climb the organizational ladder. They thrive on innovation. You can expect them to ask, "Why not?" when leadership is hesitant to try their new ideas. They like to investigate everything and question the assumptions that have created the corporate culture. They prefer to be part of a company that is seen as ethical and acting in the community interest. They also believe in justice, in the sense that they should share in the wealth that they help create.

In reality we don't totally know what the N-Geners will look like on the job. We can only make predictions at this time, because they are just beginning to enter the workforce. But in *American Generations*, an extensive organization and analysis of research facts that give insight into the generations in our society, the author states, "From the responses to the 'Class of 2001' survey, [N-Geners] appear to be well equipped to handle the challenging world they will inherit."[21]

Characteristics That Identify the Net Generation

As we look at the characteristics that identify this generation, we do see that they have drawn some character qualities from the Builders. Their desire to work together for the benefit of others, take on big tasks, and face a future that is somewhat in question is similar to the values of their grandparents. They also share some characteristics with the Baby Boomers, particularly their spirit of adventure and their desire to have fun in whatever they do. There are even some Gen-X characteristics evident in this group: their desire for current media and love of technology.

But some characteristics seem to be uniquely theirs. The first and foremost would be tolerance. They don't seem to get uptight about or feel threatened by some of the issues that previous generations struggled with. Take divorce, for example. If their parents break up, they don't feel they have to take one side or the other. They feel they can be on both sides. When you ask them about home, they may ask, "My mom's home, my dad's home, or my grandparents' home?" They seem to be able to accept the unusual configuration of people that make up the blended or fractured families so common today. They have the ability to live with all sorts of contradictions in their life, but being tolerant, they don't feel they have to solve all of the contradictions. They are very accepting of people who differ from them, and most actually prefer diversity. They tend to have a "live and let live" attitude toward those who choose alternative lifestyles.

While a certain level of tolerance is necessary in a diverse society such as ours, the downside of extreme tolerance is that if you don't stand for something, you may fall for anything. One real question for N-Geners is, do they have any beliefs that are strong enough to stand up for at any cost? This is something that will unfold as they get older and take their position in society.

Another identifying characteristic of the Net Generation is their fear. Most young generations do have fears as they leave adolescence to enter into adulthood because they don't know what the future holds. But it seems that this generation has more to fear than those who came before them. They are fearful about what the future will bring. Will they be able to get good jobs? They have great concerns about AIDS and whether they or a friend will contract the disease. They are concerned about the suicide rate, which has quadrupled in the last four decades. They fear being alienated, not having friends or family to turn to when they need them. And they certainly have concern for what their own family life will look like in the future. Will they find someone to marry? Will they have a family? Will they end up divorced? Will they be able to afford the things they have now?

Christine Yount expresses a theory about these kids' fears, and acknowledges a paradox:

> Boomers are working hard to shield Millennial children from the diet of media sex, violence, and profanity that the generation before them was weaned on. The negative side of parental concern is that children's fears are heightened.
>
> However, the awesome benefit of such protective concern, according to Strauss and Howe, is that a valued, protected generation grows up believing in its ability to make a difference. This is an idealistic, hopeful generation.[22]

Here again we see a paradox. Although this group has much to fear (and people constantly warning and reminding them of it), they also seem to feel more support from adults in their lives and gain confidence from that.

All these factors contribute to a final distinguishing characteristic of the Net Generation, and that is they are a group of people who have grown up with stress. This is one of the first generations who, as children, had to carry around their own Day-Timers to keep track of all their activities. Their busy schedules, plus the issues they are forced to face in this world, take a toll on them.

What They Value

As we have examined this new group, we have seen that this generation has grown up in a unique time and has developed unique values. Now that we are more aware of the issues that have helped to shape their values, we can, hopefully, better understand them and better relate to them. Knowing all that, it's helpful to realize that they won't operate in society the way past generations have. In his book *Generation Next,* Barna lists 15 rules that this generation will play by.

New Rules

New Rule #1: Personal relationships count. Institutions don't.
New Rule #2: The process is more important than the product.
New Rule #3: Aggressively pursue diversity among people.
New Rule #4: Enjoying people and life opportunities is more important than productivity, profitability, or achievement.
New Rule #5: Change is good.
New Rule #6: The development of character is more crucial than achievement.
New Rule #7: You can't always count on your family to be there for you, but it is your best hope for emotional support.
New Rule #8: Each individual must assume responsibility for his or her own world.
New Rule #9: Whenever necessary, gain control—and use it wisely.
New Rule #10: Don't waste time searching for absolutes. There are none.
New Rule #11: One person can make a difference in the world—but not much.
New Rule #12: Life is hard and then we die; but because it's

the only life we've got, we may as well endure it, enhance it, and enjoy it as best we can.

New Rule #13: Spiritual truth may take many forms.

New Rule #14: Express your rage.

New Rule #15: Technology is our natural ally.

(George Barna, *Generation Next*)

These rules, as well as other statistics we have quoted, are the results of various studies with various techniques. Some things seem to be contradictory; others are a paradox. Some results may be influenced by the optimism and enthusiasm of youth who have not yet experienced the reality of life on their own.

Although this Net Generation is still pretty young, there are some whose names you will recognize: Shannon Miller, Liv Tyler, Kerri Srug, A. J. McLean, Andrew Keegan, Brandy, Keshia Knight Pulliam, Claire Danes, Rider Strong, Chelsea Clinton, Venus Williams, Michelle Kwan, Macauley Culkin, Ben Savage, Elijah Wood, Jonathan Taylor Thomas, LeAnn Rimes, Mary-Kate and Ashley Olsen, and the McCaughey septuplets.

We've given you a lot of information in the previous chapters, and, hopefully, some insight into the value development of the four generations. These generational portraits are generalizations that are attempting to give a picture of who this new group of people are. And like all generalizations, not every quality applies to every person in the generation. Kids that are raised in a strong religious environment are more likely to believe in absolute truths than those who are not. Those raised in financial comfort are more likely to have optimistic views of the future than those raised in poverty are. Those who grew up in a secure, stable family situation are more likely to believe that they can count on their family than those who have experienced a divorce. But these are trends that we can take into consideration as we try to understand other generations.

/ Chapter 19 /

The Clash of Values

Thanksgiving dinner was over. It was an amazing day in many ways. For the first time in years, almost all the family had managed to get together (except, of course, for the ones who had been eliminated because of divorce and a couple of grandkids who ended up spending the holiday with the ex-spouse's families). Everyone was on his or her best behavior, and a lot of communication occurred as they tried to catch up on the details of each other's lives. Now they were parting—some to drive home, others to various guest rooms or sofa beds where they would sleep during the rest of the holiday weekend before their flights home on Sunday. Their thoughts were full of the day's conversations, some of which were amusing and some of which caused great concern.

As Grandma and Grandpa retired to their bedroom, they were exhausted as much by the emotions of the day as they were the physical exertion of hosting the event. They didn't say anything, because they didn't want to spoil the day, but they were concerned about how much time their Boomer children were spending on their careers and how far in debt they were getting. Did they really need to buy those new Jet 'Skis? It seemed that all the time and financial pressures they were putting themselves under were really taking a toll on the kids and their marriages. If Mike didn't spend so many weekends at the office, he might be able to work things out with Susan. Didn't they realize what a blow a divorce would be to the grandkids, who already saw precious little of their workaholic parents?

These Builders just couldn't understand the selfishness of the kids they had raised. The Boomers may have been well educated, but they certainly didn't seem to understand what was important in life. If they'd only go back to attending church, the way they had been raised to, there might be some hope for the grandchildren to turn out okay. These grandparents were concerned about the values, or apparent lack of them, that they saw developing in their Xer and N-Gen grandkids. The older ones, now graduated from college, seemed to lack the skills or initiative to get a decent job, and the younger ones seemed to spend all their time on the Internet. That just couldn't be good for them. And they all looked so bizarre!

The Boomers of the family were relieved that the day had gone as well as it had. They still remembered the Thanksgivings when they had been more outspoken about issues where their values differed from their parents' traditional views, and arguing had spoiled the day. If only Dad wasn't so set in his old-fashioned morals. He just wasn't in touch with what it took to survive in the real world today. Even though he didn't say anything, they could see the disapproval in his eyes. Especially when he heard about the Jet Skis. He didn't understand that they need these things to keep in touch with their kids, keep them wanting to come on vacation with them. And Mom never gave up on the church thing. She still believed it was the answer to all their family's problems, but life was so busy now, and it didn't meet their needs.

The older grandkids, the Xers in the family, enjoyed spending time with their grandparents, even though they saw them as very old-fashioned and set in their ways. They were both amused and shocked by statements their grandparents had made during the day that sounded so prejudiced, so politically incorrect—and they didn't even realize it! They'd be surprised to meet some of their grandkids' friends whose nationalities and lifestyles they had unwittingly insulted throughout the day. But the Xers enjoyed hearing their grandparents' stories of how they survived hard times in the past. These young adults respected them for sticking to their values, even if they didn't believe in them themselves. They were quite aware of the tension when the topic of finances came up. They knew that Grandpa didn't approve of how their parents bought so much on credit. These kids didn't struggle so much with the fact that their parents bought the stuff; after all, they liked having all the newest and latest stuff, too. They just wished they had the ability to qualify for a credit card themselves! But what got to them was their parents' justification for going into debt for those new Jet Skis. They said it was to bring the family together, to give them something to do together. What a joke! If they wanted to have more family time, why didn't they just work less overtime and hang out with their families more?

The youngest of the grandkids, the N-Geners of the family, spent most of the day on their grandparents' new computer. After dinner they gave their grandma a tour of the Internet and gave her lessons on how to send E-mail. They also talked Grandpa into bringing out his collection of swing albums so they could show off some of their newly acquired swing dance moves. But they really couldn't believe that you actually had to turn the records over to hear the rest of the songs! They enjoyed spending time with their grandparents and really respected their advice, even though they could be really narrow-minded on some things, especially when it came to people who were different than them. They didn't quite understand why Grandpa was questioning the wisdom of buying the new Jet Skis. They had helped to shop for the best prices on the Internet, and they were able to find a really good deal. If they had waited, they would have missed it!

Just like this family, we are constantly faced with differences that divide us. In our families, our workplaces, our churches, and our communities, we are constantly in relationships with people who have values different than ours because of the decades we were each raised in. These conflicting values lead to

The CLASH of Values

VALUES IN...	BUILDERS	BOOMERS	XERS	N-GEN
MOTHER	Homemaker Mother	Working Mother	Single Mother	Single Mother/ Single Father
FAMILY	Close Family	Dispersed Family	Latchkey Kids	Comfortable with Looser Family Structure
MARRIAGE PATTERNS	Married Once	Divorced/ Remarried	Single Parent	Undetermined
HAIR	Short Hair	Long Hair	Any Style Hair	Bleached/Spiked
CLOTHES	Formal	Casual	Bizarre	Anything Goes
MUSIC	Big Band/Swing	Rock 'n' Roll	Alternative/ Rap	Ska/Swing (Very Diverse)
MONEY	Save It Now	Buy It Now	Want It Now	Get It Now (Online)
PURCHASING	Purchasing with Cash	Purchasing with Credit Card	Struggling to Purchase	Purchase Online
MARKETING	Ford Marketing Concept	GE Marketing Concept	Ignored Market	Interactive Global Market
HIGH-TECH	Slide Rule	Calculator	Computer (Games)	Internet
WORK STYLE	Team Work & Commitment to Work	Personal Fulfillment	Tentative / Divided Loyalty	Networking
WAR	Win a War (WW II patriotism)	Why a War? (Vietnam War demonstrations)	Watch a War (Desert Storm live on TV)	Winless War (Iraq conflict)
MORALS	Puritan Ethics	Sensual	Cautious	Tolerant

misunderstanding, tension, and outright conflict between people of different generations. Now that we've looked at each decade and generation independently, let's compare them with each other to further our insight and understanding.

To help us with this comparison, we have created the chart above that summarizes some of the key issues of conflict so that we can better understand where and why our values clash.[1]

Some of the items listed in the chart describe trends, attitudes or value preferences that are unique to each generation. Others list the circumstances that created the differences, but they all contribute to the clash that exists between each of the groups.

A Closer Look

For the sake of discussion, let's tackle just a few related topics at a time. The first three topics relate to family issues.

Mothers and Families

As we look at the first and second lines, we see the typical trends/patterns relating to the situations of the mothers of each generation and the resulting effects on their families. When the Builder Generation was growing up and starting their own families, by and large, mothers stayed home to raise their children and were homemakers. This contributed to establishing a close family unit. Extended families also were more likely to live near each other. The tendency was to marry only once, and the divorce rate was relatively low.

As the Boomers grew up and became parents, more mothers began to work outside of the home. This added to the hurried lifestyle of the family, with people going every which way. We also saw that the divorce rate began to increase significantly. Often the immediate families were dispersed because of divorce, but the extended family also became more dispersed as mobility increased and young families moved to follow careers or to relocate in the suburbs.

The divorce rate continued to climb and really took its toll on Generation X. There was an increase in the number of single mothers, as well as both parents working, resulting in many children coming home from school to an empty house or apartment. There wasn't a parent around to give them the attention that previous generations had had, and many children had to lock themselves into their homes until their mothers returned from work.

The Net Generation, while still dealing with an abundance of families led by single mothers, has also seen the rise of family situations that involve joint or shared custody of the children, resulting in kids growing up in multiple households (spending time with each parent). There has also been an increasing number of children living with their single fathers. "There are now several million single fathers in the U.S., and a large chunk of them—1.5 million men—are custodial fathers. 'Father-only families are rare, but they are arguably the fastest-growing family form,'" notes Adam Shapiro, a University of North Florida sociologist who studies single fatherhood.[2]

Having had less contact or experience with the traditional nuclear family, the Net Generation is more comfortable with looser family structures that result from divorced and blended family situations.

When it comes to the role of mothers, there are differences in values. Most Builders would share the view that mothers should stay at home with the children and work there. The Boomers certainly feel that mothers should have the option to go out and work. In many cases the mother needs to work. There is a serious clash between the Builders and Boomers on this. The Boomers, the Xers, and the Net-Geners, however, seem to view this issue similarly.

There are also differences in values and expectations related to the family. The Builders think the extended family should all live near each other, and they are quite frustrated that Boomers move away and seem to be scattered all over the place. Builders often question how Boomers run their families. It concerns them that Boomer families don't all sit down and eat together at the same time.

Generation X was the first to basically raise themselves. With single moms at work, latchkey kids were left to come home alone to deal with homework, feed pets, and do chores on their own. This group generally felt abandoned by the adults in their world. Many have not known their families as a source of support, so they usually don't expect the family closeness the Builders long for and the Boomers neglect.

Even though the Net Generation is still dealing with a lot of single-parent households or blended families, their situation is different than that of Xers because parenting trends have changed. Parents have become better educated about the needs of their children and are being more intentional about their parenting. They are making more sacrifices and working harder at building relationships with their kids than the parents of Xers did, resulting in closer relationships between N-Geners and their parents. Also, fractured and blended family situations have become more common, and N-Geners seem to be better able to accept living with a mom, a dad, or a grandparent, or switching back and forth among all three.

Marriage Patterns

Perhaps the biggest clash of values results from the differences in each generation's view of marriage. The Builders, of course, felt that once married, you should be married until "death do you part." The Boomers, with their fast-paced lifestyle, rejection of traditional values, and focus on their own needs, saw divorce as a solution when relationships became difficult. That brought great pressure and tension within their families, particularly from their parents, the Builders. For many Xers, the marriage pattern they saw as they were growing up was divorce. That scared them to the degree that they tend to wait longer to get married and are hesitant to get into a marriage situation that could end in divorce. The trend of couples living together without being married (started by the Boomers) continues to be a real option in many Xers' minds. The Net Generation, because of their young age, have yet to establish a typical marriage pattern.

The next group of issues on our chart has to do with styles and preferences, which, through the years, have been responsible for a lot of judging, misunderstanding, and arguments between generations.

Hair

These are some of the issues where the clashing of values between the generations is most easily seen. Hairstyle is one of the most visible. According to Builders' values, good guys and "real men" had short hair. Their heroes came back from World War I and World War II with short hair, and they thought that was the way to go. As the '60s were ushered in, the Boomers decided to let their hair grow, partly because of the influence of the Beatles, but also as part of their rejection of the values of the establishment. This really irritated the Builders. For some reason, they seemed to take this more personally than many other clashes that we will talk about. In the '70s, young men's hairstyles, although still longer than the Builders liked, at least became more styled and socially acceptable. Then, after the Boomers went to all the trouble of getting long hair accepted, the Xers came along, often preferring a short hairstyle (which seemed to irritate some Boomers). But long hair was also still in. In fact, creative new styles emerged, combining long and short in the same style. In the '90s, men and boys often shaved some parts of their heads, leaving ponytails on other parts. Now an emerging trend of the Net Generation is to have hair a bit shorter, but to bleach it and spike it. They certainly don't alienate Generation X with these styles, but the Boomers and Builders do question why guys would bleach their hair or, as some do, add bright colors like orange, green, or blue. Many families struggle to decide how much creative freedom to allow their teens in their appearance.

Clothes

It's quite easy to see how clothes also caused division in generational values. The Builders always felt that formal clothing was better. Many of us can still remember Ozzie Nelson mowing his lawn wearing a tie and a cardigan sweater. The Boomers, always quick to reject the values of their parents, preferred casual clothing. The Boomers' desire to dress casually at work when they could arrange it, and certainly more and more in public places, seemed to irritate the Builders.

And if the Boomers irritated the Builders with their casual clothes, the Xers, with their bizarre dress, have caused the Builders to really get uptight. Baggy clothes, chains, studded leather—all of this has gone to alienate both the Builders and the Boomers. One day I (Rick) was sitting with Kathy's sister, Patti, who was in the fashion industry, when one of these Xers came by in a totally bizarre outfit. "There goes another fashion victim," she commented, shaking her head.

The Net Generation is a group who loves diversity. They enjoy dressing up, being casual, and borrowing from all the previous generations. You can see them going to school with slacks and a dress shirt, in army fatigues, flared jeans and T-shirts, baggy clothing, or whatever else strikes their fancy. They like being individuals. They borrow styles from the '40s, the '60s, the '70s—whatever they like.

Music

Music is always an indicator of how values change. The Builders enjoyed the big band sound, and swing dancing was one of the big crazes. Boomers are known for their love of rock 'n' roll, even to this day. There has been great tension between the Builders and the Boomers over rock 'n' roll music—the lyrics, the beat, the style, and the values it represented.

That clash certainly continued to grow with Generation X as they got into rap and alternative music, with even more extreme sounds, performances, and lyrics, which previous generations considered to be immoral and hostile toward society

The Net Generation loves diversity and variety. They enjoy music of the past, like their parents' rock 'n' roll. There is a serious re-emergence of the popularity of the big band/swing sound, and even swing dancing. One of the "new" sounds becoming popular with the youth is ska, which combines reggae and rap and includes brass instruments. Alternative music is also high on their list. In our survey of high school students, every type of music imaginable was listed. In fact, a large number gave us answers like "everything but . . ." and listed only one or two styles that they didn't enjoy. But there was no consistent trend in what they didn't like. Basically, the Net Generation seems to enjoy all types of music, which gives them common ground with the other three generations.

Money

You can tell an awful lot about people if you get a chance to look at two books in their possession—their appointment book and their checkbook. What a person does with his or her money is a chief indicator of what that person's values are.

The Builders are true to form when it comes to money. They grew up in a time when money was scarce and sacrifices were necessary. After the Depression and World War II, the economy greatly improved and the financial situation of many of the Builders improved with it. Most, however, kept the values that they had developed during their youth, which basically was "Save money because you can never tell when there's going to be another depression." Their main money-related value is to save.

They have a serious clash of values with the Boomers, who were raised in a time of economic prosperity. If they get money, they tend to want to spend it now. This really irritates their Builder parents. When things get financially difficult, the Boomers (who tend to spend and get themselves into debt) know they can go back to their parents (who have saved their money) for financial help. This is perhaps one of the greatest clashes of values that does exist.

Generation X was raised in a more difficult financial time. They have all the desires that the Baby Boomers have. They just haven't been able to get the quality of jobs that produce the income to get what they want, since the Boomers have the good jobs and are not ready to give them up. This actually creates tension between Xers and Baby Boomers because Xers feel they are being excluded from financial prosperity.

The N-Geners, like the Boomers, have grown up in a prosperous economic time. They believe they can get things and get them now, just like the Boomers before them. They also have a new tool to find whatever they want—the Internet. There's an increasing trend toward on-line buying. This appeals not only to the N-Geners but also to Xers and Boomers, all of whom share the value of immediate gratification. This value, however, does clash with their Builder grandparents' value of delayed gratification and saving for the future.

Purchasing

How a person makes purchases is closely related to how he values money. The security-minded Builders obviously want to pay cash to avoid building up debt. They believe in waiting until you have the money to pay for something before you buy it.

As the Boomers were leaving college, credit cards became a new trend. Many of them were sent credit cards as college students, without the money to back them up or the maturity to use them. A high percentage of Boomers have gotten into serious financial difficulty with the misuse of credit cards. There's a serious clash of values between Builders and Boomers in their views of paying cash versus using credit.

The Xers have a similar view to that of Boomers. They prefer immediate gratification—they just don't have as much discretionary money to spend. They are forced to delay gratification for financial reasons, but they don't feel good about it like the Builders do.

Although the Net Generation is not yet financially independent because of its youthfulness, we are predicting increasing use of the Internet for purchasing in the future. This group is so Internet-savvy that it makes sense that they will take advantage of the convenience and immediate gratification it provides. It doesn't even require a trip to the store. If you want it, you can find it on the Net, order it, and it will be at your house within days, and in many cases, overnight.

Marketing

Marketing provides an interesting generational study. Those in the marketing business study the different generations so they can more effectively motivate (or manipulate?) them. As the Builders became consumers, they weren't particularly catered to. Henry Ford made the comment that you can have a car any color you want, as long as it's black. The Ford marketing concept stated, "We have a product. If you want it, you can buy it."

The GE marketing concept, aimed at the Boomers, has more to do with meeting specific needs. It says, "Find out what people want, and then give it to them." We have seen this throughout the Boomers' lives, starting when they were children and continuing now as they're on their way to becoming senior adults. Industries have always specifically targeted Baby Boomers. Marketers want to find out what their needs are and then present products to meet those needs. For example, focus groups would come and ask mothers, "What kind of appliances do you need?" And mothers would say, "Well, I have four people in my family. We have breakfast together. We all like to eat toast. We'd all like to eat it at the same time, and we'd like it to be hot." These focus groups would go back with the conclusion that families needed a four-slice toaster and would develop a product to meet that need.

When it comes to being the target of marketing, the Xers have not received near the attention that the Baby Boomers have. Again, they have just a little over half the numbers of Boomers. They don't represent as significant a purchasing power, so there haven't been as many products geared toward the Xers. To some extent, they are the ignored market.

We're seeing a major change in marketing as the Net Generation arrives on the scene. First, we again have a larger target population—over 80 million. Second, there is a new way to market to them through the Internet. It's not restricted to a local store, a region, or even a country. There is a global marketing concept that makes products available on the Internet from anywhere in the world, and these can be advertised on web sites that cater to very specific interest groups.

The clash in values or perspectives on this issue of marketing is one of expectations. The Builders feel that you should just go out and buy what is available without making a big fuss about it. The Boomers believe that they should have things specifically made for them to meet their needs and their tastes. They are also willing to spend more for it. The N-Geners expect to find whatever they need through the Internet.

High-Tech

We certainly see differences in what was considered "high-tech" in each generation. It's interesting that the Builder generation, who earned that title by building our airline systems, railroads, dams, and basically the whole infrastructure of our country, did it without many of the high-tech devices we have today. Their main tool was a slide rule. I'm sure that if you held up a slide rule in a tenth grade class today, most students would not be able to identify it. Using a slide rule involved considerable knowledge and hard work, but the Builders thrive on hard work, so it suited them fine.

For Boomers, high-tech took the form of calculators when they were in college. Calculators could do all the functions of a slide rule and more, but it didn't take near the work. That was quite appealing to the Boomers, who like things quick and easy.

Xers' version of high-tech arrived while they were still young. They were first introduced to computers through computer games like Pong, Pac-Man, Atari, and Nintendo. Now they have interactive video games that they can play on the Internet. Because they were introduced to computers while they were young, they have greater understanding and skill than many from the older generations, which is probably their biggest contribution to the job market. It's interesting to note that with all the things computers are used for today, this group still sees the computer as a major source of entertainment, and they still spend a lot of time playing computer games.

High-tech for the Net Generation is the Internet. This is the generation that has been raised with it, and they seem to have a natural, innate ability to understand and use it. It's as normal to them as a pencil and a pad of paper. Their ability to use this technology will be one of the greatest assets they have.

In terms of a clash of values, there is great concern on the Builders' part about how much time the Net Generation spends on their computers and the Internet. They wonder if it's retarding their social skills because they're not meeting with people face-to-face, but on-line. They're concerned about the physical ramifications of kids sitting at their computers instead of getting out and playing and being active. Perhaps the greatest concern is the access they have to questionable material on the Internet.

Although they are concerned about the misuse of technology, the Builders are slowly joining in the high-tech movement. One of the fastest-growing populations buying computers today are Builders. They want to be able to E-mail their kids and their grandkids.

Work Style

How people operate in the workplace is another observable behavior that shows differences in values. The Builders have the "old-country" work ethic. They work as teams. They are committed to fulfill a task. They work until the job is done. That's what helped to build this country and helped to get us through difficult times like the Depression and World War II.

As the Boomers came along, just getting the job done wasn't enough. They wanted to find personal fulfillment in work. This was a serious clash of values between the Builders and the Boomers. The Builders didn't understand why Boomers couldn't just get down to work and get the job done for the sake of doing it. Builders aren't opposed to personal fulfillment at work, as long as that fulfillment comes from getting the job done.

As the Boomers have matured and risen to the level of senior leadership positions around the country, they are taking on more of the Builder work characteristics. Now that they're becoming responsible for the bottom line, they realize they need to see the job get done, whether they are finding total fulfillment or not.

There is certainly a clash of values between the Boomers and Generation X when it comes to work style. Xers have seen how the Boomers can become addicted to work and find so much fulfillment and meaning from their jobs that they neglect other areas of their lives. Xers don't want to get into this work style. They've seen the negative side of becoming workaholics— what it does to families and personal health—and they don't want to have anything to do with it. They question the work ethic of the Boomers and don't have a problem questioning it right to their faces. Because Xers are unwilling to sacrifice family or personal time for the sake of their jobs, they have divided loyalties and appear to the Boomers to have a lack of commitment or lack of initiative.

Another work-related clash stems from the frustration that Xers feel about the limited job market available to them. There are so many Boomers in the workforce that there are few good jobs left for the Xers. Because Boomers are not yet vacating positions of leadership, they are not allowing for upward mobility for Xers. In many cases, highly educated Xers have to take jobs lower than what their qualifications would merit.

I heard one Xer say, "I went to college and ended up with a job at McDonald's. Then I went back for a graduate degree and become a manager at McDonald's." This causes more than a little bit of tension between Boomers and Xers. To spend all the time, effort, and expense required to earn a degree, and then end up in a job that doesn't utilize your education, is a little hard to swallow.

When it comes to the Net Generation's work style, we don't have a totally clear picture yet because they're just now beginning to enter the workforce. But if we take into consideration how they work at school and relate socially, we can predict that they're going to have a highly networked, high-tech work style. They don't seem to care a great deal for bureaucracy or authority. They respect competency, not position. They want to be able to work quickly and creatively, and they want to do it their way. This could lead to serious clashing in the workforce if the Builders and Boomers cannot adjust to this different work style, and if the Net Generation cannot accommodate some of the established work systems.

War

Attitude toward war is another indicator of one's values. The Builders' view of war is consistent with other values they hold dear. It certainly is coming together as a team, being committed to a common cause, and being in this thing to win. The values promoted were patriotism, camaraderie, and the importance of team effort.

When the Boomers came along, they had reasonable questions about the validity of the war they were asked to fight. They demonstrated; they asked hard questions; they accused the government. This created a serious values clash with their Builder parents, who were loyal to the government that had helped to lead the world to victory in World War I and World War II. How could you possibly question what the government was doing in Vietnam?

That kind of clash didn't take place between the Boomers and the Xers. Few Xers were called on to fight in a war. Their view of war is something that happens over a period of weeks or months, like Desert Storm. Those who didn't go were able to watch it on TV, and they could always change the channel when they lost interest.

The Net Generation has no real life experience with war.

Their knowledge is from history books and a report they might notice on the evening news that we have bombed one country or another. We fly in, we drop bombs, and we leave. It's not a personal war. There never seem to be any winners or lasting solutions. Unless they have a family member involved, it has little effect on their lives. In our own survey of high school students, we asked, "What is the word or phrase that best describes your feelings, attitudes or involvement with current wars in the world?" Eighty percent of the responses were negative toward war. The most common responses were "I don't know" and "I don't care," but also included were answers like "I don't like them," "Stupid," "A waste," and "Rather not get involved." Only 20 percent were supportive of war, with responses like "They help the rest of the world," "Win," "Whatever is best for the country," and "Nuke 'em." It makes sense that this generation, which is known for tolerance and involved internationally through the Internet, would be unfavorable toward war.

Morals

The final area of comparison on our value system clash chart is morals. These words sum up each generation's values pretty concisely. The Builders had a very puritan, moral ethic. That isn't to say that everything that generation did was puritanical, moral, or ethical. But it was the accepted standard for their generation. Anyone who stepped outside of that standard was considered wrong.

As the Boomers emerged, they challenged these ethics, just as they basically challenged anything that Builders or "the establishment" valued. "Freedom" from traditional standards led to the sexual revolution and a much more sensual society. These changes showed up in our fashions, our language, the media, and especially our relationships. That's not to say that all of the Baby Boomers embraced these morality changes, but the majority of our society began to consider these changes acceptable.

This has been a major source of clashing with the Builders.

Some of the other differences in values we have talked about are more a matter of preference or viewpoint. But many of the Builders believe these differences in values are downright immoral and, in many cases, should be considered illegal.

We currently see this clash of moral values as a hot topic of national debate, particularly in our nation's capital. There doesn't seem to be a consensus of what is morally acceptable or unacceptable. "As long as it doesn't hurt anyone else, and you don't get caught, you can do what you want" seems to be a prevailing attitude. The Builders, by and large, do not believe this and have great tension with their Boomer children.

Generation X would like to embrace the freer values of the Boomers, but situations like the fear of AIDS have required them to be much more cautious about their behavior and perspective on sexual relationships. Their more careful lifestyle is a result of concerns about health issues and personal protection, rather than a change in moral convictions. Many Xers believe there aren't any absolutes in life to live by, but you have to take care of yourself.

As the decades have progressed, there has been a gradual but continual loosening of moral standards. As we look at the Net Generation, we see the development of the most tolerant generation yet. Being raised in a politically correct, everybody-is-entitled-to-choose-their-own-lifestyle-and-be-accepted social environment does not lend itself to strong moral convictions. About the only thing they stand against is a judgmental attitude.

The Potential for Relational Disaster

As our chart shows, any multigenerational situation is a potential relational "clash site." Combine any two generations and you will find areas of conflicting values. Try blending three or four generations together and, unless everyone is really working at understanding and accepting each other, expect some spontaneous combustion to occur.

Consider a few potentially explosive situations:

Your extended family is having a huge reunion in honor of

Grandma and Grandpa's 50th wedding anniversary. There will be relatives you haven't seen for years there, and lots of family portraits taken. Now you have to agree what everyone in your family will wear (including how many tattoos and body-piercings to expose, and what style and color of hair are acceptable).

Your church has outgrown its present facilities, and a committee has been appointed to propose a solution, including how to finance it. To make sure the needs of all age groups are considered, representatives from all four generations are included on the committee. The Builders on the committee believe in having cash in hand before they build, while the younger generations see nothing wrong with taking out a loan.

Your office management has decided that playing music over the intercom would improve the office environment. Now the question is, what kind of music should be played? Muzak? Classical? Oldies? Instrumental? Current popular artists?

Your family has decided to plan the "ultimate vacation," where everyone gets to vote on what he or she wants to do.

Your company has decided to revise its policy manual, and has put together a committee with representatives from every level in the organization, which also includes representative from every generation.

See any potential for value clashes here? In addition to decision-making situations like these, conflicts are frequently experienced as we live our lives in proximity to each other. Whether it's being subject to someone else's choice of music, being irritated by what you consider to be an unreasonable or unnecessary rule, or having to share the consequences of someone else's behavior, none of us can escape the effects of the generational clashes. We all need to learn how to understand and overcome the differences that divide us. Hopefully the previous chapters have helped us to understand how our values differ and why. In the next and final section of chapters, we'll look at some ways to overcome these differences and some steps to take to help lessen the generational tensions in our lives.

OVERCOMING THE DIFFERENCES THAT DIVIDE US

Chapter 20

Identifying the Differences

A s you read through your own decade and generation chapters, you were given a description of values that were considered "normal" or typical of people your age. You may have agreed with some of the value descriptions that were presented, but other values considered to be normal for your group might not line up with your personal set of values. For instance, when teaching this in Christian groups, we often hear from Boomers, Xers, and even N-Geners that, in some areas, they relate more to the Builder values. This would be because Builders tend to have more traditional values, which would more closely resemble the biblical values that Christians of all ages tend to have.

The purpose of this chapter is to help you identify what your values are and how you developed those values. We have developed an assessment tool to help you figure out what your values are in specific areas. We encourage you to use this same assessment tool to help you identify the values of someone else in your life with whom you seem to clash. This could be a family member, friend, or coworker. It would be ideal for you each to answer the assessment questions, but if the other person is either unavailable or unapproachable, you can answer for him or her as you think that person would respond.

After you've defined your values, we've given you some questions to think about and discuss to help you understand where your values came from and why. Our goal here is increased understanding, both of yourself and of others. We're convinced that the more people understand each other, the more easily they can accept each other and get along.

Your Personal Value Assessment

As you read each question and its selection of responses, choose and mark the response that most closely resembles your beliefs, attitudes, or preferences. If there is nothing listed that represents your views, write your personal response in the box labeled "other." When you are finished, total the number of responses in each column and write that total in the box at the bottom of each column. The higher the number, the more you relate to the typical values of the generation represented by each column. More importantly, as you look over your responses, you can see what your values are and how they differ from typical values of those from other generations, or even values typical of your own generation. Keep in mind that the purpose of doing this is not to put you into a category or box, but to help you understand what your unique values are and give you something to compare and discuss with others in your life.

The Value Assessment of Others

We encourage you to have others you know complete this assessment (or you can fill it out according to your best understanding of how they would respond). Then you'll have a basis for comparing your values with theirs. You can use this as the starting point for an enlightening conversation. Such communication has the potential of leading you to a better understanding and acceptance of those you find difficult to comprehend. Following this assessment, you'll find questions that will help you discover the reasons you developed the values you did, and also help you understand why that other person's values are so different from yours.

Personal Value Assessment

					Other:
1. Which would best describe your beliefs about family relationships?	Families should stay together at all costs.	If family relationships aren't working for you, get out of the relationship.	You can't count on families staying together—whoever is close to you becomes family.	Keep families together—but if not possible, accept whatever family you have.	☐
2. Which best describes your beliefs about marriage?	Marriage commitments are forever.	Marriages are for as long as they are fulfilling and meet each others' needs.	Marriage is optional for those living together and commitment levels are uncertain.	Marriage commitment is important, but if divorce is necessary, don't judge.	☐
3. Which best describes your beliefs about sex?	Sex is for married partners only.	Sex outside of marriage is somewhat acceptable.	Sex outside of marriage is common but dangerous. Use caution.	Abstinence until marriage is a good option—but at least practice safe sex.	☐
4. Which best describes your attitudes toward your parents when you were a teenager?	Respected and obeyed them.	Thought I knew more so I challenged their authority and did my own thing.	Felt abandoned by them, so I did what was best for me and looked for other significant relationships.	Respected them and wanted their advice for my life.	☐
5. How do you typically respond to people with a background or lifestyle vastly different from yours?	Uncomfortable being around them, try to avoid them.	Try to be sensitive to their differences, but prefer to be separate and with people like me.	Treat them in politically correct ways—enjoy building relationships with them.	Hardly notice the differences—enjoy the differences—don't judge.	☐

6. If you received an unexpected bonus of $1000, what would you most likely do with it?	☐ Save it for a rainy day.	☐ Spend it on something fun and exciting now.	☐ Pay bills with it.	☐ Save some and spend some on clothes, music, a car, etc.	☐ Other:
7. In addition to making a living, which factor do you find most motivating in your work?	☐ Financial gain and security.	☐ Self-fulfillment and meaning.	☐ Meeting financial needs without too many demands on personal time.	☐ Having fun while doing helpful, meaningful work.	☐ Other:
8. When it comes to longevity in careers, which best describes your expectation or preference?	☐ Stick with career—few career changes.	☐ Willing to change careers to find better or more meaningful job.	☐ Expect to change careers several times.	☐ Looking for a career. May need to change careers to find the best one for me.	☐ Other:
9. Which best describes your top priority in your job?	☐ Loyalty to the company.	☐ Loyalty to my own personal needs.	☐ Loyalty to my family's needs and my personal beliefs.	☐ Loyalty to my need to do something I enjoy.	☐ Other:
10. Which best describes your preferred work style/environment?	☐ Team work: self-sacrifice for the company goals.	☐ Doing it my way: individualistic, competitive.	☐ Fulfill the basic requirements of the job.	☐ Networking: working in cooperation with others, sharing knowledge and ideas.	☐ Other:

11. Which style of clothing would you consider to be appropriate for an office work environment?	☐ Sports coats and ties; dresses.	☐ Nice casual.	☐ Comfortable casual; jeans and T-shirts.	☐ Anything comfortable, from jeans to dressy.	☐ Other:
12. Which of the following best describes your relationship to the current high-tech society?	☐ Seems good, but I find it somewhat intimidating.	☐ Important part of our current lifestyle, both at home and work. But it's a challenge to learn.	☐ Important to daily life, both for work and entertainment. Feel comfortable with the technology.	☐ Hard to imagine life without it. Use it for entertainment, and to connect with people on the Internet.	☐ Other:
13. Which best describes your feelings about the presence of absolutes in our lives?	☐ There are many things in life that are definitely right and wrong.	☐ In some cases there are absolutes, but you have to do what's best for you.	☐ Everything is relative—no real absolutes.	☐ I have my beliefs about what is right and wrong, others are welcome to their own beliefs.	☐ Other:
14. Which best describes your attitude toward rules and traditions?	☐ Rules/traditions are good and should be followed.	☐ They should be challenged, and irrelevant ones should be ignored or changed.	☐ Tell me the rationale behind them and I will decide whether to follow them.	☐ I choose the rules that make sense to me, and you may follow different rules.	☐ Other:
15. Which best describes your feelings about the U.S.'s role in the wars of your lifetime (those we sent troops to)?	☐ Patriotism—the U.S. has played an important part in helping the world.	☐ Protesting—if there is no clear and valid reason for being involved.	☐ Uninvolved—it's something we see on TV, but nothing seems to get resolved.	☐ Unaware/indifferent—not sure what is going on, but generally opposed to the concept of war.	☐ Other:

	Typical Builder Responses	Typical Boomer Responses	Typical Generation X Responses	Typical Net Generation Responses	Your Own Unique Responses
16. Which best describes how you relate to the government?	☐ Patriotic/supportive.	☐ Skeptical/distrustful.	☐ Prefer local to national government.	☐ Waiting to see how the government will meet my needs.	☐ Other:
17. Which best describes your musical preferences?	☐ Swing, big band jazz.	☐ Rock 'n' Roll.	☐ Alternative/rap/heavy metal.	☐ Most kinds of music/ a variety.	☐ Other:
18. During your teens, which type of male hairstyle did you prefer?	☐ Short and neat.	☐ Longer/styled.	☐ Short-long combos, bizarre haircuts.	☐ Short and neat or unique haircuts, including shaved, bleached, and spiked.	☐ Other:
19. Which best describes your view of suicide?	☐ An unthinkable reaction to problems.	☐ A tragic and desperate response to life.	☐ A reasonable choice/ alternative to a difficult life.	☐ A sad but understand-able reaction to a hard life situation.	☐ Other:
Total the number of responses in each column.	Total _____	Total _____	Total _____	Total _____	Total _____

As you look at your results, remember that the purpose is not to get you to fit into a particular category but to understand what your unique values are so that you can better understand yourself and also explain your values to others in your life. Many of you will find that you have some answers in each column. It's a rare person who would completely line up in one column. As we mentioned before, Christians of all ages often end up with some Builder responses because of their adherence to biblical values, which are closer to the more traditional Builder values. There are also many other reasons why your values might not line up with those typical of your generation because of your unique experiences as you grew up. That's why we have asked you to go through this exercise. As you look at your set of values and compare them with others, you may start to ask yourself why you have these values, or why your values differ from (or are similar to) those of the person to whom you're comparing yourself.

We have given you a list of questions to help you think through your own value development. If you share your answers with others, you'll help them understand where you are coming from. As others share their answers with you, you'll better understand why they think and act the way they do.

Any of these questions could lead to lengthy times of reflection and discussion. They will bring up memories and stories from your past. Don't rush through them, but enjoy the process. If you are using these with a group of people (like your family members or a group at work), you may want to address only a few questions at a time to allow for adequate sharing.

If you use these questions with others, it's important to be committed to listening with an open heart and mind. Your goal should be to understand, not to censure or judge the other people's values. Give them the freedom to be different. This is not the time to try and convince them of the errors of their ways or to win them over to your way of seeing things. You want to know why they believe and act the way they do, to help eliminate misunderstandings and misinterpretation of their motives in your relationship with them. As you understand them better, you should find it easier to accept them, even if you can't always agree with them. At least you'll know *why* you are different if you find you have to "agree to disagree" in some areas.

Questions to Reflect on and Discuss

1. Where did you grow up during your childhood and teen years? Did your location have any particular impact on your values? How?

2. What was your family situation like during your growing-up years?
   - What was the status of your parents' marriage?
   - Describe your siblings and how you related to them.
   - Did you have any extended family members closely involved in your life?
   - How would you describe the emotional climate in your home?
   - How was discipline handled in your family?
   - What was your family's economic situation? What was your family's attitude toward money? How has that affected your values?
   - What was your relationship with your parents like when you were a teenager?

3. What role did religion/church/faith play in your upbringing and value development?

4. Were there any significant people in your life (outside your family) who had a significant influence on you? Who were they, and what did you learn from them?

5. What events in your growing-up years had an impact on you (personal, political, social, economic, inventions/new technology, etc.), and how did it affect you?

6. What were the schools you attended like? What factors in your school environment had an impact on your values, and how did they affect you? (These could be educational

methods, racial mix, economic factors, teachers, extra-curricular activities, your personal success or lack of it, etc.)

7. When you were about 10 years old, who were your heroes (or who impressed you)? What did you want to be when you grew up?

8. What forms of media were you exposed to most in your growing-up years? What types of TV shows, movies, music, etc. did you enjoy most? What were some of your favorites? How do you think they have influenced you?

9. Who or what in your life most influenced your attitudes or beliefs about the following?
    • Marriage/family
    • Money
    • God
    • Work
    • Education
    • Government/authority

10. Have you had a significant change in any of your values as you've grown up? What caused that change?

Hopefully, going through this process with the value assessment and questions has been enlightening. Ideally, we would want it to be a delightful perusal of your past, filled with fond memories. But we realize that most people's pasts involve both good and bad memories. In any case, we hope it gave you insight, both into your own values and those of others.

In some cases you may realize, as you look into where certain values came from, that your values may be based on faulty information or influenced by someone who you now know to be less than reliable or knowledgeable on the topic. This could be your chance to reconsider a particular value and exchange it for a more appropriate one. In other cases, it may reinforce your values, making you feel that their source was solid and right, in spite of those who see things differently.

Now that you've identified how your values differ from

others in your life, what are you supposed to do with that knowledge? How can knowing how your values differ from those of your parents or kids or coworkers help in those relationships? That's the topic of our next chapter. We'll be looking at the concepts of understanding, acceptance, and forgiveness as they relate to value differences. It's the next step in overcoming the generational differences that divide us.

/ Chapter 21 /

Resolving the Differences

Ralph, a vice principal at a California high school, sat at his desk, thoughtfully observing the student he had just invited into his office. Jason was sullen and slouched in the chair as he stared out the window, waiting for what was to come. Just a few months ago, Jason had looked like a typical high school student—hair cut short, but bleached and spiked on top, T-shirt, baggy pants, high-priced tennis shoes. There was nothing particularly remarkable about him. He was pretty quiet, got along okay, stayed out of trouble. But recently a dramatic change had taken place. Now he dressed all in black and wore black eye makeup. He had become more outspoken, more confrontational, and now was referred to Ralph for trying to start a fight—again.

What's going on in this kid's life and in his mind? Ralph wondered. *How much anger is pent up inside him, and where will it lead him?* These questions were particularly sensitive ones considering the timing of this incident. You see, this was April 22, 1999, just two days after a pair of angry high school students in Littleton, Colorado, tried to carry out the massacre of their schoolmates and the destruction of Columbine High School. Through guns and homemade bombs, they attacked, killing a teacher, 12 other students, and themselves. The whole nation was still in shock, wondering how something like this could happen, why it did happen, and what it was telling us about the youth of our country.

Just minutes before, as Ralph met Jason in the waiting area outside his office, he had asked Jason, "What's going on with the way you look? The changes I've seen in you lately are causing me some concern. What's up?"

"The way I look doesn't express who I really am," remarked Jason, shrugging.

"Well, your appearance seems to be getting you into some trouble. If you went back to looking like you used to, maybe people wouldn't confront you so much," suggested Ralph.

"Hey, last year I was quiet and normal-looking, and I needed to say something, but nobody would listen. I kept everything inside. So this year I'm being more outspoken, trying to get more attention by the way I look, and now you're telling me that still nobody is going to listen? Then I guess it doesn't matter."

The anger and despair behind Jason's words really caught Ralph's attention. He was experienced at working with students and had become aware that many high school students today are feeling that no one is listening to their opinions or valuing them, even though they believe that they have something to say. He knew that right now Jason needed to be listened to and understood more than anything else.

"Mrs. Smith, will you reschedule my next appointment and hold my calls?" Ralph called to his secretary. "Jason, please come into my office. I want to hear what you have to say."

So here they were, in the privacy of Ralph's office. He could have sent Jason home from school for three days without listening to his side of the story. That was how this issue would have been dealt with in the past. But Ralph sensed that Jason desperately needed an adult to listen to him, to understand him. "You have my undivided attention, Jason. I'm willing to listen to whatever you want to tell me."

As Jason started talking about some of the things that were on his mind and realized that Ralph was really interested in understanding him, he opened up quite a bit. After Jason left, Ralph knew that he hadn't shared everything and suspected there were some deep hurts in his past he wasn't ready to reveal, but he had felt Jason's appreciation that he was willing to listen. It seemed to help defuse his anger. In fact, the next day Jason sought out the student whom he had wanted to fight and attempted to resolve the conflict.

Ralph plans to continue to keep an eye on Jason, making himself available to listen and offer him advice. This administrator's understanding of the N-Geners' need to be listened to enabled him to build an accepting relationship and help a young man through a difficult situation. He could have suspended Jason, causing Jason more trouble at home, possibly leading to even deeper feelings of being misunderstood, ignored, and angry. Instead, he has created a relationship that has the potential of having a continuing positive influence on Jason in the future.

As this story illustrates, understanding why a person acts or believes the way he or she does can make a big difference in a relationship. As people understand each other better, they can usually more easily accept each other, and this can lead to forgiveness, which is often needed in a difficult relationship.

Now some of you are nervous about this, thinking that if you accept people, you are condoning their beliefs and actions, and sometimes these people in our lives are doing things that go against our deeply held beliefs. It's very important to make the distinction between accepting someone as a person who has value and approving of what he or she does, says, or believes. It doesn't mean we don't make a stand for what we believe or, as parents, we abandon our role to teach and discipline our children. It does mean that we don't reject people in our lives because they don't agree with our values.

A well-known story that illustrates this principle is the biblical account of the prodigal son. The son, who demands his inheritance from his father early, goes out and squanders it, doing things totally opposed to his upbringing and his father's values. When he returns to his father's home after total failure, before he even has a chance to speak, his father sees him coming and accepts him back with open arms, in spite of the son's actions. We sense that the father understood something about the son's need to go off to do his own thing. He accepted him back, in spite of the fact that he had rejected his father's values and acted in ways that shamed the family. He forgave him and restored the relationship.

These three important concepts—understanding, acceptance, and forgiveness—are the main points of this chapter. We consider these to be the three key elements we need in order to overcome the differences that divide us. Let's take a closer look at each of these key concepts.

Key #1: Understanding

The concept of understanding, as we are using it, is not merely to comprehend or grasp the meaning of something, but it also involves having a sympathetic or tolerant attitude toward something or someone (both are dictionary definitions of *understand*). Morris Massey, in *The People Puzzle*, shows us how understanding can work in the context of generations and value differences:

> The gut-level value systems are, in fact, dramatically different between the generations that presently exist simultaneously in our society. The focus should not be so much on how to change other people to conform to our standards, our values. Rather, we must learn how to accept and understand other people in their own right, acknowledging the validity of their values, their behavior. American Indians believed that "to know another man you must walk a mile in his moccasins." This is a classic challenge for understanding others. If we can understand and respect other people and their values, then we can interact with them in a more effective manner.[1]

The more we understand each other's points of view and allow for differences, the better we can communicate and relate to each other. The more accurately we're able to interpret someone's motivation or understand his or her values, the less likely we are to misconstrue the intentions and either overreact or react inappropriately. For instance, if I, as a Boomer, understood that my (hypothetical) Xer son, who is still in debt from student loans that paid for his college education, values relationships more highly than getting ahead financially, I would understand why he turns down an offer to work weekends for extra pay. It may not be because he is lazy or unconcerned about his financial situation, which might be my instinctive conclusion without knowledge of the values that motivate his decisions. It could be because he values having time with his friends and family more, and is unwilling to sacrifice that time.

On the other hand, it could be that he really is lazy. (Value differences don't explain away every problem.) But I won't know that unless I discuss it with him and find out what he's thinking. If I do find out that his motives are better than I feared, while I may not agree with the choice that he made, I can more easily accept it because I understand his values and have not made a hasty judgment that he is lazy, which could lead to conflicts in our relationship.

The problem with hasty judgments is that, once you have decided that something is true, you look for evidence to support your opinion, even ignoring evidence to the contrary. If you believe someone is dishonest, you will look for more signs of dishonesty, even to the point of misconstruing honest mistakes as supporting evidence. You will have a tendency to overlook or ignore things that might actually indicate honesty in that person. This is where the concept of prejudice, or prejudging, comes into play.

This is one reason why understanding each other's values is so important. When we understand someone's reason for believing or acting a certain way, we're less likely to make inaccurate judgments about that person and react in ways that harm our relationship with him or her.

Sometimes it comes down to a matter of expectations. We probably all have mental pictures of how things should be: what the ideal family should be like, how our relationships should work, what should happen to us at work, how people should relate to each other at church, at the club, and so on. These are expectations we form out of our values. If we expect others to live by our values and they don't, we can feel disappointed, confused, angry, betrayed, and generally make negative judgments about the person who hasn't lived up to our standards. But if we adjust our expectations to be more realistic, based on a more accurate understanding of the other person and his or her values, there's less tension, better communication, and more acceptance in the relationship, as each person is given the freedom to be himself.

Think of a two-year-old. It's common knowledge that two-year-olds go through a developmental stage when they say no to everything, sometimes even to the things they want. When our daughter was two, we understood this, expected it, and weren't overly concerned by it. In fact, it was a sign to us that our daughter was developing normally. Our understanding that this was a normal, temporary phase helped us to deal with Cora's negative responses more patiently, since we didn't expect her to willingly respond to our every instruction (although, like any parent, we found dealing with her strong will frustrating at times!). We adjusted our expectations to fit our understanding of her stage of development.

Now she's a teenager, and it's time to adjust those expectations again! Like all teenagers, she has moved from being dependent upon us, her parents, for most everything to making many of her own choices and taking care of most of her own needs. She has her own taste in music, clothing, hairstyles, and entertainment. It's important for all parents of teenagers to understand that a significant task during adolescence is to move from dependence on their parents to independence. They all need to do this to develop into healthy, self-sufficient adults. The question is how painful will it be for our families in the process? If we understand their need, we can help them along in the process, minimizing the pain, or we can fight the process, creating more conflict than necessary. Understanding their need to question, to find out for themselves, to make poor choices, and to experience the consequences, we need to give them the freedom to do so (within legal and safety limits). They need to distinguish themselves as unique individuals, with values and tastes of their own. They need to look at the family's values and see if they really believe them.

Understanding all this helps us align our expectations with reality. If we realize that this is a necessary part of growing up, we won't be fighting them each step of the way, trying to control them, when what they need is our understanding and the confidence that we'll still love them through the process. Once they have achieved independence, with our blessing, it's easier for them to move on to the next stage of *inter*dependence, when as adults, they come to us for advice yet feel free to make their own decisions and live their own lives.

This concept of lining up our expectations with reality also applies to values. If we don't expect everyone to value the same things that we value, we'll be less dismayed or confused by their actions or choices. The more we understand about the reasons they have the values that they do, the less personal the differences between us become. We're less likely to feel like they're rejecting our values when we realize that their values are a result of the very different worlds we each experienced as we grew up. As we better understand the people in our lives and why they have the values that they do, we can adjust our expectations of them to a level that promotes acceptance rather than judgment.

Key #2: Acceptance

As we mentioned before, our goal of understanding how values develop is not merely to enlighten us to the process and explain why those people in our lives are so difficult. The goal of our understanding is to better enable us to accept each other and create better relationships that will allow us to overcome the differences that divide us.

Acceptance, our next key to resolving differences, is a crucial part of every relationship, as well as being a basic need for a healthy self-esteem. Those who experience acceptance feel more loved, secure, confident, and are able to have healthier, more positive relationships. Those who don't feel accepted feel less valuable, insecure, judged, and defensive. They also often feel that they need to prove themselves. These feelings often lead to strained relationships. As you consider the strained relationships in your life, whether with your kids, your parents, your coworkers, or others, try looking at the situation from their point of view. This is their unspoken plea:

A Plea for Acceptance

Just because I'm different from you, please don't reject me or discount my worth. Don't assume I am wrong and try to change me.

If I see things differently than you do, please try to consider why (or even ask me). What was different about the world that I grew up in than the one you experienced?

If my passions are stronger—or weaker—than yours, take time to discover the reason rather than judging me as radical, immoral, lazy, or indifferent.

Please don't assume that, because we have different values, one of us has to be wrong. Be open to the possibility that many issues are more a matter of preference than morality.

Try not to take it personally when I don't see things or do things the way that you do. Please realize that my values are deeply ingrained from my past (as are yours), and my actions aren't necessarily a rejection of your values, but an expression of mine.

When you accept me in spite of our differences, you

are telling me that I am worthy of your respect, friendship, and love.

Your acceptance of me tells me that our relationship doesn't depend on me always agreeing with you or being just like you. I can be free to be me, and you can be free to be you.

We may have to agree to disagree on certain issues—but disagreeing doesn't mean we value each other less.

If my beliefs conflict with beliefs you hold to be absolute moral truths, please realize that you can still accept me as a valuable person without agreeing with and approving of my values and actions. As I feel secure in your unconditional acceptance of me, I'll have the freedom to listen to you without being defensive. You can help me understand why you believe the way you do, and who knows, . . . I just may be able to see your point of view and even come to the discovery that you just might be right—but that has to be my choice.

Acceptance is a powerful tool in a relationship. Feeling accepted frees a person from the quest for acceptance and gives her a sense of security and value that encourages her to grow and accomplish more. Acceptance is a gift we can give to the people in our lives that will encourage them and also improve our relationship with them.

Remember that acceptance of someone doesn't mean that we approve of what he or she does or believes. We can accept someone as a person of worth even if we can't agree with his or her attitudes or behavior. This is easier to do when the person involved is somewhat removed from us and his actions don't reflect upon us directly, as with a coworker.

As parents, it's much harder to accept a child whose behavior goes against our values and can be a source of embarrassment to us. This usually happens during the socialization period when, as teens, they're trying out their values in society to see which ones will hold up. This is a time when they're striving for independence and an identity apart from their parents, but they still need to know they are loved and accepted, no matter what. We can't abandon our role as teachers and guides. Our acceptance of our children as valuable individuals needs to be accompanied by providing them with acceptable standards and accountability. But we also need to recognize them as the unique people they are becoming and realize that they probably will make choices that grate against our value systems (like wearing blue hair and a nose ring to church or the company picnic). At times like these, we should pause, take a deep breath, and ask ourselves, "Is this issue worth the battle? Is this a matter of preference or a moral issue?" Remember that if your kids are convinced that you accept them in spite of your differences, they're more likely to allow you to impact their values than if they feel you're rejecting them.

Children desperately need to feel accepted by their parents. It is part of their self-worth. When 100,000 children between the ages of eight and 14 were asked what they wanted most in their parents, these were the top 10 items mentioned. Look at this list and notice how many of them involve acceptance in some form:

1. Parents who don't argue in front of them.
2. Parents who treat each family member the same.
3. Parents who are honest.
4. Parents who are tolerant of others.
5. Parents who welcome their friends to the home.
6. Parents who build a team spirit with their children.
7. Parents who answer their questions.
8. Parents who give punishment when needed, but not in front of others, especially their friends.
9. Parents who concentrate on good points instead of weaknesses.
10. Parents who are consistent.[2]

As we mentioned in chapter 18, there is an encouraging trend with the teens today that gives us hope as parents. For the first time in many years, we have a generation that seems to respect their parents more than in the past and seems to want their parents' input in their lives. This is quite different, for the most part, from Boomers who, as a group, tended to reject their parents' establishment values, and the Xers who largely felt abandoned by their parents' quest for success and self-fulfillment. Kids today are reaping the benefits of parents who are returning their focus to the needs of their children. As they are feeling more accepted by their parents, they seem more ready to accept parents' advice in return.

Sometimes acceptance involves trust and even some risk, especially in a work situation. When I (Rick) worked at the conference center, I was responsible for the programming of the various conferences that were held. Sometimes I would delegate the programming for certain conferences to others who worked under my authority. We had a father-son conference, and since I only had a daughter, and the majority of the fathers that were coming were younger than I, I decided to delegate the programming for that conference to Jack, who works out of an Xer frame of reference and also has a son. It turned out that Jack had some different philosophies about how he'd like to see the conference run. He wanted to make some changes to our typical time schedule. He wanted to have shorter messages and more fun. He wanted to do some things that sounded crazy to me. But I liked and respected Jack and decided to let him go with his ideas, even though I had some doubts about the results. I was willing to take a risk and trust his decisions.

When we delegate responsibility to someone, we also need to give the proper authority for that person to carry out the responsibility. That often means allowing him or her to make decisions based on values that may be different than ours. Jack's conference was a success. It turned out that Jack had his finger on the pulse of this younger group of dads and sons and understood them in ways that I didn't. My acceptance of Jack and his values led to more effective programming that better met the needs of our guests. It also enhanced our working relationship, increasing the trust and respect between us.

Acceptance can be the key that unlocks the door to more open communication and more positive relationships. As we learn to understand each other's frame of reference or point of view, based on how our values were developed, we should be able to more easily accept one another, even if we can't always agree. But sometimes there are things that still get in the way—past hurts, unresolved conflicts, misunderstandings, hurtful actions or attitudes that are a source of bitterness or anger. These things need to be dealt with before a relationship can move ahead. That brings us to our next key to resolving differences: forgiveness.

Key #3: Forgiveness

Forgiveness is a powerful force that can do enormous good. Lack of forgiveness can be a weapon of destruction. The problem with this weapon is that the one who is holding it against another is likely to do as much injury to himself as to the one he is aiming at. It's even possible that the unforgiven person is unaware he is the target, and all the damage is being done in the life of the person holding the grudge through bitterness and anger.

Sometimes differences in values can lead to conflicts that require forgiveness to repair the breach in the relationships. As values clash, tempers flare, and words and actions build walls that need some help in coming down.

A great resource for people who want help repairing damaged relationships is a book called *Dr. Rosberg's Do-It-Yourself Relationship Mender,* by Dr. Gary Rosberg, a marriage and family counselor. This helpful book (published by Focus on the Family/Tyndale House Publishers) gives practical steps for resolving conflict based on his "closing the loop" concept.

Through years of counseling people through their problems, he has identified a pattern that occurs when conflicts arise. If you are struggling with conflicts in relationships, we strongly recommend getting his book. But for the sake of our current discussion of forgiveness, let us give you a quick overview of his concept of what happens when conflicts occur in relationships:

1. A conflict begins with an offense. Person A does something to Person B (perhaps based on a clash in values).
2. This offense leads to some kind of emotional reaction. Person B is hurt.
3. Person B's hurt turns into anger. That anger is often dealt with by attacking Person A verbally or physically, by burying the anger and letting it simmer, or by compromising and letting Person A have his or her own way. In any of these cases, Person B does not resolve the conflict, but leaves "the loop" open. Many people leave open loops in their lives. These unresolved conflicts lead to smoldering anger and bitterness that cause the people involved to grow more isolated from each other.

Dr. Rosberg gives hope for damaged relationships by recommending steps to "close the loop" and resolve those conflicts.

1. **Heart Preparation**—Before approaching the other person, you need to be ready to reach out and respond. For our application, this means wanting to understand where the other person is coming from, value-wise. It means being willing to explore the reasons for the differences and willing to accept the other person with those differences.
2. **Clear Communication**—You need to honestly describe your thoughts and feelings about the offense. Using Your Value Assessment Tool and the discussion questions from chapter 20 could be a good way to help accomplish this.
3. **Loving Confrontation**—Talk openly, but with sensitivity,

about your desire to remedy the problem, and plan together how to make the situation better. How can you compromise, and if needed, agree to disagree?

4. **Forgiveness**—Forgiveness starts the healing process, and true conflict resolution is impossible without it.

5. **Rebuilding Trust** (which closes the loop)—Once the relationship is back on track through forgiveness, it often takes time and continual effort to keep the communication open and growing again.

Dr. Rosberg says that forgiveness is the most important step in conflict resolution. Here are some of his main points relating to forgiveness:

Forgiveness is choosing to release the offender. It's giving up the control of revenge and retribution, canceling the debt, being willing not to pay them back for what they did to you.

Forgiveness is validating the offense. To forgive someone doesn't mean you have to deny that they hurt you. As Dwight Carlson, in his book *Overcoming Hurts and Anger,* says: "Forgiveness means that we actively choose to give up our grudge despite the severity of the injustice done to us. It does not mean that we have to say or feel, 'That didn't hurt me,' or 'It didn't really matter.' Some things may hurt very much, and we must not deny that fact, but after fully recognizing the hurt, we should choose to forgive."[3]

Forgiveness is giving up resentment. It means giving up our right for revenge. Resentment feeds anger and keeps conflicts unresolved. It impairs our understanding and hampers the healing of our hearts. When we forgive someone, it doesn't mean we are letting them "off the hook" as far as their own need to work through the situation and whatever natural consequences may result from their actions. But it means we let them off of our hook, and we are freed from the entangling negative emotions that lack of forgiveness binds us with. Thus . . .

Forgiveness sets a prisoner free. As you forgive, you are set free from hatred, anger and bitterness. These emotions do you far more damage than they do the offender you don't forgive.

Forgiveness is an act of grace. We don't offer forgiveness with any conditions. We don't offer it because we feel like it, or because the person earned it. We forgive, in spite of the fact that they may not deserve it (as others forgive us when we don't deserve it).

Forgiveness gives us second chances. Philip Yancey once wrote: "Forgiveness breaks the cycle. It does not settle all questions of blame and justice and fairness: to the contrary, often it evades those questions. But it does allow relationships to start over."[4]

Lest we give the impression that forgiveness is as easy as 1-2-3, let us assure you that we recognize the difficult challenges that are often involved, especially if the hurts are very deep and have accumulated over time. We have found that our ability to forgive others is greatly helped by our faith and our recognition that we have been forgiven everything by a gracious God, through our relationship with Jesus Christ. This not only motivates us to forgive others, but also gives us the power to do so.

Forgiveness provides great freedom, both for the forgiver and the forgiven. As we work toward resolving the differences that divide us, it may be the most important of the three key elements we have looked at, but probably comes more easily after the other two: understanding and acceptance. All three are vital for building and maintaining good relationships, especially when generational differences are involved.

Are there people in your life you need to forgive? Some you need to ask to forgive you? Have you gained some understanding that will help you to accept them more easily now? We encourage you to take the necessary steps to resolve those conflicts and free up and restore those relationships.

It's also possible that we need to apply these principles to ourselves. Most of us can benefit from a better understanding of who we are, what values we hold, and why. Hopefully the last chapter helped with that. Sometimes we need to accept who we are, gaining a more realistic picture of ourselves. (Some need to see themselves in a more positive light; others need to recognize their weaknesses more.) There also may be things we need to forgive ourselves for—failures, disappointments, not living up to our own standards, or having unrealistic expectations. Feel free to serve yourself a dose of our key elements—understanding, acceptance, and forgiveness—to improve your relationship with yourself and others.

What's next? you might wonder. We've seen how values develop, in theory and over the course of the decades. We've looked at the four generations and now have a better understanding of why we tend to clash. We've assessed our own values, thought about them, and possibly discussed how we got them. Now we've seen what we need to do to resolve the differences we are experiencing in our relationships. But now what?

How about being a little proactive? For those of you who are parents, future parents, or grandparents, in the next chapter we'll be exploring ways you can use your new knowledge of the value development process to encourage positive values in your kids and grandkids. Perhaps you'll be able to lessen some generational tensions by being aware and intentional about value development in your family.

Chapter 22

Encouraging Positive Values

We've just spent the last two chapters identifying differences in values that we may have with others and understanding how to resolve conflicts through understanding, accepting, and forgiving. There are many relationships in which value differences can affect us, whether it's with people we work with in the community, those at our jobs or most importantly, our family members. For most relationships, it's a matter of understanding and adjusting to the other person's value system.

As we have mentioned before, once people reach adulthood, values are set unless some Significant Emotional Event causes them to exchange a value they have for another. You can be part of an event that affects someone else's value system. If you are in a position of teaching others (formally or informally), you may open their eyes to new truths or information that gives them a whole new perspective and results in a change in values and behavior. For example, many, after learning about the health risks associated with smoking, have changed from valuing smoking to trying to quit their smoking habits.

Also, being in a relationship where you are respected and trusted may allow you to influence another person's values. As you live your values out and others see the effectiveness of your values compared to theirs, they may choose to exchange their values for yours. Say, for example, you have a strong marriage relationship due to making your spouse a priority, and that is evident to those around you through your words and actions. A coworker or friend who is struggling in his marriage may become convinced that your priority system is a better way to go and change his actions as a result.

If we want to influence the values of other adults in our lives, we can best accomplish that through living out our values effectively, sharing our beliefs and the reasons behind them, and at the same time keeping the communication-lines open through a climate of acceptance in our relationships. We can't force our values on others. They must see the benefits and decide to adopt them of their own free will.

But for those who have children who are still developing their values, there's great potential for influencing them in ways that would encourage values that you'd like them to have. This could help avoid future conflicts in our families. As we pointed out earlier in the book, there are many factors that come into play as a child develops values. Now that you're aware of what they are and their potential influence on your children, you have an opportunity to evaluate and make changes, if necessary. As you understand how values are developed at different stages, you can be more intentional about what your child is exposed to and what kinds of environments and people make up his or her world.

Kathy has shared a value with me (Rick)—a love of reading. I remember that, when we were first dating, she used to tell me how she enjoyed lying in bed on Saturday mornings and reading for hours. That was definitely not a value I shared. In fact, that would probably be the last thing in the world that I would ever do. I'm not sure I actually read a book all the way through until I reached high school—and never just for fun. I didn't enjoy reading, and to think that someone would spend a Saturday morning lying in bed reading, and actually enjoying it, really amazed me. After dating and then being married to Kathy for a number of years, I caught this value of hers and really grew to love reading. I knew that when we had children, I wanted to pass that value on to them.

When Cora was just a baby, we started reading her stories and showing her books. As soon as she started to learn to read (and she read at a very early age), we got her all the types of books that she enjoyed. That was our way of showing her that we valued reading, but we wanted her to own that value herself.

I (Rick) was in graduate school when my daughter was born, and I happened to be studying the importance of reading and what it does for a child as he or she grows up. We wanted to make sure that reading was important to Cora, so we came up with a little plan. We told her that we would give her a penny a page for every book that she finished. The catch was that she could only spend this money on more books.

At first she started reading and looking through books that were only about 30 pages long and had lots of pictures, so she would get 30 cents. Then she started reading more books and bigger books. Soon they were 100 pages, and I would owe her a dollar. Then 200 pages and 300 pages, and, before long, Cora would read two, three, or sometimes four books a week. And for all the pages she read, she got a penny, and the money mounted up. I remember, even when she was a young child, at times having to give her $5, $10, or even $15 for book money that she had earned. And again, she could only spend that money on more books. As a result, she truly has developed a love for books and reading and even a passion and skill for writing. (You actually have read some of her work. Since she grew up in the '90s, we had her write the story for that decade in chapter 13.)

We really knew that we'd been successful in instilling a love for reading in Cora when a few years ago we took a summer vacation with Kathy's sister, Jody, and her family. We went to a lake and had all the fun toys and options you could want. We could go swimming, we could go fishing, and we had Jet Skis. There were all these possibilities, and some of them we did for a while. But we have a picture that shows all these fun things just sitting idle on the beach. Lined up along the water's edge are all of our family and all of Jody's family in beach chairs—

reading. There are a lot of fun and exciting things to do in life, and reading is one of them. We're glad we've been able to pass that value on to Cora.

When it comes to encouraging positive values, the whole idea is to be intentional. The first step is knowledge. You need to know how values develop and what factors are influencing your kids. (You should have that down by now!) You need to know what values you are aiming at and have some ideas about how to encourage those values. You need to be aware of what your children are dealing with and experiencing in order to know what values they may be picking up, so you can intervene and influence in another direction if necessary.

In chapter two, we talked about the three different stages of value development. It's important to be aware of which stage of the value-development process your child is in. If it's the first stage of imprinting (until about age seven or so), you need to know that your child is going to observe, absorb, and follow what you do. Being intentional might mean making sure your actions are those you want your child to imitate and realizing that "do as I say, not as I do" doesn't work.

If it's the second stage of modeling or hero worship (approximately ages eight to 13), you know that your child is going to look at others for role models, choosing what qualities she would like to imitate and which values she would want to take as her own. Being intentional might mean looking around at the people who have influence in your child's life and making sure they are people you would like your child to imitate and admire.

If you have teenagers in the socialization stage, you need to be aware that they are really going to look at and compare the values you have taught them at home with those of others in the outside world. This often means questioning, challenging, experimenting, evaluating, sometimes rejecting, but also often confirming the family values. Being intentional might mean taking the time to communicate why you do and believe the things you do, helping them to understand the reasons for your values, and why you think they're important.

Knowing what stage of development your child is in is the first important step toward encouraging positive values. It's also important to be aware of what is influencing your child in his or her daily life so you can better understand what you are up against and can more effectively respond to and influence your child's values.

Be Aware

One of the key elements in encouraging positive values in our kids is being aware of what they're dealing with in their lives. If we're aware of what's going on with them, we can be more intentional about influencing certain values and addressing issues that our children need to deal with. This, quite frankly, takes a lot of work. Keeping up with the current issues in their lives—how things are going at school, who their friends are, what might be bothering them, what dreams or goals they have—can be challenging and a full-time job in its own right. I know a lot of us think that we have enough trouble staying in touch with our own situations in life and find it difficult to keep up with the kids, too, particularly if we have two, three, or even more children. But it can be done.

Doug is a friend of mine who runs a very successful video production company. This isn't just a nine-to-five type of job. He has to fly all over the place to tape events for his productions. It requires long hours of creating, writing, and filming. The editing and actual production of the videos takes even more time, often requiring him to work until two or three in the morning. A while back, I spent a week with Doug. He was helping to produce a video for the organization I work for. By the end of the week, I was totally exhausted after keeping up with him and his schedule. The thing that surprised me was how often he was in touch with his three kids. He would call them, or they would call him at work virtually anytime during the day or night, just to talk to him, see how he was doing, and share with him how things were going in their lives. I remember one day we took a break in our busy schedule to drive over to pick up his son from football practice.

When Robert got into the car, the first thing Doug asked him was "How did the election go?"

What election is he talking about? I wondered. It turned out that this was the day they voted on class officers in Rob's high school. "Who won senior class president?" Doug asked. When Rob told him, Doug was quite surprised. Then he went on and asked about the other officers. Doug knew all the students who were running and which ones he really thought would get those offices. It surprised me that Doug, with his busy schedule and all that was going on in his business world, would stay so in touch with his son that he even knew who was running for class offices at Rob's high school. I don't think I know anyone who has a more hectic life than Doug, and I was incredibly impressed by his level of awareness of what was going on in his kids' lives.

Often in our lives we use our busy schedules and our own agendas as excuses for not knowing what's going on in our children's lives. Doug is a great example of how even busy people who have demanding schedules, if they choose to, can be aware of what's happening with their kids. And I might add that Doug's three children, now all young adults, grew up to be people that he is very proud of and that share many of the same values that he and his wife, Emily, have.

Being aware is not just a matter of knowing our kids' schedule and knowing what's going on at school. It's also a matter of being aware of what they are up against in our current society. Here are some statistics from the 1997 Youth Risk Behavior Survey of 16,262 high school students in 151 schools, conducted by the Centers for Disease Control and Prevention:

- 20.5 percent of students had seriously considered attempting suicide during the 12 months preceding the survey; 15.7 percent had made a specific plan to attempt suicide; and 7.7 percent actually attempted suicide.

- 48.4 percent of students had had sexual intercourse during their lifetimes; 34.8 percent had experienced it during the three months preceding the survey (i.e., were currently active). Among these, only 56.8 percent reported that a condom was used during their last sexual intercourse. 16.0 percent of students had had sexual intercourse with four or more sex partners during their lifetimes.

- Before 13 years of age, 24.8 percent had smoked a whole cigarette; 31.1 percent had first drunk alcohol (more than a few sips); 9.7 percent had tried marijuana; 7.2 percent of students had initiated sexual intercourse.

- 79.1 percent of students had had at least one drink of alcohol during their lifetimes, 50.8 percent within the 30 days preceding the survey; 33.4 percent had had five or more drinks of alcohol at one time during the previous 30 days.

- 70.2 percent of students had tried cigarette smoking; 35 percent had smoked cigarettes during the previous 30 days.

- 14.8 percent of students had been in physical fights on school property one or more times during the previous 12 months.

- 32.9 percent had had property (e.g., a car, clothing, or books) stolen or deliberately damaged on school grounds during the previous 12 months.[1]

We need to be aware of the intense pressure that our kids are under to get involved in these types of things. It is up to us to help give them the ability to handle these pressures successfully. Being aware of the environment they are in, helping them to make wise choices about avoiding tempting and compromising situations, and talking openly about rationales and consequences are good steps in the right direction.

As we attempt to be aware of what's going on in our children's lives, there are two areas to focus on—what's going on in the outside world and what's going on inside our own homes or families. Staying in touch with society today takes a little focused effort. Articles and books are available to help you be informed. In the notes section in the back of our book, you'll find some sources that we've used to find out what youth and teens are currently dealing with.

In addition, there are reports in newspapers almost daily, giving us analyses of what is taking place in the youth culture. There are also TV reports that give us an evaluation of where our youth and teen culture are today. John Stossel recently did a report on ABC called "Teens: What Makes Them Tick." It gave an interesting perspective of what's going on in a certain segment of the teen population. These reports, on topics like the rate of smoking, teen pregnancies, drug and alcohol abuse, and average test scores, inform us about trends and fads so we can be aware of what is currently popular and communicate with our kids on these topics.

You need to be intentional about increasing your awareness, but the most important part of being aware is simply communicating with your child. That requires a time commitment on your part. It's going to take more than just a few minutes a day. You don't want to be part of this statistic published in the Family Research Council's *Washington Update* of April 21, 1999: "20 percent of 6th- through 12th-graders say they haven't had a good conversation lasting at least 10 minutes with a parent in over a month."

You have to have a plan to communicate with your kids. If you just briefly talk to them as they're on their way out to school, or you chat with them for a moment or two before they go bed, you may not get the full picture. You need to have time when you and your child can be alone together, no matter what age he or she is. And if you can create an environment where it's enjoyable and relaxed, and you give them your full, undivided attention, you're more likely to get your kids to talk. If you show real interest, by actively listening and asking them questions to show you really want to understand, you'll find them more likely to open up to you. If you talk about the things they want to talk about, what's going on in their world becomes quite evident. Once you hear what they're going through and you better understand their feelings, you're in a better position to be intentional about the values that you want to influence.

You may remember back in chapter three that we mentioned eight major factors that influence value development. You're not the only one who is shaping your kids' values. Family is important in the early years, but as time goes along, peers have more and more influence. The media, school, music, and textbooks all have a significant impact, as well as the other factors we mentioned in chapter three. So, to become more aware of what your kids are experiencing, you also need to be aware of these other areas that are influencing their values. As they get into the teen years, peers tend to be even more influential than parents are, and you may feel somewhat helpless because of that. But being aware of this can help you guide your children's decisions about who to hang around with.

In many cases, you have to live in a certain area based on your job, but there are often choices about the neighborhood you choose to live in. Based on your neighborhood, your children usually have to go to a specific school, but sometimes you can choose the schools your children attend. If you are worried about the peer influence at the local public school, you can send them to private school, you can get permission to have them attend a different school, or you can homeschool them.

In this mobile society of ours, most of us, at some point, find ourselves in a situation where we need to move. When faced with relocation, one of the key factors in determining where you move to certainly can be the type of school that your children will attend. Some schools are better for value development than others. It may take some effort to investigate, but I would suggest that could be a key factor in influencing your children. Of course, picking the best school situation for your child is not the end of your parental responsibility. You still need to be aware of what is being taught and what is going on at the school.

Other ways of being intentional about influences on your kids' values involve things like getting your kids into team sports, reading clubs, dance programs, youth groups, or a number of other types of extracurricular groups. Activities like these can help to teach good values like teamwork, commitment, discipline, unity, and getting along with others. These are all intentional choices that we can make to help our children develop positive values.

Broken Homes

Another area is incredibly significant in understanding what our children are going through. It relates to our marital status. Now we want to be very careful here, because we realize that there are many reasons why children end up in single-parent homes. Sometimes there are difficult situations in marriages, involving various forms of abuse, that force a parent to divorce a spouse for the sake of the child. What I am about to say is difficult to hear and may seem like we are placing even more guilt on the single, or even remarried, parent, but that is not our intent. Rather, we intend it to be a list of areas to be aware of, that have been proven to be areas of concern if a child is growing up in a home with one or both natural parents absent. Your increased awareness can help you look for ways to try and compensate for, or at least address, the issues that come with the situation. The information on this list should also be strongly considered by parents who may be considering a divorce. As you look at it, you'll see that the signs of at-risk behavior are significantly increased for kids in this situation.

According to George Barna, in his book *Generation Next: What You Need to Know About Today's Youth,* who has gleaned this information from several studies, a child growing up in a home in which one or both natural parents is absent is more likely to (in contrast to kids from intact families):

- Receive less parental attention.
- Receive less discipline.
- Be less adept at playing with peers.
- Have more frequent and more serious health problems.
- More frequently exhibit emotional problems, sexual problems, and antisocial behavior.
- Get divorced.
- Be more pessimistic about the future.
- Lack role models.
- Experience bouts of depression and a deep sense of loneliness and rejection.
- Commit crimes.
- Struggle with low self-esteem, anger, guilt, and lower levels of achievement.
- Be expelled or suspended from school and repeat a grade.
- Develop a mental illness. (Four out of five adolescents in psychiatric hospitals come from broken homes.)[2]

You can see that the potential difficulties for children growing up in single-parent homes, or even homes with stepparents, can be overwhelming. You may be in this situation and desire a better life for your child, and this list can help you be more aware and intentional about dealing with some of these issues. The first step to solving a problem is being aware that there is one. It's possible that you're already aware and dealing with some of these issues. We encourage you to increase your awareness through interaction with your kids and becoming more educated about possible solutions, and be intentional about planning value development strategies that can counteract these effects.

For instance, make sure your kids are getting plenty of quality parental attention. Plan one-on-one time with each child to make sure they are getting the attention from you that they need. Evaluate the discipline situation. Are you handling things effectively? Do you need to get ideas from other parents who seem to have an effective strategy in this area?

If you want to make sure they have good role models, get involved in organizations where they'll have positive relationships with adults other than you (Scouts, a church group, a sports team, etc.). (Again, you need make sure these relationships are, indeed, positive. You should be involved enough yourself to be aware.) You may also want to build relationships with and do things with other families who have older kids with positive values. These kids could also be good role models for your kids. You may want to "adopt" some local grandparent-type people for your kids if your parents aren't readily available (or are not a positive influence).

It's also important to the emotional health of your kids to understand that the divorce was not their fault. So many children of divorce believe that somehow they were to blame. Talk honestly with your kids, and put the responsibility for the decisions that were made on the adults, where they belong. When appropriate, talk about the real causes, helping them to understand and maybe even learn from your experiences. Help them to learn to forgive those who have hurt them (this means you will need to forgive, too, and model it for them). Anger and bitterness always do more damage to the one who is feeling them than to the target of the feelings.

Your kids need to know that you love them, not just when they are behaving or living up to your expectations, but all the time, no matter what. Security, which everyone needs, comes from knowing you are loved unconditionally. Work at communicating that, especially during the rough times. Allow your ex-spouse to show them love, too (assuming the relationship is positive and he or she is available). Don't let the problems between you and your spouse rob your kids of the love they need to feel from both parents.

Being aware and intentional about meeting these internal needs of your kids can help prevent some of the outward effects on our list. Kids who get plenty of parental attention and appropriate discipline and who have a sense that they are truly loved and not to blame for their parent's divorce will most likely be less prone to have problems, such as committing crimes, being expelled, or developing a mental illness. They should have less depression, less loneliness, and fewer self-esteem problems. Rather than being overwhelmed and discouraged by this list, we want you to head off these possible effects by being aware and intentional in your parent-child relationships.

Are You Aware?

The purpose of this section is to help all parents become more aware of what their children are going through. Some parents think they have a pretty good handle on it and believe that they're in touch with their kids and what they're dealing with. Walt Mueller, in his book *Understanding Today's Youth Culture,* presents the results of a survey that show that adults may not know as much about what their kids are doing as they think they do. The point is that many parents don't really know which values, attitudes, or behaviors their children are adopting. As you'll see in the chart on page 348, the parents' beliefs about their kids' actions are quite different from what the kids say they're doing.[3]

As you read this section, you might have been a bit skeptical about whether you needed to get more involved in your children's lives. Based on the following chart, we can see that what we understand our children's beliefs to be and what their actions actually are may be quite different. The more involved with them we become, the better our communication with them and the more aware we will be.

Being Intentional

Once we are more aware of what our children are experiencing, we need a game plan to help influence them toward the values

QUESTIONS	TEENS' RESPONSE	PARENTS' RESPONSE
1. Have you had one or more alcoholic drinks?	66% say yes	34% think they have
2. Have you considered suicide?	43% say yes	15% think they have
3. Have you ever smoked?	41% say yes	14% think they have
4. Do you tell your mom about boyfriends and sex?	36% say yes	80% think they do
5. Have you ever used drugs?	17% say yes	5% think they have
6. Have you lost your virginity?	70% say yes	14% think they have
7. Have you thought about running away from home?	35% say yes	19% think they have

that we want them to have. Whether it's working with our children or working on our own values or behaviors that need to change, the whole concept of being intentional comes into play. Being intentional is not just letting things happen to you; it's actually having some plans about how you want things to develop or what outcomes you want to see happen.

When it comes to intentionally taking control of life, there are three kinds of people: (1) those who watch things happen; (2) those who make things happen; and (3) those who ask, "What happened?"

There are some people who just sit back and watch what's going on in the world and hope that things don't affect them too negatively. There are more assertive people who understand what they want to have happen and they go after it. And then there are definitely those who are clueless, who don't even know that things are happening around them. When it comes to taking control of our lives and influencing our kids, first being aware and then being intentional are definitely key steps. We need to be the kind of parents who make things happen in the value systems of our children.

The story of John Goddard is the best example that I've ever heard of a person being intentional about life. When he was only 15, as he was sitting in his room on a rainy day, he started thinking about how many times he had heard adults talking about all the things they wished they had done. "If only I had done that," he'd hear them say. Or "I always wanted to go to see such and such." After hearing so much regret in their statements, he made a decision about his own life. He determined that, as he grew up, he was going to make things happen in his life. He set goals, made plans, and was intentional. At that young age he set 127 goals for his life.

He wanted to go mountain climbing, so he set a goal to climb 16 of the highest mountains in the world, including the Matterhorn, Fuji, McKinley, Everest, Ararat, and Kilimanjaro. (At the time of the printing of the *Life* magazine article reporting this, at age 47, he had climbed all but four.) He planned to explore eight of the world's rivers, including the Nile, Amazon, Congo, and Yangtze. (He only had three more to go.)

He also determined to carry out a career in medicine, visit every country in the world, study Navajo and Hopi Indians, learn to fly an airplane, retrace the travels of Marco Polo and Alexander the Great, and ride a horse in the Rose Parade. (Of these, he was only lacking in visiting 30 countries.)

Other goals that he set and achieved include becoming an Eagle Scout; diving in a submarine; landing and taking off from an aircraft carrier; riding an elephant, camel, ostrich, and bronco; playing flute and violin; typing 50 words a minute; making a parachute jump; learning water and snow skiing; going on a church mission; studying native medicines; learning to fence; learning jujitsu; teaching a college course; writing a book; publishing an article in *National Geographic;* learning French, Spanish, and Arabic; reading the Bible from cover to cover; becoming proficient in the use of a plane, motorcycle, tractor, surfboard, rifle, pistol, canoe, microscope, football, basketball, bow and arrow, lariat, and boomerang . . . the list goes on and on. John Goddard, at age 47, had accomplished 103 of his 127 goals, and he was still working on them.[4]

You can see that John Goddard had goals. He was intentional about his life. He wasn't content to just let things happen to him. He wanted to determine what and how things were going to occur in his life. Being intentional about your kids' futures and values doesn't just happen. It takes effort and planning.

Our friends, Doug and Emily Momary, wanted to encourage their kids to work hard in school, so they came up with a plan. Emily recently shared their plan with us: "To encourage our kids to work hard in school, we offered them a 'Day Alone with Mom' toward the end of each semester. We never tied it to grades, just to effort. If we felt they were working hard in their classes and doing their best (no matter what the grades happened to be), they could stay home for a day with me. On that day, we would just be together doing fun things—baking cookies, going out for lunch, having a picnic at the park, Christmas shopping—each child planned the day when it was his or her turn. It seemed to be a wonderful incentive to take their schoolwork seriously and was a big treat for both of us! We did this from kindergarten all the way through high school."

Henry and Margie Janowski, friends and coworkers of ours, have also been intentional about developing certain values in their three kids. One of those values is "If it's worth having, it's worth working for." To teach this value, they encourage their kids to work to earn the extra things they want, rather than just giving things to them. They allow them to earn money by doing extra jobs around the house, such as washing cars, cutting grass, and weeding. They've also earned money by starting a soft drink business at our office and doing housecleaning for others. Not only have these kids learned the value of working, but they've also become very capable and responsible young people.

Here's a list of some intentional things you can do to encourage the development of character qualities and values that you desire in your kids.

1. Have your children read (or read to them) good books about people who have the character qualities and values that you want your children to have.
2. Watch movies and videos that illustrate and honor good values and character. Discuss them with your family.
3. Cultivate relationships with people of admirable character and values, including those who have overcome and learned from difficult circumstances. Have them in your home. Learn about their lives. Allow them to influence you and your kids.
4. Talk to your kids about situations in your life, and let them experience the process of decision making and problem resolution with you. Help them understand the "whys" of how you react and what you do.
5. Provide experiences for your family that will help them see positive values in action: community service projects, helping those in need, mission trips, visiting historic sites that remind us of people who lived admirable lives, visiting countries less fortunate than ours to gain some perspective about our material possessions and our country.

These ideas should get you started, but as you get into the mode of becoming aware and intentional, you'll probably come up with your own creative ideas that suit your family and your particular goals.

So, have you caught the vision? Do you see the potential for shaping your kids' values? We hope you'll make the effort to take some of those ideas that are swimming around in your head and put them into practice. We truly believe that the combination of being aware of what your child is experiencing, plus putting some intentional plans into practice, can help you to encourage positive values in your child's life. Remember the time and effort you put into this is an investment in the future. You are influencing the kind of adult your child will grow up to be. It's a high calling and a big responsibility, but it's what parenting is all about. We urge you to take on the challenge, armed with your new knowledge, and make a difference in your child's life.

Chapter 23

Some Final Thoughts

"My sisters and I always wondered why my parents were so nonverbal. Why didn't they give us more direction through our teen years? We seemed to always be hiding behind humor or talking about the weather rather than talking about our feelings. We wanted our mum to share with us on a deeper level and show us more affection. But she didn't, and we didn't understand why. I decided to love her, in spite of my hurt, but one of my sisters especially resented this and has really pulled away from spending much time with our mum," explained a British friend of ours. But then she went on to explain about an event that provided her with insight into her mother's behavior that helped her to understand, forgive, and accept her.

"When Princess Diana died, we went to sign the Book of Remembrance at our local cathedral. As we stood waiting, my friend and sisters and I were going on about Charles and how uncommunicative, untouchable, and unfeeling he was to Diana, compared to how relational she was. After a time, my mum spoke up.

"'Don't be too hard on him,' she said. 'He is of the old school of Brits. His parents are like Daddy and I. Our generation was taught the stiff upper lip. We wouldn't have survived two terrible wars if we hadn't learned to push our emotions down and keep quiet since careless talk costs lives. We had to just endure. As Churchill said, 'Never, never, never, never, never give up!'"

"The others just shrugged and went on with their conversation, but I was deeply touched by this insight my mum had just revealed about herself and others her age. I have always been amazed by the war stories I heard while I was growing up. I don't think that I could have endured the way they did. Now I realize that even though this generation of Brits drives us up the wall because they seem so shallow, superficial, and unaffectionate, they are actually living out the effects of being brave and uncomplaining during the wars—sometimes to a fault!

"I still try to get my mum to talk on a little deeper level, but now I understand why this is difficult for her and others her age, and I don't get so offended by it or take her lack of emotions so personally. This insight has helped to ease some tension in our relationship."

Our friend has experienced with her mother what we hope you'll experience as you apply the principles in this book. Now that you understand how values are developed and some of the factors that influence them, look at those difficult relationships in your life and see where those value clashes are occurring. Through communication, find out why the other person's values are different from yours and seek to understand them, accept them and, if necessary, forgive them.

You might say, "This was a nice book to read. I enjoyed the stories, I enjoyed learning about history." Or you might choose to do something about the conflicts that have been in your life for a very long time. As you attempt to resolve past conflicts or help your children establish the values that you want them to have, you may be a bit perplexed about what to use as a standard, what values to promote. Well, let me tell you, you're not alone in that confusion.

A few years ago, I was asked to go to Russia to help a camp there determine what their teaching curriculum should be. These "pioneer" camps were originally established for the purpose of promoting communism. Children who did well earned the privilege of going to these camps. There are thousands of camps all over Russia that were established for this purpose. When communism was eliminated, these camps lost a great deal of their reason for existence. At that time, I was working for a very successful camp and conference center and was asked to help determine how they could develop programs that were more intentional in their outcome.

When I arrived in Russia and toured the camp, I was amazed by the facility. This conference center could house 3,000 children, had a space museum, had a dock for an ocean-going ship, and had five subcamps within the property. This was a well-developed complex. As I explored their programming, I found their problem. Communism was not just a political way of life; it was also their moral standard and the direction for their society. With communism gone, they simply had nothing to teach. They had no basis from which to teach morals and ethics. They had the structure, they had the facility, they had the teachers, and they had the students. What they didn't have was moral content or values.

Many in our country today feel that we are headed in a similar direction. The shootings and bombings that have occurred in the high schools of our nation have people pointing fingers of blame in many directions. Several have blamed the elimination of prayer and the lack of instruction in moral values in our schools as contributing factors to the apparent decline of our youth today. Kids being raised without morality in a society full of deviant and harmful influences are like sponges ready to soak up things that are exciting or seem fulfilling to the void in their lives. Kids need direction. If we don't give them direction to good values, someone else will influence them, and we may be distressed by where they end up.

You may find yourself in a confusing situation. You may want to teach or adopt good values but aren't sure what the basis of your values should be. By now you've probably figured out that we have a strong commitment to our Christian faith in God. As Kathy grew up with her faith, and as Rick changed to a life of faith as a young adult, we have learned to use God's Word, the Bible, as our standard for the values that we have established in our life. If you're confused about what standard to use for your values, if you're not sure what it is that you should be teaching your children, we'd like to strongly encourage you to consider the Bible as a basis.

Some feel that biblical values are too restrictive or too difficult to follow. We have found that the restrictions keep us from doing things that bring about difficult or painful consequences. Rather than losing our freedom to do what we want, we find we are free to live as we should, free to enjoy life without the consequences of immoral or hurtful behavior. As for the difficulty factor, we couldn't agree more. Not only is living by biblical standards hard, but it is downright impossible if we are left to our own devices. That's why it should not be attempted without the help of the One who set the standard.

We were designed to live in a relationship with God in such a way that His Spirit would work in us and through us to accomplish what God requires of us. But because God is holy and perfect, and we are imperfect, a separation has developed between us and God that we cannot overcome because of our imperfections. But God, in His wisdom and love, overcame our imperfections through the giving of His Son, Jesus Christ, as the solution to our separation from God through His life on earth, sacrificial death on our behalf, and resurrection. If we believe this and accept God's solutions to our separation problem by expressing our faith to Him in prayer, we become qualified to have His Spirit working in us and through us to help us live the way He asks us to. Not only does He give us the guidelines to live by, but He also gives us the motivation and the ability to live by those guidelines. The seemingly impossible becomes very doable.

We have found that the principles we have learned from the Scriptures have helped us as we raise our daughter, as we make choices in our personal lives, and as we do our work. They are practical and lead to positive relationships, peace of mind, and a sense of well-being. It's a time-proven standard, and we challenge you to consider these principles as a reliable source of quality values.

Understanding the Generational Differences

It's our hope that, as you have learned more about Boomers, Xers, and other strangers, you have developed a practical understanding about the generational differences that divide you from others in your life. You are now better equipped to relate in a more insightful, intentional, and accepting way. Go out into your families and communities and use your new knowledge for good, as you build bridges of understanding and communication.

Notes

Chapter 3

1. Timeline printed off the Internet, gopher://gopher.well.sf.ca.us:
70/00/community/60sTimeline/1st00-60.nrf, page 23 of 49.
2. Harry Stein, "Benjamin Spock's Baby Bible," 50 Who Made the
Difference," *Esquire* (December 1983), p. 525.
3. Family Research Council, *Free to Be Family: Helping Mothers and
Fathers Meet the Needs of the Next Generation of American Children*
(Washington, D.C.: Family Research Council, 1992), p. 65.
4. James Dobson, monthly newsletter (May 31, 1990): 3.
5. Family Research Council, *The American Family Under Siege: An
Analysis of Social Change Affecting the Family 1950–1990* (Washington, D.C.: Family Research Council, 1989), pp. 22-23.
6. Steven D. Stark, *Glued to the Set: The 60 Television Shows and
Events That Made Us Who We Are Today* (New York: Free Press,
1997), p. 54.

Chapter 4

1. Britta Waller, "Norris, Texas Ranger," *Delta Sky* (August 1998): 58.
2. Descriptions of these theories of development were drawn from
The Gale Encyclopedia of Psychology, Susan Gall, exec. ed. (Detroit:
Gale Research, Inc., 1996).
3. Morris Massey, *The People Puzzle: Understanding Yourself and
Others* (Reston, VA: Reston Publishing, 1979), p. 12.
4. Robert M. Goldenson, *The Encyclopedia of Human Behavior: Psychology, Psychiatry, and Mental Health*, vol. 1 (Garden City, NY:
Doubleday, 1970), p. 591.
5. Details of Eisenhower's and Armstrong's life from "50 Who Made
the Difference," *Esquire* (December 1983).
6. Details of Namath's and Maravich's life taken from Fred Katz's
book *American Sports Heroes of Today* (New York: Random
House, Inc., 1970).

Chapter 5

1. Joseph A. Slobodzian, *Philadelphia Inquirer On-line* (July 10, 1998).
2. Adaptation of the bell curve concept from Massey, *The People
Puzzle.*

Chapter 6

1. Marc McCutcheon, *The Writer's Guide to Everyday Life from Prohibition Through World War II* (Cincinnati: Writer's Digest Books, 1995), pp. 41-42.
2. Lois and Alan Gordon, *The Columbia Chronicles of American Life 1910–1992* (New York: Columbia University Press, 1995), p. 190.
3. Janet McDonnell, *America in the Twentieth Century: 1920–1929* (New York: Marshall Cavendish, 1995), p. 335.
4. Carolyn Kott Washburne, *America in the Twentieth Century 1930–1939* (New York: Marshall Cavendish, 1995), p. 439.
5. Ibid., p. 447.
6. Ibid, p. 178.
7. Ibid., p. 269.
8. Judith S. Baughman, ed., *American Decades 1920–1929* (Detroit: Gale Research, 1996), p. 268.
9. Peter Jennings and Todd Brewster, *The Century* (New York: Doubleday, 1998), pp. 123-4.
10. Baughman, *American Decades*, p. 143.
11. Washburne, *America*, p. 439.
12. Ibid., p. 439.
13. Baughman, *American Decades*, p. 143.
14. Ibid., p. 42.
15. Ibid., p. 43.

Chapter 7

1. McCutcheon, *Writer's Guide*, p.62.
2. Washburne, *America*, p. 456.
3. Karen Rood, ed., *American Decades 1930–1939* (Detroit: Gale Research, 1995), p. 302.
4. Washburne, *America*, p. 464.
5. Ibid., p. 467.
6. Ibid., p. 457.
7. Ibid., p. 467.
8. Rood, *American Decades*, p. 302.
9. Ibid., p. 304.
10. Washburne, *America*, pp. 472-3.
11. Ibid., pp. 474-5.
12. Rood, *American Decades*, p. 436.
13. McCutcheon, *Writer's Guide*, p. 172.

14. Rood, *American Decades*, p. 305.
15. Ibid., p. 306.
16. McCutcheon, *Writer's Guide*, p. 172.
17. Rood, *American Decades*, p. 302.
18. Ibid., p. 329.
19. Washburne, *America*, p. 569.

Chapter 8

1. Kelly Peduzzi, *America in the Twentieth Century: 1940–1949* (New York: Marshall Cavendish, 1995), p. 609.
2. Ibid., p. 616.
3. McCutcheon, *Writer's Guide*, p. 81.
4. Jennings and Brewster, *Century*, p. 266.
5. Karen Rood, ed., *American Decades 1940–1949*, (Detroit: Gale Research, 1995), pp.465-6.
6. Ibid., p. 328.
7. Jennings and Brewster, *Century*, p. 247.
8. Rood, *American Decades*, p. 331.
9. John Cheever, "Moving Out," *Esquire* (June 1983), pp.107-111.
10. Rood, *American Decades*, pp. 449-50, 458.
11. John E. Findling and Frank W. Thackeray, eds., *Events That Changed America in the Twentieth Century* (Westport, CT: Greenwood, 1996), p. 127.
12. Rood, *American Decades*, p. 328.
13. Ibid., p. 133.

Chapter 9

1. Richard Layman, ed., *American Decades 1950–1959* (Detroit: Gale Research, 1994), p. 262.
2. Ibid., p. 266.
3. David Wright and Elly Petra Press, *America in the Twentieth Century: 1950–1959* (New York: Marshall Cavendish, 1995), p. 765.
4. Gordon, *Columbia Chronicles*, p. 426.
5. Ibid., p. 471.
6. Wright and Press, *America in the Twentieth Century*, p. 750.
7. Layman, *American Decades*, p. 262.
8. Ibid., p. 272.
9 Ibid., p. 137.
10. Stark, *Glued to the Set*, p. 25.

11. Wright and Press, *America in the Twentieth Century*, p. 811.
12. Layman, *American Decades*, p. 134.

Chapter 10
1. Jennings and Brewster, *Century*, p. 382.
2. Layman, *American Decades 1960–1969* (Detroit: Gale Research, 1995), p. vii.
3. Ibid.
4. Gordon, *Columbia Chronicles*, p. 559.
5. Layman, *American Decades*, p.vii.
6. Gordon, *Columbia Chronicles*, p. 565.
7. David Wright, *America in the Twentieth Century: 1960–1969* (New York: Marshall Cavendish, 1995), p. 978.
8. Layman, *American Decades*, p. 326.
9. Wright, *America in the Twentieth Century*, pp. 933-36.

Chapter 11
1. Victor Bondi, ed., *American Decades 1970–1979* (Detroit: Gale Research, 1995), pp. 345-46.
2. Ibid., p. 347.
3. Gordon, *Columbia Chronicles*, p. 632.
4. Ibid., p. 578.
5. Ibid., p. 587.
6. Ibid., p. 605.
7. Janet McDonnell, *America in the Twentieth Century 1970–1979* (New York: Marshall Cavendish, 1995), p. 1083.
8. Gordon, *Columbia Chronicles*, p. 587.
9. Bondi, *American Decades*, p. 349.
10. Ibid., p. 348.
11. Gordon, *Columbia Chronicles*, p. 632.
12. Ibid., p. 659.
13. Bondi, *American Decades*, p. 334.
14. Gordon, *Columbia Chronicles*, p. 659.
15. Bondi, *American Decades*, p. 328.
16. Gordon, *Columbia Chronicles*, p. 641.
17. Bondi, *American Decades*, p. 335.
18. McDonnell, *America in the Twentieth Century*, pp. 1060-62.
19. Gordon, *Columbia Chronicles*, p. 623.
20. McDonnell, *America in the Twentieth Century*, pp. 1021-22.

21. Ibid., p. 1015.

22. Gordon, *Columbia Chronicles*, p. 587.

23. Bondi, *American Decades*, p. 152.

24. McDonnell, *America in the Twentieth Century*, p. 1081.

25. Bondi, *American Decades*, p. 330.

26. Gordon, *Columbia Chronicles*, p. 650.

27. Ibid., p. 659.

28. Bondi, *American Decades*, pp. 321, 323.

29. Ibid., p. 336.

30. Ibid., p. 327.

31. Ibid.

32. Ibid., p. 321.

33. Ibid., p. 342.

34. Ibid.

Chapter 12

1. Gordon, *Columbia Chronicles*, p. 672.

2. Ibid., p. 726.

3. Victor Bondi, ed., *American Decades 1980–1989* (Detroit: Gale Research, 1996), p. 374.

4. Ibid., p. 146.

5. Ibid., p. x.

6. Gordon, *Columbia Chronicles*, p. 708.

7. Ibid., p. 744.

8. Ibid., p. 672.

9. Ibid., p. 744.

10. Bondi, *American Decades*, p. 395.

11. Gordon, *Columbia Chronicles*, p. 672.

12. Ibid., p. 708.

13. Bondi, *American Decades*, p. 173.

14. Ibid.

15. Ibid., p. 177.

16. Gordon, *Columbia Chronicles*, p. 735.

17. Ibid., p. 681.

18. Ibid., p. 690.

19. Bondi, *American Decades*, pp. 431-32.

20. Gordon, *Columbia Chronicles*, p. 744.

21. Bondi, *American Decades*, p. 400.

22. Ibid., p. 178.

23. Gordon, *Columbia Chronicles*, p. 753.

24. Ibid., p. 708.

25. Ibid., p. 726.

26. Ibid., p. 753.

27. Bondi, *American Decades*, p. x.

28. Ibid., p. 381.

29. Gordon, *Columbia Chronicles*, p. 735.

30. Bondi, *American Decades*, p. 176.

31. Ibid., p. 539.

32. Ibid., p. 557.

33. Ibid., p. 387.

Chapter 13

1. Gordon, *Columbia Chronicles*, p. 775.

2. Ibid., p. 776.

3. John W. Kirshon, ed., *Chronicle of America* (New York: Dorling Kindersley, 1995), p. 908.

4. Gordon, *Columbia Chronicles*, p. 775.

5. Gini Holland, *America in the Twentieth Century: 1990s* (New York: Marshall Cavendish, 1995), p. 1312.

6. Ibid., p. 1357.

7. Gordon, *Columbia Chronicles*, p. 766.

8. Bureau of Labor Statistics, http://stats.bls.gov/wh/cpsbref3.htm.

9. Holland, *America in the Twentieth Century*, p. 1312.

10. Jennings and Brewster, *Century*, pp. 564-67.

11. Holland, *America in the Twentieth Century*, p. 1357.

12. Ibid., p. 1324.

13. Ibid.

14. Jennings and Brewster, *Century*, p. 539.

15. Promise Keepers Web site, www.promisekeepers.org.

16. March for Jesus Web site, www.mfj.org.

17. Don Tapscott, *Growing Up Digital: The Rise of the Net Generation* (New York: McGraw-Hill, 1998), p. 163.

18. Maximov On-line, Mir Space Station, www.maximov.com/Mir/index.html.

19. Rick Hicks and Kathy Hicks, unpublished survey of 1,110 teenagers, November 1998.

Chapter 14

1. The concepts for this chart, which have been expanded by the authors, from Massey, *The People Puzzle.*
2. William J. Bennett, "Quantifying America's Decline," *Wall Street Journal* (March 15, 1993).
3. Ted Baehr, *The Media-Wise Family*, (Colorado Springs, CO: Chariot Victor, 1998), p. 140.
4. J. Walker Smith and Ann Clurman, *Rocking the Ages: The Yankelovich Report on Generational Marketing* (New York: Harper-Collins, 1997), p. 274.
5. Christine Yount, "Reaching Millennial Kids," *Children's Ministry* (1998).

Chapter 15

1. Diane Crispell, "Where Generations Divide: A Guide," *American Demographics*, (May 1993).
2. William Strauss and Neil Howe, *Generations: The History of America's Future, 1584 to 2069* (New York: William Morrow, 1991), p. 265.
3. Ibid., p. 268.
4. Ibid., p. 271.
5. Ibid., p. 273.
6. Ibid., p. 281.

Chapter 16

1. Smith and Clurman, *Rocking the Ages*, p. 46.
2. Stark, *Glued to the Set*, p. 14.
3. Ibid., p. 18.
4. Brandon S. Centerwall, MD, MPH, "Television and Violence: The Scale of the Problem and Where to Go From Here," *Journal of the American Medical Association* 267, no. 22 (1992): 3059-63.
5. Susan Mitchell, *American Generations: Who They Are, How They Live, What They Think* (Ithaca, NY: New Strategist, 1998), p. 85-86.
6. Smith and Clurman, *Rocking the Ages*, p. 22.

Chapter 17

1. George Barna, *Baby Busters: The Disillusioned Generation* (Chicago: Northfield, 1994), pp. 72-74.
2. Ibid., pp. 34-38.
3. Ibid., p. 75.

4. George Barna, *Generation Next: What You Need to Know About Today's Youth* (Ventura, CA: Regal, 1995), p. 24.

5. Barna, *Baby Busters*, p. 105.

6. Smith and Clurman, *Rocking the Ages*, pp. 88-89.

7. Barna, *Baby Busters*, p. 64.

8. Henry Beard and Christopher Cerf, *The Official Politically Correct Dictionary and Handbook* (New York: Villard Books, 1992)

9. Barna, *Baby Busters*, p. 114.

Chapter 18

1. Multiple Internet sources

2. Don Tapscott, *Growing Up Digital: The Rise of the Net Generation* (New York: McGraw-Hill, 1998), p. 282.

3. Centers for Disease Control, "Youth Risk Behavior Trends," www.cdc.gov/nccdphp/dash/yrbs/trend.htm.

4. "Adults Possess a Radically Different View of Teenagers Than Teens Have of Themselves," www.barna.org/PressTeens.htm.

5. Ibid.

6. Ibid.

7. Barna, *Generation Next*.

8. Mike Woodruff, Kids Today column: "The Coca-Cola Company's Take on Generation Y," *YoungLife Magazine* (Spring, 1998), p. 19.

9. "11th Annual Special Teen Report: Teens and Self-Image: Survey Results," *USA Weekend* (May 1-3 1998), p. 18.

10. Mitchell, *American Generations*, p. 84.

11. Dyan Machan, "A More Tolerant Generation," *Forbes* (September 8, 1997), pp. 46-47.

12. Cheryl Russell, "What's Wrong with Kids?" *American Demographics* (November 1997), www.demographics.com.

13. "11th Annual Special Teen Report," *USA Weekend*, p. 18.

14. Hicks, unpublished survey of 1,110 teenagers, November 1998.

15. Yount, "Reaching Millennial Kids."

16. Alexander W. Astin et al., *The American Freshman: Thirty-Year Trends, 1966–1996* (Los Angeles: Higher Education Research Institute, UCLA, 1997), pp. 12-13.

17. Yount, "Reaching Millennial Kids."

18. Susan Mitchell, "The Next Baby Boom," *American Demographics* (October 1995), www.demographics.com.

19. Tapscott, *Growing Up Digital*, p. 40.
20. Barna, *Generation Next*, p. 46.
21. Mitchell, *American Generations*, p. 83.
22. Yount, "Reaching Millennial Kids."

Chapter 19

1. This chart was conceptually based on Massey, *The People Puzzle*. His book addresses the Builders (whom he calls Traditionalists) and the Boomers (whom he calls Challengers). His work does not include Generation X or Net Generation values.
2. "'Pop' Culture," Family Education Network, 1998. http://familyeducation.com.

Chapter 21

1. Massey, *The People Puzzle*, p. 21.
2. "Parental Behavior," *Coral Ridge Encounter* (April 1990): 41.
3. Dwight L. Carlson, *Overcoming Hurts and Anger* (Eugene, OR: Harvest House, 1981), p. 126.
4. Philip Yancey, "An Unnatural Act," *Christianity Today* (April 18, 1991): 37.

Chapter 22

1. Centers for Disease Control, "1997 Youth Risk Behavior Surveillance System (YRBSS)," www.cdc.gov/nccdphp/dash/yrbs/natsum97.
2. Barna, *Generation Next*, pp. 56-57.
3. Walt Mueller, *Understanding Today's Youth Culture* (Wheaton, IL: Tyndale House, 1999), p. 49.
4. Mark Lee, *How to Set Goals and Really Reach Them* (Portland, OR: Horizon Books, 1978), pp. 9-11.

Acknowledgments

First, we'd like to thank Morris Massey. His original presentation of the concepts that form the basis of this book caught Rick's attention and led him to many enjoyable years of teaching seminars on the topic.

Thanks, also, to Norm Wright who, after hearing the seminar several times, encouraged us to put it into book form as a helpful tool for others.

To the Focus on the Family staff who made it possible: To Al Janssen, thanks for believing we could do it, giving us the chance, and being patient about our deadlines. To Larry Weeden, our patient editor, thank you for your critical eye and suggestions throughout the process. We also appreciate Christina Harrell for her diplomacy and hard work on the cover concept, and Maureen Kimmell for her artistic contributions to our graphics.

We are also grateful to all our friends and coworkers who helped us in very specific and practical ways: Lane Powell, for her editing skills; Rita Haywood, for typing and tabulating survey results; Dave Hoffman, for original graphic designs and research; Margie Janowski, for proofing and typing; Connie and Rob Taylor and Aimee Wells, for tabulating survey results; Shannon Boehm and her group, for their input; Lisa Hopkins, Don Davis, and Tony Pattiz, for facilitating the distribution of our surveys; and Dave Hopkins, for assistance in research.

A special thanks goes to our daughter, Cora Hicks, who helped with distributing surveys and tabulating survey results. She also wrote the story in chapter 13 from her N-Gener perspective. We greatly appreciate her positive attitude, support, and patience through this whole process.

We are also indebted to those who shared their personal stories with us to use as examples: Dina Nelson, Rita Haywood, Doug and Emily Momary, Henry and Margie Janowski, Ralph and Don and others who wished to remain anonymous. (You know who you are!) In addition, we appreciate the many other friends and family members who allowed us to use scenes from their lives as illustrations, and those who have supplied us with a steady stream of articles and E-mails to enhance our research on the topic.

A big thanks to all of you, and especially to our Lord and Savior, Jesus Christ, through whom we find our purpose, strength, and fulfillment in life.

More Faith-Strengthening Stories
From Focus on the Family®

Molder of Dreams

When Guy Doud was named National Teacher of the Year in 1986, he seemed the picture of success. But few knew the hard road that had led Guy to develop an unusual compassion for his students. In this compelling account of his often-troubled childhood, Guy shares a moving message about the extraordinary difference love and encouragement can have on those around us. *Also available on video.*

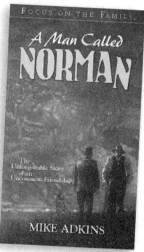

A Man Called Norman

Mike Adkins's belief in "loving your neighbor as yourself" was put to the test when he found himself across the street from an eccentric neighbor named Norman. Through the years, however, Mike learned to minister to his neglected, elderly neighbor and found himself learning what it really means to reach out to another. This unusual story of an uncommon friendship will stay with you long after you've turned the last page. *Also available on video.*

• • •

Look for these special books in your Christian bookstore or request a copy by calling 1-800-A-FAMILY (1-800-232-6459). Friends in Canada may write Focus on the Family, P.O. Box 9800, Stn. Terminal, Vancouver, B.C. V6B 4G3 or call 1-800-661-9800.

Visit our Web site (www.family.org) to learn more about the ministry or find out if there is a Focus on the Family office in your country.

FOCUS ON THE FAMILY®

Welcome to the Family!

Whether you received this book as a gift, borrowed it from
a friend, or purchased it yourself, we're glad you read it! It's just
one of the many helpful, insightful, and encouraging
resources produced by Focus on the Family.

In fact, that's what Focus on the Family is all about—providing inspiration, information, and biblically based advice to people in all stages of life.

It began in 1977 with the vision of one man, Dr. James Dobson, a licensed
psychologist and author of 16 best-selling books on marriage, parenting,
and family. Alarmed by the societal, political, and economic pressures
that were threatening the existence of the American family, Dr. Dobson
founded Focus on the Family with one employee—an assistant—
and a once-a-week radio broadcast, aired on only 36 stations.

Now an international organization, Focus on the Family is dedicated
to preserving Judeo-Christian values and strengthening the family
through more than 70 different ministries, including eight separate
daily radio broadcasts; television public service announcements;
11 publications; and a steady series of award-winning books,
films, and videos for people of all ages and interests.

Recognizing the needs of, as well as the sacrifices and important
contribution made by, such diverse groups as educators, physicians,
attorneys, crisis pregnancy center staff, and single parents,
Focus on the Family offers specific outreaches to uphold and
minister to these individuals, too. And it's all done for one purpose,
and one purpose only: to encourage and strengthen individuals
and families through the life-changing message of Jesus Christ.

• • •

For more information about the ministry, or if we can be of help to your
family, simply write to Focus on the Family, Colorado Springs, CO 80995
or call 1-800-A-FAMILY (1-800-232-6459). Friends in Canada may write
Focus on the Family, P.O. Box 9800, Stn. Terminal, Vancouver, B.C. V6B 4G3
or call 1-800-661-9800. Visit our Web site—www.family.org—
to learn more about the ministry or to find out if there is a
Focus on the Family office in your country.

We'd love to hear from you!